T0321903

Design and Use of Virtualization Technology in Cloud Computing

Prashanta Kumar Das
Government Industrial Training Institute Dhansiri, India

Ganesh Chandra Deka
Government of India, India

A volume in the Advances
in Computer and Electrical
Engineering (ACEE) Book Series

Published in the United States of America by
    IGI Global
    Engineering Science Reference (an imprint of IGI Global)
    701 E. Chocolate Avenue
    Hershey PA, USA 17033
    Tel: 717-533-8845
    Fax: 717-533-8661
    E-mail: cust@igi-global.com
    Web site: http://www.igi-global.com

Library of Congress Cataloging-in-Publication Data

Names: Das, Prashanta Kumar, 1981- editor. | Deka, Ganesh Chandra, 1969-
  editor.
Title: Design and use of virtualization technology in cloud computing /
  Prashanta Kumar Das and Ganesh Chandra Deka, editors.
Description: Hershey, PA : Engineering Science Reference, 2017. | Includes
  bibliographical references.
Identifiers: LCCN 2017010716| ISBN 9781522527855 (hardcover) | ISBN
  9781522527862 (ebook)
Subjects: LCSH: Virtual computer systems. | Cloud computing.
Classification: LCC QA76.9.V5 D43 2017 | DDC 004.67/82--dc23 LC record available at https://
lccn.loc.gov/2017010716

This book is published in the IGI Global book series Advances in Computer and Electrical Engineering (ACEE) (ISSN: 2327-039X; eISSN: 2327-0403)

British Cataloguing in Publication Data
A Cataloguing in Publication record for this book is available from the British Library.

For electronic access to this publication, please contact: eresources@igi-global.com.

Advances in Computer and Electrical Engineering (ACEE) Book Series

ISSN:2327-039X
EISSN:2327-0403

Editor-in-Chief: Srikanta Patnaik, SOA University, India

MISSION

The fields of computer engineering and electrical engineering encompass a broad range of interdisciplinary topics allowing for expansive research developments across multiple fields. Research in these areas continues to develop and become increasingly important as computer and electrical systems have become an integral part of everyday life.

The **Advances in Computer and Electrical Engineering (ACEE) Book Series** aims to publish research on diverse topics pertaining to computer engineering and electrical engineering. **ACEE** encourages scholarly discourse on the latest applications, tools, and methodologies being implemented in the field for the design and development of computer and electrical systems.

COVERAGE

- Electrical Power Conversion
- Computer Architecture
- Power Electronics
- Applied Electromagnetics
- Analog Electronics
- VLSI Design
- Qualitative Methods
- Optical Electronics
- Programming
- Digital Electronics

IGI Global is currently accepting manuscripts for publication within this series. To submit a proposal for a volume in this series, please contact our Acquisition Editors at Acquisitions@igi-global.com or visit: http://www.igi-global.com/publish/.

Titles in this Series

For a list of additional titles in this series, please visit:
http://www.igi-global.com/book-series/advances-computer-electrical-engineering/73675

Transport of Information-Carriers in Semiconductors and Nanodevices
Muhammad El-Saba (Ain-Shams University, Egypt)
Engineering Science Reference ●©2017 ● 677pp ● H/C (ISBN: 9781522523123) ● US $225.00

Accelerating the Discovery of New Dielectric Properties in Polymer Insulation
Boxue Du (Tianjin University, China)
Engineering Science Reference ●©2017 ● 388pp ● H/C (ISBN: 9781522523093) ● US $210.00

Handbook of Research on Nanoelectronic Sensor Modeling and Applications
Mohammad Taghi Ahmadi (Urmia University, Iran) Razali Ismail (Universiti Teknologi Malaysia, Malaysia) and Sohail Anwar (Penn State University, USA)
Engineering Science Reference ●©2017 ● 579pp ● H/C (ISBN: 9781522507369) ● US $245.00

Field-Programmable Gate Array (FPGA) Technologies for High Performance Instrumentation
Julio Daniel Dondo Gazzano (University of Castilla-La Mancha, Spain) Maria Liz Crespo (International Centre for Theoretical Physics, Italy) Andres Cicuttin (International Centre for Theoretical Physics, Italy) and Fernando Rincon Calle (University of Castilla-La Mancha, Spain)
Engineering Science Reference ●©2016 ● 306pp ● H/C (ISBN: 9781522502999) ● US $185.00

Design and Modeling of Low Power VLSI Systems
Manoj Sharma (BVC, India) Ruchi Gautam (MyResearch Labs, Gr Noida, India) and Mohammad Ayoub Khan (Sharda University, India)
Engineering Science Reference ●©2016 ● 386pp ● H/C (ISBN: 9781522501909) ● US $205.00

Reliability in Power Electronics and Electrical Machines Industrial Applications ...
Shahriyar Kaboli (Sharif University of Technology, Iran) and Hashem Oraee (Sharif University of Technology, Iran)
Engineering Science Reference ●©2016 ● 481pp ● H/C (ISBN: 9781466694293) ● US $255.00

For an enitre list of titles in this series, please visit:
http://www.igi-global.com/book-series/advances-computer-electrical-engineering/73675

701 East Chocolate Avenue, Hershey, PA 17033, USA
Tel: 717-533-8845 x100 ● Fax: 717-533-8661
E-Mail: cust@igi-global.com ● www.igi-global.com

Editorial Advisory Board

Table of Contents

Detailed Table of Contents

Chapter 1
Applications of Virtualization Technology in Grid Systems and Cloud
Servers..1
> *Mohammad Samadi Gharajeh, Tabriz Branch, Islamic Azad University,
> Iran*

Grid systems and cloud servers are two distributed networks that deliver computing resources (e.g., file storages) to users' services via a large and often global network of computers. Virtualization technology can enhance the efficiency of these networks by dedicating the available resources to multiple execution environments. This chapter describes applications of virtualization technology in grid systems and cloud servers. It presents different aspects of virtualized networks in systematic and teaching issues. Virtual machine abstraction virtualizes high-performance computing environments to increase the service quality. Besides, grid virtualization engine and virtual clusters are used in grid systems to accomplish users' services in virtualized environments, efficiently. The chapter, also, explains various virtualization technologies in cloud severs. The evaluation results analyze performance rate of the high-performance computing and virtualized grid systems in terms of bandwidth, latency, number of nodes, and throughput.

Chapter 2
Application of Virtualization Technology in IaaS Cloud Deployment Model 29
> *Ganesh Chandra Deka, Government of India, India*
> *Prashanta Kumar Das, Government Industrial Training Institute
> Dhansiri, India*

Virtualization is an old proven technology used for effective utilization of Servers, Storage, and Network for reducing IT expenses without compromising the efficiency and agility for all size businesses. The area of application of Virtualization is very diverse such as e-Learning, Social Networking, and Simulation are a few to be mentioned. This chapter focuses on different virtualization approaches, benefits, architecture of different open source and commercial Virtual Machine Manager (VMM) and Virtual Machines (VM) migration techniques. All the technical terms appearing in this chapter is either defined wherever they appear or explained in the Key Terms and Definitions section of the chapter. The hardware requirements of all the hypervisiors are discussed for hassle free implementation and smooth reading of the chapter.

The essence of Cloud computing is moving out the processing from the local systems to remote systems. Cloud is an umbrella of physical/virtual services/resources easily accessible over the internet. With more companies adopting cloud either fully through public cloud or Hybrid model, the challenges in maintaining a cloud capable infrastructure is also increasing. About 42% of CTOs say that security is their main concern for moving into cloud. Another problem which is mainly problem with infrastructure is the connectivity issue. The datacenter could be considered as the backbone of cloud computing architecture. As the processing power and storage capabilities of the end devices like mobile phones, routers, sensor hubs improve we can increasing leverage these resources to improve your quality and reliability of services.

Invention of new computing techniques like cloud and grid computing has reduced the cost of computations by resource sharing. Yet, many applications have not moved completely into these new technologies mainly because of the unwillingness of the scientists to share the data over internet for security reasons. Applications such as Next Generation Sequencing (NGS) require high processing power to process and analyze genomic data of the order of petabytes. Cloud computing techniques to process this large datasets could be used which involves moving data to third party distributed system to reduce computing cost, but this might lead to security concerns. These issues are resolved by using a new distributed architecture for De novo assembly using volunteer computing paradigm. The cost of computation is reduced by around 90% by using volunteer computing and resource utilization is increased from 80% to 90%, it is secure as computation can be done locally within the organization and is scalable.

Chapter 5

    Chitresh Verma, Amity University, India
    Rajiv Pandey, Amity University, India

Mobile computing is a critical technology area which is actively integrated with field of cloud computing. It is broadly an application of virtualization technology at both ends of client server architecture. The mobile and cloud computing is a natural combination as mobile devices have limited computing and storage capacity, thus to reap the benefits of high end computing, cloud is the answer. Thus, amalgamation of mobile platform with cloud platform is inevitable. This chapter shall deliberate on the various aspects of mobile computing, mobile cloud computing and its relationship with virtualization technology. The detailed integration aspects and virtualization shall be signified through case study and suitable real time examples. The chapter shall envisage a case study, modeling the virtualization in the context of mobile cloud.

Chapter 6

    Wolfgang Mexner, Karlsruhe Institute of Technology (KIT), Germany
    Matthias Bonn, Karlsruhe Institute of Technology (KIT), Germany
    Andreas Kopmann, Karlsruhe Institute of Technology (KIT), Germany
    Viktor Mauch, Karlsruhe Institute of Technology (KIT), Germany
    Doris Ressmann, Karlsruhe Institute of Technology (KIT), Germany
    Suren A. Chilingaryan, Karlsruhe Institute of Technology (KIT),
        Germany
    Nicholas Tan Jerome, Karlsruhe Institute of Technology (KIT),
        Germany
    Thomas van de Kamp, Karlsruhe Institute of Technology (KIT),
        Germany
    Vincent Heuveline, Heidelberg University, Germany
    Philipp Lösel, Heidelberg University, Germany
    Sebastian Schmelzle, Technische Universität Darmstadt (TUD),
        Germany
    Michael Heethoff, Technische Universität Darmstadt (TUD), Germany

Modern applications for analysing 2D/3D data require complex visual output features which are often based on the multi-platform OpenGL® API for rendering vector graphics. Instead of providing classical workstations, the provision of powerful virtual machines (VMs) with GPU support in a scientific cloud with direct access to high performance storage is an efficient and cost effective solution. However, the automatic deployment, operation and remote access of OpenGL® API-capable VMs with professional visualization applications is a non-trivial task. In this chapter the authors demonstrate the concept of such a flexible cloud-like analysis infrastructure within the framework of the project ASTOR. The authors present an Analysis-as-a-Service (AaaS) approach based on VMware™-ESX for on demand allocation of VMs with dedicated GPU cores and up to 256 GByte RAM per machine.

    Khaleel Ahmad, Maulana Azad National Urdu University, India
    Ahamed Shareef, Maulana Azad National Urdu University, India

In this chapter, we will discuss in the introduction to KVM, how to create KVM, both command line and using GUI, briefly on KVM management. This chapter also describes the pre-requisites and a brief introduction on all the pre-requisite software. KVM utilizes the CPU virtualization technology on modern AMD and Intel processors, known as AMD-V and Intel-VT. KVM a is free virtualization solution and does not require any licensing, but if your CPU does not support virtualization KVM will be a waste of time. Linux OS, which is used in this chapter, is Cent OS.

    Srinivasa K. G., CBP Government Engineering College, India
    Aahan Singh, M. S. Ramaiah Institute of Technology, India

VirtualBox is a cross-platform virtualization application. What does that mean? For one thing, it installs on your existing Intel or AMD-based computers, whether they are running Windows, Mac, Linux or Solaris operating systems. Secondly, it extends the capabilities of your existing computer so that it can run multiple operating systems (inside multiple virtual machines) at the same time. So, for example, you can run Windows and Linux on your Mac, run Windows Server 2008 on your Linux server, run Linux on your Windows PC, and so on, all alongside your existing applications. You can install and run as many virtual machines as you like—the only practical limits are disk space and memory.

    Khaleel Ahmad, Maulana Azad National Urdu University, India
    Masroor Ansari, Maulana Azad National Urdu University, India

A vagrant is a freeware tool that facilitates to easily manage and configure multiple virtual machines. The main goal of its creation is to simplify the environment maintenance in a large project with multi technical tasks. It provides the better manageability and maintainability for the developers and prevents needless maintenance and improve the productivity for development using simple functions. Vagrant supports almost all main languages for the development, but it is written in the Ruby language. Vagrant was initially supported by Virtual Box, but the version 1.1 has the full vital support for VMware, KVM and other virtualization environment as well as for the server like Amazon EC2. It supports many programming languages such as C#, Python, PHP and JavaScript to enhance the project efficiency. Recently, version 1.6 may serve as a fully virtualized operating system due to the added support for Docker containers.

Xen is an open source virtualization framework in distributed system based on rapid elasticity on broad network access. It is a cost-effective platform for resource pooling and allows easy access to run any code any time from everywhere by any user. It is a hypervisor using a microkernel design, provides services that allow multiple operating systems to execute on the same computer concurrently. In other words, the hypervisor was made accessible to the world directly from any location, anticipating a fully virtualized cloud base environment, which is turned into cloud computing.

CloudStack is an Apache open source software that designed to install and handle large virtual machine (VM) networks, designed by Cloud.com and Citrix. This application is written in Java and was released under the terms of Apache License 2.0. This chapter discusses the easy availability and effortless scalability of CloudStack, which is an Infrastructure-as-a-service (IaaS) cloud computing platform software. We explore how CloudStack can either be used to setup public cloud services, or to provide a private cloud service.

OpenStack is a cloud operating system that controls large pools of compute, storage, and networking resources throughout a data center. All of the above components are managed through a dashboard which gives administrators control while empowering their users to provision resources through a web interface. OpenStack lets users deploy virtual machines and other instances which handle different tasks for managing a cloud environment on the fly. It makes horizontal scaling easy, which means that tasks which benefit from running concurrently can easily serve more or less users on the fly by just spinning up more instances.

With Open source virtualization software like VMware Player and Virtualbox, it is easy to install and run Virtual machines (VMs) in a home desktop computer. Endian Firewall provides a service called VPN (Virtual Private Network); it offers a secure communication between two different networks by using internet connection. In this chapter, we will install an Endian Firewall Community OS in one of the virtual machines (VM) and network it with the other VM for creating a firewall/router/proxy/VPN.

Virtual Routing and Forwarding (VRF) is a technology that allows multiple instances of IP (Internet Protocol) routing table to co-exist within the same Router at the same time. The routing instances are independent, allowing the same or overlapping IP addresses to be used without conflict. Using VRF technology, users can virtualize a network device from a Layer 3 standpoint of creating different "Virtual Routers" in the same physical device. Internet Service Providers (ISP) often use VRF technology to create separate routing table in a single physical Router which are completely isolated one from the others. This chapter discusses about the configuration of VRF-Lite in GNS3 (Graphical Network Simulator-3) on RIP/v2, EIGRP and OSPF protocols.

Foreword

I got an opportunity to go through the abstract of the chapters for this new book on the path-breaking virtualization paradigm and hence I think I have gained the required competency to write the foreword for this book. Yes, the virtualization idea definitely has brought in the much-needed tectonic shift for the IT industry. With the virtualization, the automation level is getting deeper into our everyday systems and in their operations and offerings. We hear, read and even experience the programmable, virtualized, sharable, interoperable, portable, and composable infrastructures. Once upon a time, the IT infrastructures (server machines, storage appliances, and network solutions such as load balancers, firewalls, switches, and routers, etc.) are massive, monolithic, closed, inflexible, underutilized, expensive, etc. Now with the virtualization tricks, tips and techniques are gathering the critical mass, the IT infrastructures steadily are becoming programmable, extensible, open, modular, productive, etc. Further on, IT products are remotely discoverable, usable, monitorable, measurable, manageable, and repairable. The virtualization concept has purposefully penetrated into every element so that we increasingly hear about service, application, data, and OS virtualization concepts.

The editor of the book has meticulously chosen the chapter titles for the book. This book covers everything about the virtualization technology and how it is impacting the various computing models such as grid and cloud computing. The application domains and use cases of the powerful virtualization principles are vividly illustrated through a few chapters. There are several chapters exclusively ordained for practical information and tutorials. Increasingly the computing becomes virtual and voluntary and there is an exclusive chapter on this in order to portray how virtual supercomputing is being made possible through the smart application of the proven and potential virtualization technology. Mobile virtualization is also explained in a chapter. There are chapters for virtual networks, routers, and firewalls. Definitely, this book is going to be an informative and inspiring one for the prospective readers as the book is stuffed with a lot of right and relevant information for cloud engineers, evangelists, exponents, and experts.

Pethuru Raj
Reliance Jio Cloud Services (JCS), India

Preface

Virtualization Technology is an old proven technology used for effective utilization of Servers, Storage, and Network for reducing IT expenses without compromising the efficiency and agility for all size businesses. The area of application of Virtualization Technology is very diverse such as e-Learning, Social networking, Simulation are a few to be mentioned.

This book discusses various Hypervisors (VMM) for creating the IaaS (Infrastructure as a Service). The book concludes with Network Virtualization.

Grid and Cloud servers are two distributed networks that deliver computing resources via a large and often global network of computers. Virtualization technology can enhance the efficiency of these networks by dedicating the available resources to multiple execution environments. The First Chapter of the book titled *Applications of Virtualization Technology in Grid Systems and Cloud Servers* describes applications of virtualization technology in Grid systems and Cloud servers.

Second chapter titled *Application of Virtualization Technology in IaaS Cloud Deployment Model* focuses on different virtualization approaches, benefits, architecture of different open source and commercial Virtual Machine Manager (VMM) and Virtual Machines (VM) migration techniques. All the technical terms/ definition appearing in this chapter is either defined wherever they appear or explained in the Keyword and Terminology. The hardware requirements of all the Hypervisiors are discussed for smooth reading of the chapter.

Chapter 3 is about Fog Computing. Fog computing will help businesses be more agile and efficient in their operations, help in decluttering and reduces information overload at the highest decision making levels. Fog computing is an extension of the cloud bringing the virtual resources called fog nodes nearby the data generation and consumption. It is application areas are as vast as IoT deployment, 5G network deployment, SDN, Personal Area network, Plant management. Cisco IOx platform is a pioneer in this domain providing a production level platform for the companies to introduce fog in their environments. The major research challenges include the deployment of Fog nodes, International device communication protocols. Chapter

3 titled "Fog computing and Virtualization" deliberates upon prospects of fog Computing.

Many applications have not moved completely into Cloud or Grid mainly because of the unwillingness of the scientists to share the data over the internet for security reasons. Applications such as Next Generation Sequencing (NGS) require high processing power to process and analyze genomic data of the order of Petabytes. Cloud computing techniques to process this large datasets could be used which involves moving data to third party distributed system to reduce computing cost, but this might lead to security concerns. These issues are resolved by using a new distributed architecture for De novo assembly using the volunteer computing paradigm. The cost of computation is reduced by around 90% by using volunteer computing and resource utilization is increased from 80% to 90%, it is secure as computation can be done locally within the organization and is scalable. Chapter 4 titled *Virtual Supercomputer Using Volunteer Computing* discusses about the concept of Virtual Supercomputer using volunteer computing.

Mobile computing is a critical technology area which is actively integrated with field of cloud computing. It is broadly an application of virtualization technology at both ends of client server architecture. The mobile and cloud computing is a natural combination as mobile devices have limited computing and storage capacity, thus to reap the benefits of high end computing, cloud is the answer. Thus, amalgamation of mobile platform with cloud platform is inevitable. Chapter 5 titled *Mobile Cloud Computing Integrating Cloud, Mobile Computing, and Networking Services Through Virtualization* discusses the various aspects of Mobile Cloud computing and its relationship with virtualization technology.

Modern applications for analyzing 2D/3D data require complex visual output features which are often based on the multi-platform OpenGL® API for rendering vector graphics. Instead of providing classical workstations, the provision of powerful virtual machines (VMs) with GPU support in a scientific cloud with direct access to high performance storage is an efficient and cost effective solution. However, the automatic deployment, operation and remote access of OpenGL® API-capable VMs with professional visualization applications is a non-trivial task. In Chapter 6, the authors demonstrate the concept of such a flexible Cloud-like analysis infrastructure within the framework of the project ASTOR. The authors present an Analysis-as-a-Service (AaaS) approach based on VMware™-ESX for on demand allocation of VMs with dedicated GPU cores and up to 256 GByte RAM per machine.

Chapter 7 is a *Hands-On Kernal Based Virtual Machine (KVM)*, where the author of the Chapter describes a brief introduction of KVM and pre-requisites for installation of open source *Kernal Based Virtual Machine*.

VirtualBox is a cross-platform virtualization application. Chapter 8 is a hands-on guide to VirtualBox.

Chapter 9 is *Hands-On Vagrant*. Vagrant supports almost all main languages for the development, but the source code is written in the Ruby language. Vagrant has the full vital support for VMware, KVM and other virtualization environment as well as for the server like Amazon EC2. Vagrant supports many programming languages such as C#, Python, PHP and JavaScript enhance the project efficiency.

Chapter 10 is a *Hands-On Xen,* an open source virtualization framework for distributed system on rapid elasticity network.

CloudStack is an Apache software which is open source that is designed to install and handle large virtual machine (VM) networks, designed by Cloud.com and Citrix. Chapter 11 is a *A Tutorial on CloudStack.*

Chapter 12 titled *An Insight Into Openstack* discusses the installation of OpenStack Hypervisor.

The Firewall provides a service called VPN (Virtual Private Network) for a secure communication between two different networks by using internet connection. Chapter 13 demonstrates the Endian Firewall Community OS in one of the virtual machines (VM) and network it with the other VM for creating a firewall/router/proxy/VPN.

Finally, Chapter 14 titled *Hands-On Network Device Virtualization With VRF (Virtual Routing and Forwarding)* discusses about the configuration of VRF-Lite in GNS3 (Graphical Network Simulator-3) on RIP/v2, EIGRP and OSPF protocols.

Acknowledgment

We are grateful to our friends, colleagues and family members who were our source of Inspiration during the preparation of the manuscript.

Special thanks to the chapter contributors for their contribution.

Chapter 1

Applications of Virtualization Technology in Grid Systems and Cloud Servers

Mohammad Samadi Gharajeh
Tabriz Branch, Islamic Azad University, Iran

ABSTRACT

Grid systems and cloud servers are two distributed networks that deliver computing resources (e.g., file storages) to users' services via a large and often global network of computers. Virtualization technology can enhance the efficiency of these networks by dedicating the available resources to multiple execution environments. This chapter describes applications of virtualization technology in grid systems and cloud servers. It presents different aspects of virtualized networks in systematic and teaching issues. Virtual machine abstraction virtualizes high-performance computing environments to increase the service quality. Besides, grid virtualization engine and virtual clusters are used in grid systems to accomplish users' services in virtualized environments, efficiently. The chapter, also, explains various virtualization technologies in cloud severs. The evaluation results analyze performance rate of the high-performance computing and virtualized grid systems in terms of bandwidth, latency, number of nodes, and throughput.

1. INTRODUCTION

Virtualization technology is executed by a process unit (e.g., a single program and an operating system) inside a program environment, namely jail or sandbox, running in a physical machine, namely hosting machine. A powerful hosting machine can be used to provide a set of the virtual machines (VMs) interconnected by one or multiple virtual networks. A virtual network scenario emulates behaviors of the

DOI: 10.4018/978-1-5225-2785-5.ch001

same scenario implemented with real computer systems. The main advantage of virtualization technology is that the main processes running in virtual machines behave, almost, truly as they are running on a real environment (Uhlig et al., 2005; Kim & Forsythe, 2010; Sahoo, Mohapatra, & Lath, 2010; Wang, Iyer, Dutta, Rouskas, & Baldine, 2013). This approach can be used in computer networks (e.g., grid systems and cloud servers) to reduce equipment and management costs compared to real scenarios. In this case, the hosting machine is used to implement the entire network to save financial costs of all the real equipments and infrastructure (e.g., wire and hubs) (Adabala et al., 2005; Di Costanzo, De Assuncao, & Buyya, 2009; Liang & Yu, 2015; Chen, Zhang, Hu, Taleb, & Sheng, 2015; Han, Gopalakrishnan, Ji, & Lee, 2015). Figure 1 illustrates the main elements of a virtual network laboratory: backbone, headquarters, regions, and sites. Backbone is a network to transport all the traffic among headquarters and regions. Headquarters are the central sites that involve main organization servers and applications. Regions contain one or more sites to manage the activity of desirable organization. Finally, sites indicate different offices of the organization and its end-users (Galán, Fernández, Ruiz, Walid, & de Miguel, 2004).

This chapter describes various applications of virtualization technology in grid systems and cloud servers. The chapter, initially, focuses attention on network virtualization, virtualized projects of computing systems, and virtualization technology

Figure 1. A schematic of virtual network laboratory

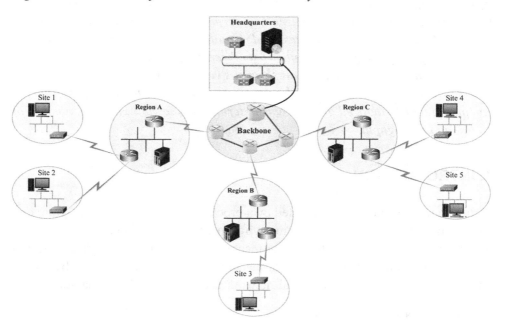

in teaching. Then, it represents virtualization technologies for high-performance computing environments including virtual machine abstraction, feature comparison between virtualized environments, a framework for high-performance computing based on virtual technology, and performance evaluation of high-performance computing. Afterwards, grid architecture for liquid computing and services, grid virtualization engine, virtual clusters for grid computing, virtualization in In-VIGO, and evaluation results of virtualized grid systems are studied in Section 3. Section 4 discusses about virtualization technology in cloud servers that involves a sample architecture of cloud computing, types and roles of virtualization in cloud servers, from virtualization to private cloud services, and virtualization in high-performance IaaS cloud. Grid virtualization into cloud environment is discussed in Section 5. Finally, the chapter is concluded by Section 6.

1.1 A Glimpse on Network Virtualization

According to the pluralist approach, network virtualization can be defined as an essential part of the Internet architecture. This definition leads multiple co-existing heterogeneous network architectures from different service providers to be supported and a common physical substrate to be shared, efficiently. Network virtualization offers flexible features for the current innovation and changes by dissociating the service providers from infrastructure providers (Anderson, Peterson, Shenker, & Turner, 2005). Figure 2 depicts a business model of network virtualization in two viewpoints: relationship between players and hierarchy of roles. The relationship workflow shown in Figure 2(a) indicates that players in the network virtualization

Figure 2. A business model of network virtualization. (a) relationship between players; (b) hierarchy of roles

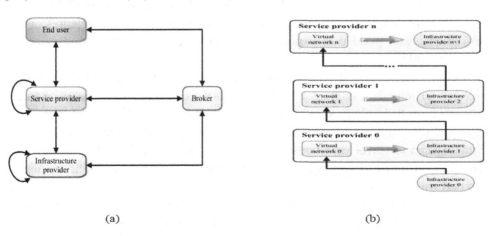

(a)   (b)

model are not the same as those in the traditional networking model. It consists of infrastructure provider, service provider, end user, and broker. Infrastructure providers deploy the fundamental physical network resources in the network virtualization environment. They conduct the operations and maintenance of physical infrastructure. Furthermore, they provide their physical resources via programmable interfaces to different service providers and do not provide directed services to end users. Service providers obtain physical resources from multiple providers to build virtual networks and deploy various network protocols. This process is carried out by programming the allocated network resources in order to provide end-to-end services to end users. As depicted in hierarchy model of Figure 2(b), a service provider can partition its resources to create child virtual networks. Afterward, the service provider leases child networks to other service providers. In the most cases, end users of the network virtualization environment act similar to end users of the Internet. The main difference between them is that end users in the network virtualization environment select a wide range of services from the competing service providers of multiple virtual networks. Finally, broker plays a major role in the network virtualization performance. In fact, it acts as a mediator among infrastructure providers, service providers, and end users in the network virtualization area (Chowdhury & Boutaba, 2009; Chowdhury & Boutaba, 2010).

1.2 Virtualized Projects of Computing Systems

There are three virtualization targets in virtualized computing systems: virtualized resources environment, virtualized tasks environment, and virtualized user environment. Virtualized resources environment combines or divides computing resources (e.g., storage disks) to service users in a good granularity and transparence way. Virtualized tasks environment builds an on-demand task execution environment to obtain the high utilization and efficiency. Virtualized user environment includes desktop virtualization applications that should have two major features: high convenience and good user experiences (Soltesz, Pötzl, Fiuczynski, Bavier, & Peterson, 2007).

Virtual user environment should be built and managed to accomplish the users' services, efficiently. As shown in the categories of Figure 3, the user-oriented virtualization technology should include three features: high performance, high manageability, and high secure. High performance indicates that a user-oriented virtualized project involves various optimization characteristics including architecture optimization, resources optimization, optimization of virtual machine manager, and performance evaluation. The high manageability features can be carried out in single virtual machine manager middleware and multiple virtual machine manager middleware based on the users' requirements. Finally, user-oriented virtualization

Figure 3. Main features of the user-oriented virtualization technology

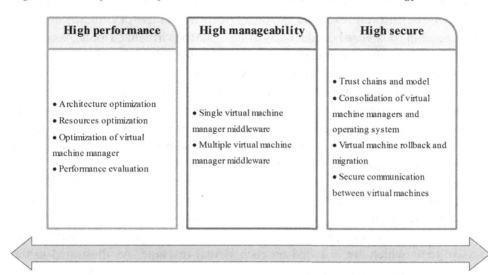

technology can be highly secured via trust chains and model, consolidation of virtual machine managers and operating system, virtual machine rollback and migration, and secure communication between virtual machines (Binge, Kaiyuan, & Weilong, 2007; Jarząb, Kosiński, Zieliński, & Zieliński, 2012).

Anywin and virtual laptop environment are two desktop virtualization projects. Anywin is a multi-platform supported virtual desktop, which focuses attention on four objectives: the on-demand use of environment tailor, collaborative backup and restore, the multi-platform supported characteristics, and the check-pointing and reply capabilities. Virtual laptop environment is another desktop virtualization that supports hardware virtual machine. By this project, there is a live switch between multiple operating systems as well as virtual machine manager is transparent for users. Furthermore, a cascaded multiple virtual machine illustrates the isolated running, free switching, and agile adjusting (Jin & Liao, 2008; Li, Jia, Liu, & Wo, 2013).

1.3 Virtualization Technology in Teaching

Implementation of teaching environments using virtualization technology contains big opportunities and benefits for educational institutes. It leads the teaching performance to be improved considerably. This subsection describes four teaching-learning applications: cost-effective platform for teaching and learning processes, availability of user accounts on remote servers, multi-platform computer labs, and tests and software validation (Fuertes, De Vergara, & Meneses, 2009).

Reduction of the infrastructure investment costs, central management, and an efficient use of hardware resources are some evident advantages of virtual technology. Hence, teaching costs can be reduced by using some the virtualized tools. According to Dobrilovic's analysis results (Dobrilovic & Odadžic, 2008), it is hardly possible to conduct the teaching computer networks without having professional network laboratories. Virtualization technology can be used to replace laboratory networks and operating systems by using modern capabilities for executing the practical teaching. Consequently, it has been used in educational institutes for teaching various courses (e.g., systems configuration, routing mechanisms, and network security attacks) in order to reduce financial costs of the teaching and learning processes.

User accounts on remote servers, which are located in the university laboratories, are utilized to offer an additional service to teachers and students. These servers contain several Virtual Box and VMware Server to organize remote capabilities. Microsoft Office, video applications, and online chat messaging are some of the massive tools which are installed on each virtual machine. As illustrated in the testing environment of Figure 4, users are able to access the Internet as well as to

Figure 4. Application environment of a remote desktop access

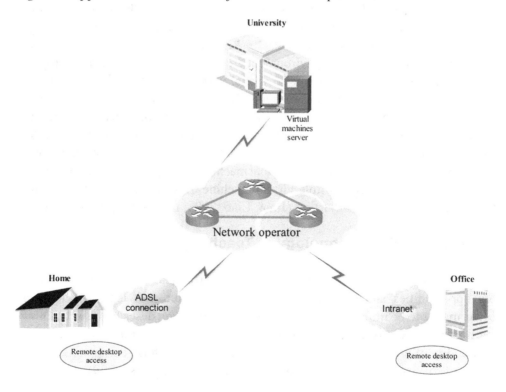

the main applications and actual services in cooperative networks. In this example, Microsoft Remote Desktop client, Linux rdesktop, or other remote connection tools are used to provide graphical interfaces to users.

In the traditional laboratory networks, multiple installations of various software packages must be installed each semester based on the requirements of different courses. Besides, software packages need efficient hardware characteristics (e. g., memory and number of processor), which increase both energy consumption and hardware financial costs. Hence, virtualizations tools can be offered to solve the above problems and constraints without depending to multi-platform computer labs. Since virtualization technology does not eliminate the need for better hardware characteristics, available hardware devices can be shared by installing the multiple virtualization machine images on a server.

Virtualization platforms are able to run the tests and software validation. In addition, they offer enormous facilities for dimensioning the network services via virtual network environments. For instance, the test process of software validation before real implementation is one of the essential phases in software engineering course. Since computer laboratories do not have an enough infrastructure similar to the complex networks of business companies, virtualization tools offer a platform for the software testing and validation. This capability can be achieved by using different networks, multiple servers, and emulation of several clients (Martignoni, Paleari, Fresi Roglia, & Bruschi, 2010).

2. VIRTUALIZATION TECHNOLOGIES FOR HIGH-PERFORMANCE COMPUTING ENVIRONMENTS

High-performance computing uses the parallel processing to execute the advanced application programs efficiently, reliably, and readily. It is sometimes applied as a synonym for the supercomputing which performs the highest operational calculations for computers. Researchers, engineers and academic institutions are the most common users of high-performance systems. Furthermore, some of the government agencies, especially the military usages, apply high-performance systems for complex applications. These systems accomplish the highest operations by using custom-made components and so-called commodity components (Armstrong et al., 1999; Egwutuoha, Levy, Selic, & Chen, 2013). This section describe various aspects of high-performance computing: virtual machine abstraction, feature comparison between virtualized environments, a framework for high-performance computing based on virtual technology, and performance evaluation of high-performance computing.

2.1 Virtual Machine Abstraction

Figure 5 show depicts the main components of virtual machine abstraction: physical machine, hardware, virtual machine monitor (hypervisor), and virtual machine. Physical machine, in fact, involves all the other components which are participated to form a virtual machine system. Hardware involves computing resources (e.g., storages disk and memory) to accomplish users' services. Virtual machine monitor (hypervisor) is a software, firmware, or hardware, which creates and executes various virtual machines. Each physical machine contains a desirable number of virtual machines that is usually determined based on hardware characteristics. Each virtual machine accomplishes users' requests independently. Moreover, it involves the simulated hardware, operating systems (e.g., Linux), and various applications (Brunthaler, 2009).

2.2 Feature Comparison Between Virtualized Environments

Since there are a wide variety of virtualization technologies, potential users have some challenges to identify which virtualization platform is the best suited for their

Figure 5. A schematic of virtual machine abstraction

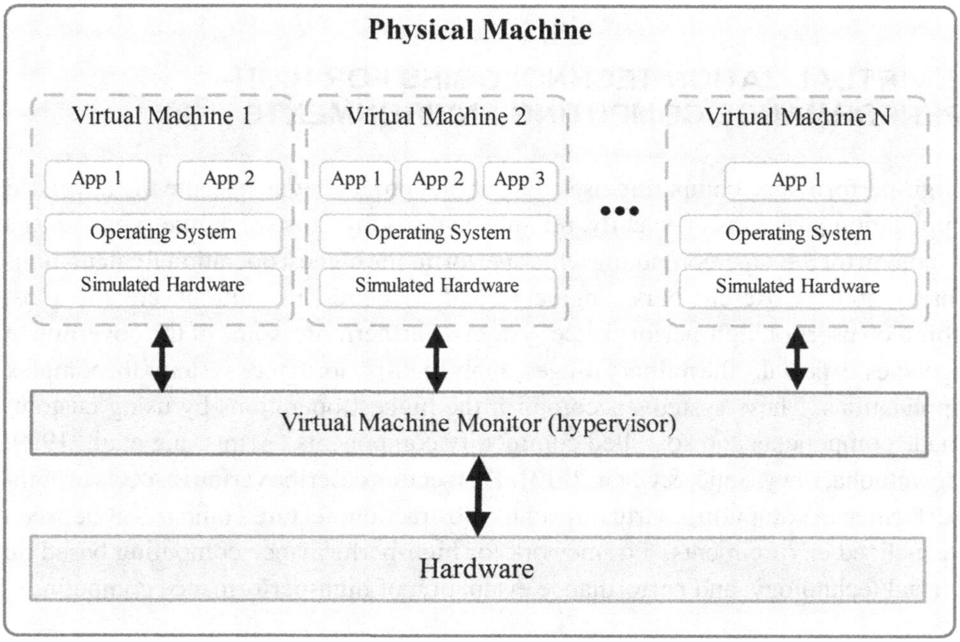

needs. As represented in Table 1, this subsection offers a comparison between Xen 3.1, KVM from RHEL5, VirtualBox 3.2, and VMWWare ESX. Hypervisors contain a desirable host and guest operating systems to support hardware within a guest environment. VirtualBox involves a variety of host operating systems compared to Xen, KVM, and VMWare. As represented in the results, all virtualized environment support a maximum number of guest operating systems. While VT-x / AMD-v are the required features in KVM, they are optional in the other environments. The Xen environment support the highest number of cores compared to KVM, VirtualBox, and VMWare. Memory in Xen and KVM is available more than the other hypervisors. Besides, all the hypervisors offer some 3D acceleration features and support the live migration capability across homogeneous nodes. Live migration is activated in all hypervisors as well as GPL is supported as the license in the most hypervisors. Para-virtualization is supported only in Xen, while full virtualization is supported in all the virtualized environments. From the host and guest CPU details, it can be concluded that the x86 and x86-64 guests are all universally supported by the hypervisors (Younge et al., 2011).

Table 1. Comparison results between Xen, KVM, VirtualBox, and VMWare (Younge et al., 2011)

Term	Xen	KVM	VirtualBox	VMWare
Host operating system	Linux, Unix	Linux	Windows, Linux, Unix	Proprietary Unix
Guest operating system	Windows, Linux, Unix	Windows, Linux, Unix	Windows, Linux, Unix	Windows, Linux, Unix
VT-x / AMD-v	Optional	Required	Optional	Optional
Number of cores	128	16	32	8
Available memory	4TB	4TB	16GB	64GB
3D acceleration	Xen-GL	VMGL	Open-GL	Open-GL, DirectX
Live migration	Yes	Yes	Yes	Yes
License	GPL	GPL	GPL/ Proprietary	Proprietary
Para-virtualization	Yes	No	No	No
Full virtualization	Yes	Yes	Yes	Yes
Host CPU	x86, x86-64, IA-64	x86, x86-64, IA-64, PPC	x86, x86-64	x86, x86-64
Guest CPU	x86, x86-64, IA-64	x86, x86-64, IA-64, PPC	x86, x86-64	x86, x86-64

2.3 A Framework for High-Performance Computing Based on Virtual Technology

A framework is presented in Huang, Liu, Abali, & Panda (2006) that works in high-performance computing environments based on virtual technology. Figure 6 shows the main elements of this framework in addition with relationship between the elements. The framework consists of front-end users, physical resources, management module, virtual machine image manager, and storage. Front-end users submit their batch job requests to the management module. Physical resources contain the cluster computing nodes which are connected via high speed interconnects. They involve a desirable number of resources to accomplish the users' services. Management module is the most important part of the framework that maintains the mapping feature between virtual machines and physical resources. Virtual machine image manager conducts available pool of the virtual machine images which are stored in the storage components. Efficiency of the storage and cluster file systems is very critical in the presented framework. It is possible that virtual machine images need to be transferred to computing nodes during the runtime process. In this case, the efficient storage and file systems can reduce the management overhead throughout then network.

Figure 6. A computing framework based on virtual technology

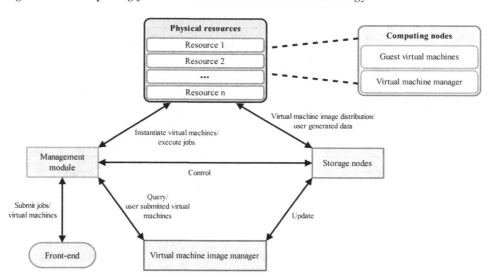

2.4 Performance Evaluation of High-Performance Computing

Performance evaluation of four popular hypervisors is represented in Table 2. The comparison results are carried out in the quantitative terms of minimum, average, and maximum based on bandwidth and latency. The results obtained for the bandwidth parameter indicates that, in total, VirtualBox has the highest bandwidth and KVM has the lowest bandwidth compared to the other hypervisors. Also, the bandwidths provided for the Native and Xen environments are near to each other. Besides, comparison results of the latency parameter represent that Xen has the highest latency and VirtualBox has the lowest latency compared to latency of the Native and KVM hypervisors. The reason is that the highest bandwidth is offered for VirtualBox. Furthermore, the Native and KVM hypervisors contain closely the same latencies according to the comparison results (Younge et al., 2011).

3. VIRTUALIZED GRID SYSTEMS

Grids have emerged as a global cyber-infrastructure system and incredible technology for the next generation of e-Science applications via integrating the large-scale, distributed, and heterogeneous computing resources. Scientific institutes (e.g., high-energy physics, geophysics, and bioinformatics) are applying grids to share, conduct, and process the large data sets. Grid computing technology provides some significant solutions for distributed and parallel computing. It can offer a reliable, cooperative, and secure access to remote computational resources, distributed data, and scientific applications. Since a great number of users access to grid systems for accomplishing their computing resources, these systems can use virtual technology to manage the defined operations simultaneously (Foster, Kesselman, Nick, & Tuecke, 2002; Wang, Von Laszewski, Chen, Tao, & Kunze, 2010). This section presents some essential information about virtualization technology in grid systems

Table 2. Comparison results between the high-performance computing environments (Younge et al., 2011)

Hypervisor	Bandwidth (GBytes/sec)			Latency (usec)		
	Minimum	Average	Maximum	Minimum	Average	Maximum
Native	4.8	5.6	6.7	0.22	0.4	0.57
Xen	2	5	7	0.22	0.77	1.5
KVM	2.8	3.2	3.7	0.22	0.4	0.6
VirtualBox	3.8	6.5	13.9	0.8	0.36	0.6

including grid architecture for liquid computing and services, grid virtualization engine, virtual clusters for grid computing, virtualization in In-VIGO, and evaluation results of virtualized grid systems.

3.1 Grid Architecture for Liquid Computing and Services

Grid computing can be, generally, defined as the pooling of information technology resources (e.g., file storages) into an available set of shared services. It should deliver on-demand computing resources to the users' requests at anytime and anywhere. The information technology department of a bank, for instance, serves many internal business departments. Because financial markets are not stable, transaction volumes can be predicted only to a given degree. Therefore, a scalable distribution of computer resources is required consequently. In this case, the business departments do not need to understand underlying technology of the resources which are requested by their users' computing services. Figure 7 illustrates the service architecture of such a departmentalized organization. Computer resources will become 'liquid' in this

Figure 7. Main layers of the grid architecture for liquid computing and services

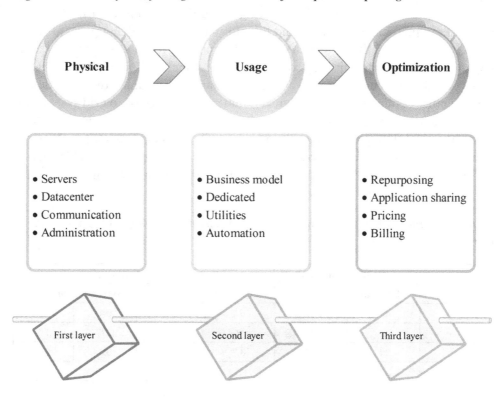

grid computing environment. Hence, they will be flexible and scalable so that the pricing and billing of resources are extremely challenging. This architecture consists of three layers: physical, usage, and optimization. The physical layer contains the most important data and components including servers, datacenter, communication, and administration. In the usage layer as the second layer of grid architecture, business model, dedicated, utilities, and automation are placed to accomplish the users' requests. Finally, the optimization layer offers some extra capabilities including repurposing, application sharing, pricing, and billing (Buyya & Venugopal, 2005; Beck, Schwind, & Hinz, 2008).

3.2 Grid Virtualization Engine

Users of the grid environments require for applying various technology-based capabilities whenever they use grid computing resources such as the qualities of service for resource provision as well as the performance isolation and customized runtime environment for grid applications. To obtain these capabilities, Grid Virtualization Engine (GVE) is presented in Wang, Von Laszewski, Tao, & Kunze (2009) to build a virtual machine provider for grid infrastructures base on Web services. The major objective of this engine is to create an abstract layer between underlying virtualization technologies and users. It, also, implements a scalable distributed architecture through a hierarchical structure. After grid infrastructures are built successfully, users can operate virtual machines via the Web service interfaces offered by GVE Site Service. Besides, the underlying GVE Agent Service is provided to deal with various virtualization products inside computing centers and offer different virtual machine resources to GVE Site Service. The presented engine is generally designed and implemented with distributed computing technologies including Web service and Grid standards.

Figure 8 shows the main components and architecture of the GVE framework. It is, generally, composed of GVE Site Service and GVE Agent Service. GVE Site Service is placed on the access point of a computer center that conducts host computing resources inside the center. It consists of GVE Web Service, User Information Service, and User Information Database. GVE Web Service is defined as the component which is responsible for the business task of GVE Site Service. It specifies the virtual machine requests which should be sent by GVE Agent Service and determines the policies of computing resource allocation. User Information Service stores the data that may be simultaneously applied by other components in the GVE. Finally, the management policies and accounting information of virtual machine usage are recorded in User Information Database. Besides, GVE Agent Service is designed as a Web Service to being executed on the host resource. It gets the defined operation commands from GVE Site Service and interacts with the specific virtual

Figure 8. Architecture of Grid Virtualization Engine

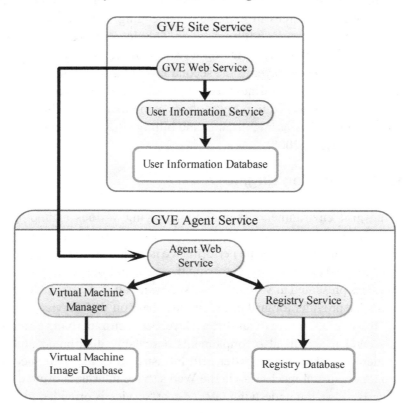

machine manager which is installed on the host resource. GVE Agent Service is, in fact, virtualization technology dependent. Consequently, a corresponding GVE Agent Service should be implemented for each type of the virtual machine manager. Registry Service operates like the User Information Service of GVE Site Service. It offers different functions to access Registry Database and stores the state of virtual machine managers (Wang, Von Laszewski, Tao, & Kunze, 2009).

3.3 Virtual Clusters for Grid Computing

The Cluster-on-Demand (COD) project is presented in Chase, Irwin, Grit, Moore, & Sprenkle (2003) to build an operating system for a large, shared, and mixed cluster. It enables the rapid and automated partitioning of a physical cluster into multiple independent virtual clusters (vclusters). Figure 9 depicts main elements of the COD framework. A site administrator determines the access ways to an external service interface for the COD area. This framework includes the Dynamic Host Configuration

Figure 9. The Cluster-on-Demand (COD) framework

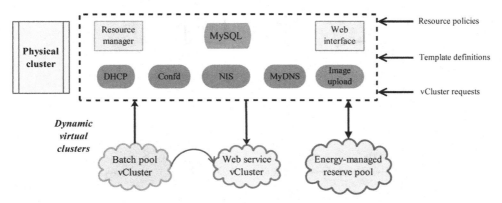

Protocol (DHCP) to manage and control the cluster nodes. It uses NIS and DNS to make each node possible to control its site based on the vCluster membership. MySQL is applied as a unifying back-end database to store node states and configurations by DHCP, DNS, and NIS servers. The COD site uses network boot, automatic configuration, and resource negotiation to carry out the defined virtual operations. Upon booting a node, the DHCP server requests its status from the database. The DHCP server loads a minimal operating system, including the x86 Linux kernel and small RAM-based root file system, to setup the user-defined software when the node is switching to a new configuration. The confd component partitions the local drives to fetch and install various software images. The MyDNS component maps between host names and Internet Protocol (IP) addresses. Afterwards, COD generates the NFS file storage volumes as groups and, also, vclusters are defined consequently. Nodes achieve an NFS amount map, which are authorized for access by the group via NIS.

3.4 Virtualization in In-VIGO

Figure 10 illustrates main elements of the In-VIGO framework. It adds three layers of virtualization technology to traditional grid-computing models. The first layer creates the pool of virtual computing resources that are, in fact, the primitive components of a virtual computing grid. It contains virtual machines, virtual applications, virtual data, and virtual networks. This layer dedicates the process of allocating applications to computing resources so that users' jobs are conducted across the administrative domains, physical machines, and local software configurations. That is, users' jobs are mapped to virtual computing resources (e.g., RedHat Linux 7.0 x86 virtual machines) in a way that just virtual resources are controlled and managed across

Figure 10. An overall view of the In-VIGO framework

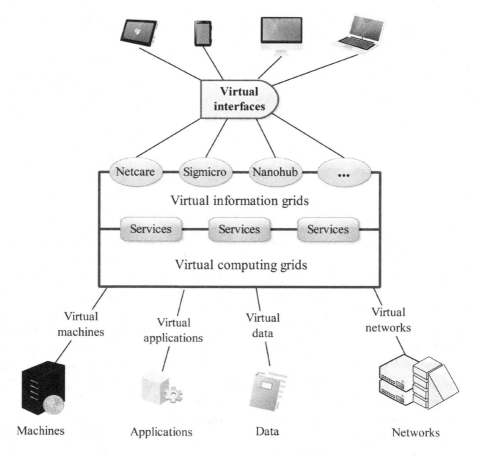

domains and physical environments (e.g., Win2000 physical systems at different locations). In the second layer, grid applications are placed as services for creating the virtual information grids. It separates the composition process of virtual services from the management process of the underlying grid applications. Various grid-computing mechanisms (e.g., Globus) can be applied to execute grid applications. However, their implementation phase is not often shown when grid applications are encapsulated and composed as services (e.g., using OGSI). The third layer exports the virtualized interfaces by using aggregated services (possibly presented to users via portals) to can be displayed by different access devices. It separates the creation process of services interfaces (e.g., XML and UIML) from the rendering process on various devices (e.g., HTML for laptop and WAP WML for a cell phone) (Adabala et al., 2005).

3.5 Evaluation Results of Virtualized Grid Systems

This subsection evaluates the simulation results of two virtualized grid systems. Table 3 represents evaluation results of the GVE network (Wang, Von Laszewski, Tao, & Kunze, 2009). The results are carried out based on the effect of memory size on system throughput. They indicate that performance rate of the GVE network is higher than that of the real network under various changes on memory sizes. While the memory size of computing resources increases, the performance of both networks enhances consequently. The reason is that a virtualized grid network can accomplish much more users' computing requests by increasing the hardware characteristics of computing resources.

Table 4 represents performance results of the COD network (Chase, Irwin, Grit, Moore, & Sprenkle, 2003) under three vclusters: Systems, Architecture, and BioGeometry. Moreover, performance of all the vclusters, namely Total, is considered too. The performance process is carried out based on priority allocation and minimum reservations when resources were limited to an extended period of time. The results indicate that Bio-Geometry involves the highest priority, Systems includes the next highest priority, and Architecture contains the lowest priority. Furthermore, the evaluation results of Total represent that number of nodes is nearly distributed as the same throughout the whole network in the range of [11, 14] days.

Table 3. Performance evaluation of the GVE network (Wang, Von Laszewski, Tao, & Kunze, 2009)

Memory Size (KB)	Throughput (MB/sec)	
	GVE Network	Real Network
1	1	2
2	3	4
4	3	4
8	12	16
16	15	19
32	18	22
64	28	33
128	48	51
256	63	67
512	66	69
1024	67	70

Table 4. Performance evaluation of the COD network (Chase, Irwin, Grit, Moore, & Sprenkle, 2003)

Time (Days)	Number of nodes			
	Systems	Architecture	BioGeometry	Total
10	5	0	63	70
11	8	12	55	80
12	20	15	48	77
13	20	15	47	80
14	8	8	68	79

4. VIRTUALIZATION TECHNOLOGY IN CLOUD SERVERS

The true, valuable, and economical contributor to cyber-infrastructure features are the key differentiating elements of a successful information technology. Cloud computing includes a service-oriented architecture, greater flexibility, decreased total cost of ownership, reduced information technology overhead for the end-user, on-demand computing services, and many other things. It is the next natural stage in the evolution of on-demand information technology services and products. Figure 11 shows the main characteristics of cloud computing. 'On-demand self-service' indicates that information technology is applied as service and is easily available on-demand without any need to manual intervention. 'Broad network access' represents that the cloud services are made available through a network independently of the users end devices. 'Resource pooling' contains the necessary computing resources, which is available to multiple consumers by using various technologies (e.g., virtualization technology). 'Rapid elasticity' represents that the computing resources can be essentially offered without manual intervention when no longer needed. Finally, 'measured service' indicates that the consumed computing service should be measurable in terms of the resources used (e.g., "pay as you go" and "pay-per-use") (Venters & Whitley, 2012; Gharajeh, 2015; Rittinghouse & Ransome, 2016). Similar to any computer network, virtualization technology can enhance the performance of cloud networks. This section describes the basic information and also various virtualization technologies in cloud servers: a sample architecture of cloud computing, types and roles of virtualization in cloud servers, from virtualization to private cloud services, and virtualization in high-performance IaaS cloud.

Figure 11. Cloud computing characteristics

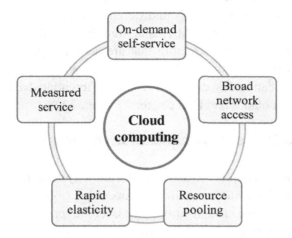

4.1 A Sample Architecture of Cloud Computing

A sample architecture of cloud computing is illustrated in Figure 12, which is implemented by Virtual Computing Laboratory. It can be available by users via a web portal or an API. Database keeps authentication, resource availability, various images, and other needed information. One or several management nodes manage and control the real and virtual resources. They can be placed within the same cloud or among different clouds in order to enable the extensive sharing of available

Figure 12. Cloud architecture of Virtual Computing Laboratory

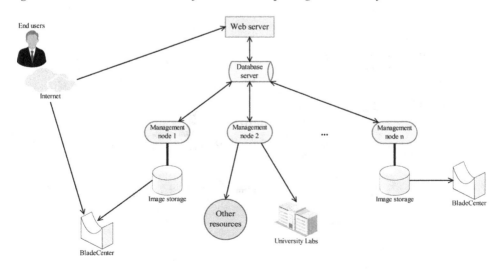

resources. End users can access to web server and desirable blades via the Internet. This architecture is implemented for undifferentiated resources of North Carolina State that contains about 1000 IBM BladeCenter blades. Teaching lab computers are the main services of this structure that are adopted into Virtual Computing Laboratory when they are not used by student (e.g., at night). It is worth to noting that this laboratory can be associated with other differentiated and undifferentiated resources (e.g., Sun blades and Dell clusters) (Vouk, 2008).

4.2 Types and Roles of Virtualization in Cloud Servers

As shown in Figure 13, types of virtualization technology in cloud servers are grouped into four categories: hardware virtualization, operating system virtualization, server virtualization, and storage virtualization. That is, cloud servers can be virtualized by these types like other computer networks. Hardware virtualization is carried out when virtual machine software or virtual machine manager is installed on the hardware system, directly. Since the control of virtual machines is much easier than the control of a physical server, this type can be applied for the server platforms. Operating system virtualization is resulted when virtual machine software or virtual machine manager is installed on the host operating system instead of the hardware system. It can be used to test various applications on different platforms. Server virtualization is made when virtual machine software or virtual machine manager is installed on the server system, directly. This type is managed on various cloud servers because a single physical server can be divided into multiple servers based on the needed

Figure 13. Virtualization types in cloud computing

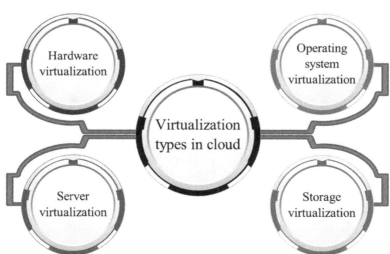

fundamentals. Finally, storage virtualization is carried out by grouping the physical storage derived from multiple network storage devices. It operates similar to a single storage device and can be implemented by software applications. A cloud server can uses one or more types of the above virtualization technologies to accomplish the users' computing services (Virtualization in cloud computing, 2017).

Server virtualization is one of virtualization roles in cloud servers. It is divided into three categories: full virtualization, para-virtualization, and OS-level virtualization. In full virtualization, hypervisor uses various components of physical cloud servers, directly. Furthermore, hypervisor does not expose all virtual servers to another operating on the same cloud server. In para-virtualization, all virtual servers have some information about each other. Hence, operating system of the virtual cloud server placed on physical cloud server is aware about needs of the other operating systems requested by the physical server. In OS-level virtualization, there is not any need to hypervisor to conduct the virtualized tasks. That is, physical operating system manages the defined roles of hypervisor along with virtualization capacity (Jain & Choudhary, 2016).

4.3 From Virtualization to Private Cloud Services

Figure 14 depicts five high-level steps and features of the virtualization to private cloud services. In Step 1, a cloud strategy is developed to establish where you want to go. The cloud strategy, obviously, specifies the benefits, procedures, and expected objectives for the technology-based investments across organizations.

Figure 14. The high-level steps of the virtualization to private cloud services

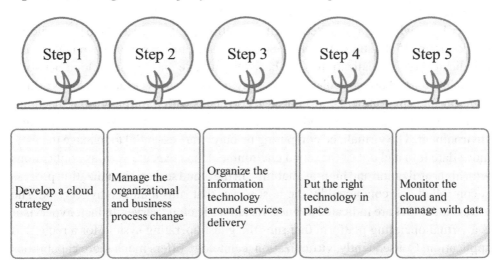

This step includes the high-level business case, implementation phases, workloads, cloud architecture, client devices, monitoring and management, and business relationships of information technology. In Step 2, the organizational and business process changes are managed to get the business on board. In order to success a cloud project, the organization should collaborate with process owners. This process leads the affected processes and tasks to be documented as well as the number of required human control points to be minimized, considerably. In Step 3, information technology around service delivery is organized via shifting the roles of information technology to a broker of cloud services. Since many users in large corporations are familiar with the concepts of information technology services, organization process of the information technology workforce around the cloud service delivery leads the business is effectively served as a cloud services broker. In Step 4, the right technology, in place, is put to set the short-term, medium-term, and long-term objectives. A cloud server cannot accurately work without using the right technology. Therefore, the technology priorities is required to set based on the implementation phases considered in the cloud strategy. In Step 5, the cloud is monitored and also managed with data by using the analytics processes to improve the defined operations. End-to-end health and efficiency monitoring of the environments are one of the requirements of cloud management. The information, which is needed to benefit from system efficiencies or measure success, cannot be accessible without using the data collection and analytics processes (Intel IT Center, 2013; Xing & Zhan, 2012).

4.4 Virtualization in High-performance IaaS Cloud

IaaS (Infrastructure as a Service) is the virtualized and multitenant infrastructure of cloud servers. It supports the private cloud and also validates various applications for business companies across the enterprise to share. A set of technologies build and deliver IaaS, which is initialized by virtualization technology as the basic building block. Figure 15 illustrates the elements of virtualization technology in IaaS cloud. It indicates that virtualization is the basis for an agile and scalable cloud network. Virtualization technology isolates the underlying hardware as virtual machines in their own runtime environments. Moreover, it correlates with multiple virtual machines for the computing, storage, and networking resources into an individual hosting environment. The virtualized computing resources are essential to manage the data, move data into and out of the cloud environment, and execute various applications with high-utilization and high-availability. In the cloud server, virtualization process is controlled and conducted by the host server that runs a unique hypervisor. The virtual machines are indicated as guest machines in cloud server. In fact, hypervisor is a virtual operating platform that runs the guest operating system for a requested application. Consequently, virtualization technology offers much more capabilities

Figure 15. Architecture of the high-performance IaaS cloud for virtualization technology

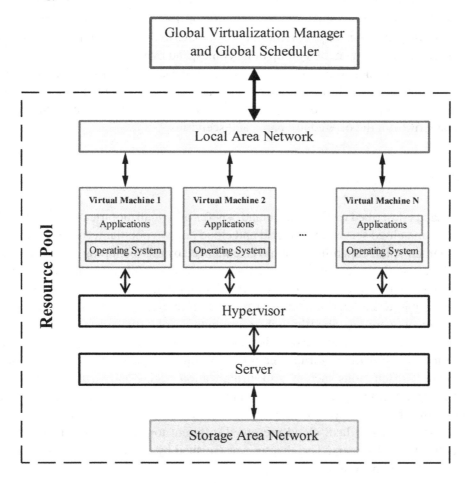

for cloud servers such as resource sharing, virtual machine isolation, and load balancing. These capabilities lead the scalability and utilization to be enhanced noticeably (Intel IT Center, 2013).

5. GRID VIRTUALIZATION INTO CLOUD ENVIRONMENT

Grid infrastructure can be virtualized by cloud resources to conduct various scientific applications (Loomis, 2010; Raboso et al., 2011). The StratusLab project (Loomis, 2010) builds a private cloud distribution to deploy grid services over virtualized cloud resources. This process is carried out to enable scientists for exploiting the e-infrastructures through a cloud-based interface. The project is created by multiple use cases and scenarios including grid services on the cloud, customized environments for virtual organizations, customized environments for users, sharing of dataset and machine images, provision of common appliances, virtual organization/user services on the cloud, deployment of a group of machines, and hybrid infrastructures. These use cases are developed by the project's partners based on their experiences with some of the existing e-infrastructures. Scientists, software scientists & engineers, community service administrators, system administrators, and hardware technicians will benefit from the offered use cases and scenarios.

6. CONCLUSION

This chapter described various aspects and benefits of virtualization technology in grid systems and cloud servers. Since grid and cloud are two popular terms in the cyber environment, their capabilities should be enhanced by this technology to serve their users' requested services efficiently. The chapter has been begun by introducing the network virtualization, virtualized projects of computing systems, and virtualization technology in teaching. Afterward, virtualization in high-performance computing environments were described through a representation of virtual machine abstraction, comparison between virtualized environments, and an efficient framework for high-performance computing. Various features of virtualized grid systems are provided by multiple discussions such as grid virtualization engine and virtual clusters for grid computing. Besides, various types and roles of virtualization in cloud servers, relationship between virtualization and private cloud services, and virtualization in high-performance IaaS cloud presented different topics and challenges of the virtualized cloud servers. The chapter was finished by a glance on using the grid virtualization into cloud servers.

Performance of virtualization methods in grid systems was evaluated on the Native, Xen, KVM, and VirtualBox hypervisors in terms of bandwidth and latency. Furthermore, evaluation results of the cloud servers were considered based on simulation results of the COD network under three different vclusters.

REFERENCES

Adabala, S., Chadha, V., Chawla, P., Figueiredo, R., Fortes, J., Krsul, I., & Zhao, M. et al. (2005). From virtualized resources to virtual computing grids: The In-VIGO system. *Future Generation Computer Systems*, *21*(6), 896–909. doi:10.1016/j. future.2003.12.021

Anderson, T., Peterson, L., Shenker, S., & Turner, J. (2005). Overcoming the Internet impasse through virtualization. *Computer*, *38*(4), 34–41. doi:10.1109/MC.2005.136

Armstrong, R., Gannon, D., Geist, A., Keahey, K., Kohn, S., McInnes, L., & Smolinski, B. et al. (1999). Toward a common component architecture for high-performance scientific computing. *Proceedings of The Eighth International Symposium on High Performance Distributed Computing,* Redondo Beach, California, USA (pp. 115-124). doi:10.1109/HPDC.1999.805289

Beck, R., Schwind, M., & Hinz, O. (2008). Grid economics in departmentalized enterprises. *Journal of Grid Computing*, *6*(3), 277–290. doi:10.1007/s10723-008-9102-3

Binge, C., Kaiyuan, Q., & Weilong, D. (2007). GridDoc: A End-User-Oriented Presentation Model for Resource Integration. *Proceedings of the IEEE Sixth International Conference on Grid and Cooperative Computing (GCC '07),* Urumchi, Xinjiang, China (pp. 261-266). doi:10.1109/GCC.2007.74

Brunthaler, S. (2009). Virtual-Machine abstraction and optimization techniques. *Electronic Notes in Theoretical Computer Science*, *253*(5), 3–14. doi:10.1016/j.entcs.2009.11.011

Buyya, R., & Venugopal, S. (2005). A gentle introduction to grid computing and technologies. *CSI Communications*, *29*(1), 9–19.

Chase, J. S., Irwin, D. E., Grit, L. E., Moore, J. D., & Sprenkle, S. E. (2003). Dynamic virtual clusters in a grid site manager. *Proceedings of the 12th IEEE International Symposium on High Performance Distributed Computing,* Seattle, WA, USA (pp. 90-100). doi:10.1109/HPDC.2003.1210019

Chen, M., Zhang, Y., Hu, L., Taleb, T., & Sheng, Z. (2015). Cloud-based wireless network: Virtualized, reconfigurable, smart wireless network to enable 5G technologies. *Mobile Networks and Applications*, *20*(6), 704–712. doi:10.1007/s11036-015-0590-7

Chowdhury, N. M. M. K., & Boutaba, R. (2009). Network virtualization: State of the art and research challenges. *IEEE Communications Magazine*, *47*(7), 20–26. doi:10.1109/MCOM.2009.5183468

Chowdhury, N. M. M. K., & Boutaba, R. (2010). A survey of network virtualization. *Computer Networks*, *54*(5), 862–876. doi:10.1016/j.comnet.2009.10.017

Di Costanzo, A., De Assuncao, M. D., & Buyya, R. (2009). Harnessing cloud technologies for a virtualized distributed computing infrastructure. *IEEE Internet Computing*, *13*(5), 24–33. doi:10.1109/MIC.2009.108

Dobrilovic, D., & Odadžic, B. (2008). Virtualization technology as a tool for teaching computer networks. *International Journal of Social, Behavioral, Educational, Economic, Business and Industrial Engineering*, *2*(1), 41–45.

Egwutuoha, I. P., Levy, D., Selic, B., & Chen, S. (2013). A survey of fault tolerance mechanisms and checkpoint/restart implementations for high performance computing systems. *The Journal of Supercomputing*, *65*(3), 1302–1326. doi:10.1007/s11227-013-0884-0

Foster, I., Kesselman, C., Nick, J. M., & Tuecke, S. (2002). Grid services for distributed system integration. *Computer*, *35*(6), 37–46. doi:10.1109/MC.2002.1009167

Fuertes, W., De Vergara, J. E. L., & Meneses, F. (2009). Educational platform using virtualization technologies: Teaching-learning applications and research uses cases. *Proc. II ACE Seminar: Knowledge Construction in Online Collaborative Communities* (Vol. 16).

Galán, F., Fernández, D., Ruiz, J., Walid, O., & de Miguel, T. (2004). Use of virtualization tools in computer network laboratories. *Proceedings of the Fifth International Conference on Information Technology Based Higher Education and Training (ITHET)*, Istanbul, Turkey (pp. 209-214). doi:10.1109/ITHET.2004.1358165

Gharajeh, M. S. (2015). *The Significant Concepts of Cloud Computing: Technology, Architecture, Applications, and Security*. Seattle: CreateSpace Independent Publishing Platform.

Han, B., Gopalakrishnan, V., Ji, L., & Lee, S. (2015). Network function virtualization: Challenges and opportunities for innovations. *IEEE Communications Magazine*, *53*(2), 90–97. doi:10.1109/MCOM.2015.7045396

Huang, W., Liu, J., Abali, B., & Panda, D. K. (2006). A case for high performance computing with virtual machines. *Proceedings of the 20th annual international conference on Supercomputing (ICS '06)*, Cairns, Queensland, Australia (pp. 125-134). doi:10.1145/1183401.1183421

Intel, I. T. Center. (2013). *Virtualization and Cloud Computing*, pp. 1-23. Retrieved January 24, 2017, from http://www.intel.com/content/dam/www/public/us/en/documents/guides/cloud-computing-virtualization-building-private-iaas-guide.pdf

Jain, N., & Choudhary, S. (2016). Overview of virtualization in cloud computing. *Proceedings of the IEEE Symposium on Colossal Data Analysis and Networking (CDAN),* Indore, Madhya Pradesh, India (pp. 1-4).

Jarząb, M., Kosiński, J., Zieliński, K., & Zieliński, S. (2012). User-oriented provisioning of secure virtualized infrastructure. In M. Bubak, T. Szepieniec, & K. Wiatr (Eds.), *Building a national distributed e-infrastructure–PL-Grid* (pp. 73–88). Berlin: Springer. doi:10.1007/978-3-642-28267-6_6

Javatpoint.com. (2017). Virtualization in cloud computing. Retrieved January 14, 2017, from http://www.javatpoint.com/virtualization-in-cloud-computing

Jin, H., & Liao, X. F. (2008). Virtualization technology for computing system. *China Basic Science, 10*(6), 12–18.

Kim, J., & Forsythe, S. (2010). Factors affecting adoption of product virtualization technology for online consumer electronics shopping. *International Journal of Retail & Distribution Management, 38*(3), 190–204. doi:10.1108/09590551011027122

Li, J., Jia, Y., Liu, L., & Wo, T. (2013). CyberLiveApp: A secure sharing and migration approach for live virtual desktop applications in a cloud environment. *Future Generation Computer Systems, 29*(1), 330–340. doi:10.1016/j.future.2011.08.001

Liang, C., & Yu, F. R. (2015). Wireless network virtualization: A survey, some research issues and challenges. *IEEE Communications Surveys and Tutorials, 17*(1), 358–380. doi:10.1109/COMST.2014.2352118

Loomis, C. (2010). *Review of the Use of Cloud and Virtualization Technologies in Grid Infrastructures, HAL-IN2P3.* Retrieved February 15, 2017, from http://hal.in2p3.fr/docs/00/68/71/59/PDF/stratuslab-d2.1-v1.2.pdf

Martignoni, L., Paleari, R., Fresi Roglia, G., & Bruschi, D. (2010). Testing system virtual machines. *Proceedings of the 19th international symposium on Software testing and analysis (ISSTA '10),* Trento, Italy (pp. 171-182).

Raboso, M., del Val, L., Jiménez, M. I., Izquierdo, A., Villacorta, J. J., & José, A. (2011). Virtualizing Grid Computing Infrastructures into the Cloud. In A. Abraham, J. M. Corchado, S. R. González, & J. F. De Paz Santana (Eds.), *International Symposium on Distributed Computing and Artificial Intelligence* (pp. 159-166). Berlin: Springer. doi:10.1007/978-3-642-19934-9_20

Rittinghouse, J. W., & Ransome, J. F. (2016). *Cloud computing: implementation, management, and security.* NY: CRC press.

Sahoo, J., Mohapatra, S., & Lath, R. (2010). Virtualization: A survey on concepts, taxonomy and associated security issues. *Proceedings of IEEE Second International Conference on Computer and Network Technology (ICCNT)* Bangkok, Thailand (pp. 222-226). doi:10.1109/ICCNT.2010.49

Soltesz, S., Pötzl, H., Fiuczynski, M. E., Bavier, A., & Peterson, L. (2007). Container-based operating system virtualization: A scalable, high-performance alternative to hypervisors. *Operating Systems Review*, *41*(3), 275–287. doi:10.1145/1272998.1273025

Uhlig, R., Neiger, G., Rodgers, D., Santoni, A. L., Martins, F. C. M., Anderson, A. V., & Smith, L. et al. (2005). Intel virtualization technology. *Computer*, *38*(5), 48–56. doi:10.1109/MC.2005.163

Venters, W., & Whitley, E. A. (2012). A critical review of cloud computing: Researching desires and realities. *Journal of Information Technology*, *27*(3), 179–197. doi:10.1057/jit.2012.17

Vouk, M. A. (2008). Cloud computing–issues, research and implementations. *Journal of Computing and Information Technology, 16*(4), 235-246.

Wang, A., Iyer, M., Dutta, R., Rouskas, G. N., & Baldine, I. (2013). Network virtualization: Technologies, perspectives, and frontiers. *Journal of Lightwave Technology*, *31*(4), 523–537. doi:10.1109/JLT.2012.2213796

Wang, L., Von Laszewski, G., Chen, D., Tao, J., & Kunze, M. (2010). Provide virtual machine information for grid computing. *IEEE Transactions on Systems, Man, and Cybernetics. Part A, Systems and Humans*, *40*(6), 1362–1374. doi:10.1109/TSMCA.2010.2052598

Wang, L., Von Laszewski, G., Tao, J., & Kunze, M. (2009). Grid virtualization engine: Design, implementation, and evaluation. *IEEE Systems Journal*, *3*(4), 477–488. doi:10.1109/JSYST.2009.2028589

Xing, Y., & Zhan, Y. (2012). Virtualization and cloud computing. In Y. Zhang (Ed.), *Future Wireless Networks and Information Systems* (pp. 305–312). Berlin: Springer. doi:10.1007/978-3-642-27323-0_39

Younge, A. J., Henschel, R., Brown, J. T., Von Laszewski, G., Qiu, J., & Fox, G. C. (2011). Analysis of virtualization technologies for high performance computing environments. *Proceedings of the IEEE 4th International Conference on Cloud Computing (CLOUD)* (pp. 9-16). Washington, DC, USA. doi:10.1109/CLOUD.2011.29

Chapter 2
Application of Virtualization Technology in IaaS Cloud Deployment Model

Ganesh Chandra Deka
Government of India, India

Prashanta Kumar Das
Government Industrial Training Institute Dhansiri, India

ABSTRACT

Virtualization is an old proven technology used for effective utilization of Servers, Storage, and Network for reducing IT expenses without compromising the efficiency and agility for all size businesses. The area of application of Virtualization is very diverse such as e-Learning, Social Networking, and Simulation are a few to be mentioned. This chapter focuses on different virtualization approaches, benefits, architecture of different open source and commercial Virtual Machine Manager (VMM) and Virtual Machines (VM) migration techniques. All the technical terms appearing in this chapter is either defined wherever they appear or explained in the Key Terms and Definitions section of the chapter. The hardware requirements of all the hypervisiors are discussed for hassle free implementation and smooth reading of the chapter.

1. INTRODUCTION

Virtualization technology was developed by IBM Corporation by creating several Virtual Machines (VMs) on a single physical mainframe computer. The terminology

DOI: 10.4018/978-1-5225-2785-5.ch002

virtualization was introduced by 1960 (R. J. Adair, R. U. Bayles, L. W. Comeau, R. J. Creasy (1966)). During those days only single application could be executed in a computer at a time. To overcome this problem the time-sharing technique was introduced to rum several applications simultaneously for effective utilization of computing resources. One major disadvantage of time-sharing approach was the isolation of applications running. Furthermore, in the event of an application develops a hardware error all the applications running was affected. To isolate the application running on a single machine, virtualization technology was introduced (Deka, G. C., & Das, P. K. (2014)).

The creation and management of VMs have been referred to as platform or server virtualization (R. P. Goldberg (1974)). A virtualization system separates the OS from the underlying platform resources. Generally, lots of VMs run on a physical machine; limited by the number of cores, processing power of the CPU and capacity of physical memory (RAM). The Guest OS need not to be in the host machine. The guest systems are capable of accessing hardware devices such as a printer, hard disk drive, network interface card, graphic and audio card and exploiting the interfaces of these devices.

VMM partitions the physical servers into multiple VMs. Multiple VMs can share a single physical server simultaneously from various locations. Each VM represents a complete computing environment with a Processor, Random Access Memory (RAM), Virtual devices, etc.. The OS and other software of the VM does not change after the execution at the remote server.

1.1 Chronology of Virtualization: (Ramses Soto-Navarro, RHCE, 2012)

- 1968: IBM CP-67/CMS for System360 (mainframe).
- 1972: IBM VM/370 (mainframe).
- 1977: IBM OpenVMS (mainframe).
- 1980: PC, Client-server, Distributed computing.
- 1997: Apple Virtual PC for (Macintosh).
- 1998: VMware Technical Patent.
- 1999: VMware Virtual Platform (IA-32, x86).
- 2000: FreeBSD jails.
- 2000: IBM z/VM (mainframe).
- 2001: VMware ESX, VMware Workstation.
- 2003: Xen.
- 2004: Solaris Containers.
- 2004: Microsoft VirtualPC (aquired from Apple), MS Virtual Server.
- 2005: VMware Player.

- 2005: Solaris Zones.
- 2005: HP Integrity Virtual Machines.
- 2006: VMware Server.
- 2006: QEMU.
- 2007: Sun Virtualbox (qemu-based).
- 2007: Linux KVM.
- 2007: Citrix XenSource (Xen-based).
- 2008: Microsoft Hyper-V (Xen-based).

2. VIRTUALIZATION APPROACHES

Virtualization follows various approaches related to the architecture of the VMM/ Hypervisor. In the Hosted Virtualization architecture, the VMM runs as an application on the Host and relies on the resource of the host OS such as Memory, Hardware devices and various drivers/libraries. VMM Starts, Stops and Manage each VM and Controls Access of VMs to the system resources (Hardware and Software). VMware Workstation follows this approach.

The Autonomous Architecture of Virtualization places the VMM directly above the hardware, making it responsible for allocation of system resources such as CPU, RAM and Hard disk etc. to each VM.

The guest OS runs with limited privileges and do not have direct access to hardware. As a result, it is difficult to virtualize some of the critical OS (System Commands) instructions because their implementation requires higher privileges.

2.1 x86 Virtualization

The term x86 refers to the 32-bit architecture and equivalent products from Intel and AMD that be present in that period. It particularly does not include the later extensions that provided 64-bit support (Intel IA32-E and AMD x86-64) or hardware support for virtualization (Intel VT-x and AMD-v). X86 Virtualization facilitates sharing of multiple operating systems simultaneously x86 processor resources in a safe and efficient manner generically known as hardware Virtualization. During 1990 x86 became the prominent server platform. During that time x86 Virtualization was achieved through complex software techniques to overcome the lack of Virtualization support for enhancing performance. However, in 2006 both Intel and AMD added processor (CPU) hardware support making Virtualization simpler (Wikimedia Foundation, Inc., 2014).

Intel 64 instruction set is the superset of IA32 (x86) instruction set. All the instructions of x86 instruction could be executed by Intel 64-bit CPUs. Thus, CPUs will natively run programs that run on x86 CPUs from Intel, AMD (AMD64 / x86_64) (Wikimedia Foundation, Inc., 2014).

The following are the three existing alternative techniques for handling sensitive and privileged instructions for Virtualization of x86 CPU architecture:

1. Full Virtualization uses Binary Translation
2. Paravirtualization or OS Assisted Virtualization
3. Hardware Assisted Virtualization *aka* Accelerated Virtualization (in *Xen* it is known as Hardware Virtual Machine (HVM))

The x86 is easier to virtualize due to:

- Built in security levels build within the x86 architecture known as rings
- The x86 Virtualization architecture is having four levels of privilege to OSs i.e.:
  - Ring "0"
  - Ring "1"
  - Ring "2"
  - Ring "3"

Most systems have the OS running in the most privileged ring i.e. Ring 0. User software runs in ring 3. Ring 1 and Ring 2 are generally not used. Xen utilizes Ring 1 to modify the OS to execute on ring 1.

These levels and application manage access to computer hardware. The user level applications usually run in Ring 3. The OS requires having direct access to memory and hardware and hence runs the privileged instructions of Ring 0. Ring 0 is associated with the kernel code (Xen, 2009).

2.2 Full Virtualization

Full virtualization simulates sufficient hardware to VMs. Full virtualization completely abstracts the guest OS from the underlying hardware. In Full Virtualization guest OS are not aware that they are being virtualized and require no modification.

Isolation, security for VMs and simple procedures for migration are some of the interesting features of Full virtualization. There is possibility that, the same VM can run virtualized or on native hardware. While the virtualization layer is executed at the application level, the ring problem is solved with the Binary Rewriting technique. The flow of the binary instructions performed by the VMs is inspected by the VMM and the privileged instructions are conveniently translated. The Binary Rewriting technique is computationally highly expensive. Recent full virtualization products

Figure 1. Full Virtualization

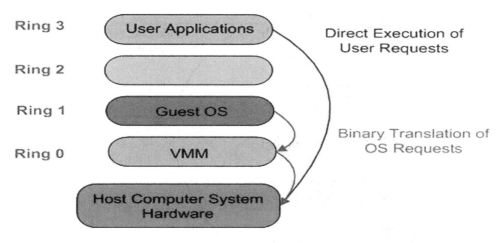

include *Parallels* (GmbH, 1999), *VirtualBox* ("Oracle VM VirtualBox," n.d.), *Hyper-V*, *VMware*, *QEMU*.

2.3 Paravirtualization

In a paravirtualized architecture, a light software layer (Hypervisor) runs directly over the hardware. The Hypervisor is able to allocate the resources needed by the VMs. A privileged *OS* instance runs over the Hypervisor in order to manage all the active VMs. Paravirtualization enables running of isolated and secure virtualized servers on a single *Host*. A paravirtualized system provides a low virtualization overhead. The advantage of paravirtualization over full virtualization can vary depending on the workload. The host and guest OSs are to be modified for replacing the privilege of Hypervisor calls (hypercalls). While the Hypervisor is executed at ring level 0, the guest OS executes at level 1. Since paravirtualization does not support unmodified OSs (e.g. Windows), its compatibility and portability is limited. Examples of paravirtualization systems are XEN (Posted & Kurth, 2013) and VMware Infrastructure (VMware, 2016).

2.4 Hardware Assisted Virtualization

In hardware assisted virtualization technique, the hypervisor/*VMM* creates VM by emulating a complete hardware environment. The OS loaded into a VM may be standard or unmodified. The hardware emulation software executes the *System Call* and sends the operating data structures provided by the *VMM* to *VM*s.

Figure 2. Paravirtualization

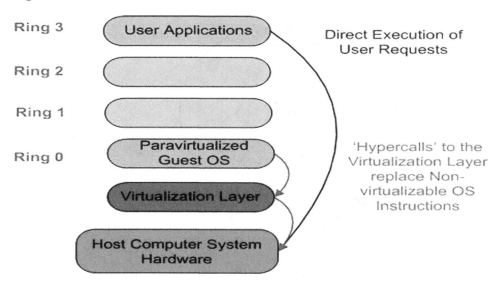

When the *VM* is in *running* state, the hardware emulated VMM changes a part of the host OS. The OS directly interacts with system hardware. The VMM translates the native binary format of the OS to the *VMM* within the areas of the OS that makes calls to hardware resources. Windows and Linux *VM*s support Hardware emulation technique.

Binary translation takes place in parts of the OS that interacts with the following resources:

1. Processor
2. Memory
3. Network, and
4. Storage

The *VMM* replaces sections of OS code, such as network device drivers, with code that interacts with the emulated hardware layer such as virtualized motherboard, within the *VMM*. The *VMM* then forwards the calls from the emulated hardware to the actual physical hardware on the Host (Server Computer).

Hardware emulation is implemented by VMware. VMware's VMware Server is installed *atop an existing OS* (Windows or one of flavors of Linux), whereas its ESX Server implements *bare-metal hardware* emulation.

Hardware vendors quickly enforced the virtualization and developed new options to create easier virtualization techniques. The 1st generation implementation consists of Intel Virtualization Technology (VT-x) and AMD's AMD-V that targets privileged instructions with a brand new CPU execution mode feature that enables the VMM to run during a new root node below ring zero. As shown in the figure below, privileged and sensitive calls are set to mechanically trap to the hypervisor, removing the requirement for either binary translation or paravirtualization. The status of a guest stored on in Virtual Machine Control Structures (VT-x) or Virtual Machine Control Blocks (AMD-V). Processors with Intel VT and AMD-V technology became available in 2006; hence tin the newer systems, these features is included as hardware assist options (VMware, Inc., 2007).

2.5 Types of Virtualization

In this section various types of Virtualization techniques will be discussed.

2.5.1 Operating System Virtualization

OS Virtualization permits installation of various types of OS such as Linux / Windows 7 as a guest OS, in addition to the existing *Host OS*. The *VMM* manages multiple OS running concurrently on the *Host*.

Figure 3. Hardware Assisted Virtualization

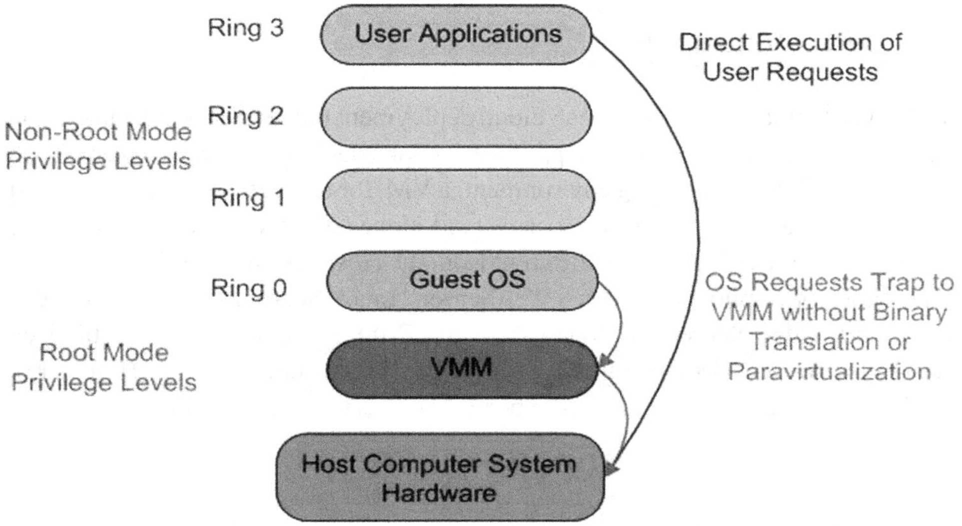

Advantage of *OS* virtualization:

- Enhanced Efficiency of hardware and software resources.
- Cost saving in terms of CapEX and OpEx.
- Optimum utilization of resources (hardware & Software).

OS virtualization is suitable where heterogeneous computing environments are required with minimum investment. Some of the software vendors offering *OS* virtualization solutions are:

- Solaris from Sun Microsystems.
- *OS* Virtualization solution from *Virtuozzo* (https://virtuozzo.com/products/virtuozzo-hypervisor/)

OS virtualization is beneficial for:

- Data Center.
- Web hosting.

The three existing forms of Virtualization are:

- Server
- Storage
- Network

2.5.2 Server Virtualization

The Server Virtualization is the IaaS cloud deployment model. Server virtualization is performed on a given hardware platform by introducing a software layer, which creates a simulated computing environment, a VM, for its guest software. The guest software runs as if it were installed on a stand-alone computer. The guest software is in many cases a complete *OS*, different from the *Host* OS. Most of the use cases a combination of Application Servers, Web Servers, Image Servers, Document Servers, Audio and Video Servers, Database Servers, Print Servers, etc. are Virtualized through the Server Virtualization in a single physical machine (Server Hardware).

The following are the some of the benefits of Server Virtualization:

- Cost reduction (CapEx and OppEx)
- Greater stability and higher availability
- Greater fault tolerance and faster Disaster recovery
- Portability in terms of server types and OS.

2.5.3 Storage Virtualization

Storage Virtualization is used to provide virtual storage with advanced data protection features. The virtual storage space is offered by either through SAN (Storage Area Network) or NAS (Network Attached Storage). The benefits of storage virtualization are:

- Easy replication of data for faster access and disaster recovery.
- Smooth storage migration.

Types of Storage Virtualization

- **Block Virtualization:** Is the abstraction of logical storage from physical storage for easy access of storage irrespective of storage structure (physical / logical). Advantage of Block virtualization is greater flexibility in managing storage for end users.
- **File Virtualization:** File virtualization facilitates optimization of storage usage and server consolidation for non-disruptive file migrations.

2.5.4 Network Virtualization

Network Virtualization is the most commonly implemented form of scalable Virtualization. In this approach the Virtualization functionalities are implemented within the network hosts and nodes. Network Virtualization potentially reduces the amount of physical space that an organization needs for hardware. The Virtual LAN (VLAN) is a Network Virtualization technique wherein two or more virtual networks can be created within the same physical network using the same IP addresses without requiring the authorization to communicate with each other. The VLAN will be operating in their own logical network having different set of processes and functions to perform.

The following are some of the popular Virtualization computing environment deployment techniques (Arunkumar Jayaraman, Pavankumar Rayapudi, (2012)).

Table 1. Virtualization Techniques

Virtualization Technique	Features
Hosted Virtualization	• VM is a replica of the **Host** machine • The **Host** and the VMs will be sharing the same system resources such as RAM, OS, processor (CPU), Storage etc.
Paravirtualization	• OS assisted Virtualization, hence does not support the OS not permitting modification of source code. • Compatibility and portability are poor. • Performance varies significantly with workload (Fanatical, n.d.)
Desktop Virtualization	• Creates a Virtualized desktop environment accessible from remote locations through the Internet. • Does not require a compatible system or any other hardware resources on the client side • Centralized IT management • Cost effective since no PC maintenance • Easy update service packs, OS patches.
Host Virtualization	• Client host connects to the server VMs through personalized desktop/random desktop assignment method. • The Client connects to the data center through remote connection using the client host login into the hosted VMs. • Provides greater security for data • Management of VMs is easy compared to traditional desktop Virtualization
Client Virtualization	• OS is working on the portable device so that the device can be carried and run on a system on a single host. • Similar to the complete Virtualization method • Greater security for data • Ease to manage the network • Reliability of data • Easy to monitor client's activity
Memory Virtualization	• Uses Virtualized memory to run applications. • Each VM share and map its memory without conflicting • An application accessing huge amounts of memory space to enhance the performance of the application accordingly
Data Virtualization	• A collection of different data storages from different places. • Provides a logical structure like a front-end application • Abstract dissimilar data sources through a single data access layer • Easily portable and easy to manage the database • Access data without interruption
Storage Virtualization	• Encapsulate a collection of storages as a single storage unit/device. • Easy to manage since storage is dynamically allocated • Facilitates addition of storage as per requirements without changing the network configuration • Two categories of Storage Virtualization are ✓ File level ✓ Block level
Network based Virtualization	• Combines entire network into a single mode and allocates its bandwidth, channels and other resources according to workloads. • Easy overall network management • Scalability to groups inside the network • Enhances the security to all devices in the network. The network Virtualization functionalities are implemented by the following scalable network Virtualization techniques i.e.: • Switches based (router) • Appliances based (servers) Actual Virtualization occurs in intelligent switch in a switch based network Virtualization. In case of appliance based network Virtualization I/O flows through an appliance which controls the Virtualization layer in an appliance based approach ("Hyper-V," 2016). Both these techniques are capable of providing the same service like Disk management, Metadata (data that is used to describe other data) lookup, Data migration and Replication.

3. BENEFITS OF VIRTUALIZATION

Lots of big organizations are implementing Virtualization technology leading to availability of a huge pool of qualified Virtualization professionals. Virtualization consolidates the Servers, isolates process beneficial for disaster recovery. Some of the features of Virtualization are discussed in details in this section.

3.1 Hardware Reusability

Virtualization ensures the efficient utilization of hardware resources in an organization. The efficient utilization of hardware reduces the necessity to buy of new hardware.

To allocate hardware for each server or application is not only time consuming, but also involves huge amount of investment for companies. Maintaining the hardware resource is another liability for the organization.

Virtualization technology consolidates the hardware resources to maximized performance (R. Uhlig, 2005).

3.2 Cost Reduction

Virtualization separates servers and applications from the hardware. It uses the server on pool for all services (A. A. Semnanian, J. Pham, B. Englert, and X. Wu, 2011) resulting in reduction of IT investment. Virtualization is the way to use a variety of **OS**s, Application, Storage and Servers at very nominal cost (C. Waltzing and S. Delgado, 2009).

3.3 Disaster Recovery

For recovering the information is a big challenge during the disaster situation such as natural calamities/Server crash. After a disaster occurs, the recovery process mainly depends on the backup from the existing back Server or Virtual server. In this scenario, Virtualization quickly copies the existing image from the servers with less downtime (T. Adeshiyan).

Double-Take protection software used in the VMware environment offers IT infrastructure protection, move and recover options. Double-Take technique provides security to existing recovery method; improve the data security and loss with less impact on down time. The Double-Take service constantly monitors the primary data. In the event of failover, Double-Take automatically switches to secondary real time backup servers for smooth functioning of services during unfavorable situation. The end-user services are not interrupted during the recovery (Inc, 2016).

3.4 Virtualized Storage Recovery

Protecting the VMs stored on virtual disks is a big challenge of Virtualization. Two types of storage techniques are used to restore the VMs in a virtual computing environment i.e.

1. Virtual disks
2. Raw disks

The Virtual disk is a group of related disk files stored on the Server/Host. The virtual disks encapsulate the VM's data on the Host, providing the benefits of Autonomy, but complexity in Protection.

The Raw disk storage method allows access a physical partition of the hard disk on the Host directly to store the VM's data to the VMs.

3.5 Server Migration

Virtualization allows migration of servers from one remote site to another, virtually without any downtime. When the server load amplifies during the time of peak load/ growing load the data center manager can move the running VMs from one server to another high capacity server or add more CPU cores to enhance the processing capability of VMs/Server.

3.6 Power Consumption

Largest and most inefficient consumer of power in the datacenter is Computer Room Air Conditioning (CRAC) systems. More than 50% of the power in the datacenter goes to cooling. Virtual network infrastructure makes organization energy efficient (G. Khanna, K. Beaty, G. Kar, and A. Kochut, 2006). The impact of various energy saving technologies on in a datacenter Virtualization is shown in (DOS FDCCI Plan) in Table 2 (Deka, G.C. 2014).

4. CHALLENGES IN VIRTUALIZATION

Virtualization is rapidly replacing physical computing infrastructures for their abilities to emulate hardware environments, share hardware resources and utilizes variety of operating systems (OS). However, there are some of the issues of Virtualization.

Table 2. Energy saving Technology in the datacenter (Source: dot net developer's Journal)

Technology	Saving
Server Virtualization	40%
Power efficient server	20%
Facilities Infrastructure such as Computer Room AC, Power Distribution Unit etc.	7%
Storage system	6%
Network Equipment	5%
Data Storage Management technique	5%
Server/ PC power management software	4%
Alternative/Renewable energy	4%
Tiered storage	4%
Others	5%

4.1 Security Issues

The VMs on the same Host (physical hardware) in isolation from each other. The VMs or the guest OS can run diverse applications without conflicting with each other or the host. The Host should guarantee that the VMs secure from threats. If the Host security fails, all VMs hosted on the physical server are at high risk. The security of the VMs is based on the network infrastructure (M. Pedram and I. Hwang, 2010).

The Virtual LAN (VLAN) are multiples virtual LANs in a single physical LAN. The failure of a VM in a LAN does not affect the operations other VMs on the same LAN but *Physical Network* fails, it will affect all the VMs hosted on the VLAN.

4.2 Physical Machine Failure

Failure of server shutdown of all the services offered from a physical server (M. Rosenblum and T. Garfinkel, 2005).

4.3 Input/Output Request

All I/O related commands need to be accessed through host machine. The I/O service commands executed uses the host resources. If a VM needs to perform any read or write operation, this command is executed through host device. The server level I/O accessing speed should be high in order to achieve better performance (J.

Kirkland, D. Carmichael, C. L. Tinker, and G. L. Tinker, 2006) (M. Rosenblum and T. Garfinkel, 2005).

4.4 Mostly Used Virtualization Software

There is lots of Virtualization Software coming from various software vendors. The following tables introduce some of the most used Virtualization Software.

5. INTRODUCTION TO VM

VMM/ hypervisor has been used on IBM mainframes since the 1970s. The virtual machines (VM) are controlled by the VMM. VMM monitor activities between OS and the hardware. A VMM can boot in few seconds, Coexists with VMs/other OS on a Host machine (Betonio, 2011). VMMs manages the guest OS running on the VM, their Storage space, RAM and other resources. The OS on the physical machine is called host OS. VMMs support multiple OS environments; isolate unreliable software such as Peer-to-peer applications. In a corporate environment, VMMs are often used on desktops to permit the use of legacy custom software based on Windows 95 alongside with modern office software based on XP/Vista/Win7.

Two types of hypervisors are Type 1 and Type 2 (Y. Chubachi, T. Shinagawa, and K. Kato)

- **Type-1 Hypervisor:** Is also known as a bare metal hypervisor or Native hypervisor. Different types of OS can run in Type-1 hypervisor irrespective of the OSs on the host machine, hence portability is achieved.
- **Type 2 Hypervisor or Hosted Hypervisor:** Is connected between the guest OS and the real machine. Type 2 hypervisor performs better than type 1 hypervisor, since VMs are coupled with physical machines. Hypervisor runs on top of the host OS. Since the hypervisor (VMM) is in between the VMs and host OS this leads to slower performance of VMs.

The inefficiency of the hosted architecture lead to the development of *Hybrid Hypervisor* where the hypervisor runs directly on hardware, but leverage the feature of an existing OS running as a guest. Microsoft's Hyper-V and Xen are examples of *hybrid hypervisor*.

Table 4 shows some of the standard Virtualization software product available in the market.

Lots of VMMs from various vendors are available in the market. The following are some of the popular VMMs:

Table 3. Virtualization products

Application	Product	Comment
Development and Testing	VMware Server	Free, good for low-density use.
	VMware ESX Server	Highly scalable, expensive for development and test environments.
	VMware ESXi Server	Scalable, Expensive for development and testing environments.
	Xen	Open source. Used in **Red Hat Enterprise Linux**, **Fedora** etc.
	KVM	Open source Suitable for **Red Hat Enterprise Linux 6** and higher version and **Cent OS** etc.
Server Consolidation	VMware ESX & ESXi Server	Commercial. Most widely deployed virtualization product, very scalable hardware emulation virtualization product.
	Xen	Open source paravirtualization product, offered in many Linux distributions. Depending on the underlying hardware, may support Windows or unmodified Linux guests High scalability.
Failover	VMware	ESX Server can be configured to automatically restart crashed virtual machine.
	Xen	Open source paravirtualization product. Contained in many Linux distributions, can be configured to automatically to restart crashed guest OSs.
High Availability (HA)	VMware ESX Server	Virtual Infrastructure provides sophisticated management services for collections of VMs.
	Xen	Provides high availability functionality.
Load Balancing	VMware ESX Server	Virtual Infrastructure provides load-balancing capacity.
	KVM	Provides load-balancing capacity.

Table 4. Some of Standard Virtualization Software

Company	Product
VMware	VMware vSphare
Citrix(http://www.citrix.com/products/xenserver/overview.html)	CITRIX (Xen)
SUN (Operating System Solaris)	SUM XVM (VirtualBox)
Microsoft	Microsoft Hyper-v
Parallels(http://www.parallels.com/products/)	Parallels
Virtual Iron (acquired by Oracle in 2009 http://www.oracle.com/us/corporate/acquisitions/virtualiron/index.html)	VIRTUAL IRON

- Open source VMMs: Xen, Kernel-based Virtual Machine (KVM) and Oracle VirtualBox
- Licensed VMMs: VMware ESXi, Hyper-v (Microsoft)

5.1 VM Implementation

The Simplest implementation of VM is to simulate the VM's instruction set in software. This is very flexible (can simulate any machine regardless of the underlying hardware), but very expensive i.e. 10 to 1000 times overhead.

The efficient implementations use emulation. This requires that the underlying real hardware has mostly the same instruction set as the VM. An emulated VM executes directly on the hardware, but when the VM uses certain instructions that require Virtualization, the machine traps into the VMM. Instructions that must be virtualized including:

- Those accessing hardware devices (device registers)
- Changes the machine state (user/kernel mode), or change the TLB or page tables.

Another form of Virtalization, i.e. *Paravirtualization* is used in most VMMs. By disallowing instructions that are hard to virtualize, simplify the VMM implementation to improve performance. An additional advantage of paravirtualization is that hosted OSs can be aware of the Virtualization. They can be made aware of the distinction between virtualized and real time, and they can yield a CPU when it has not worked to do.

Modern VMM implementations can achieve performance very close to that of the physical machine with paravirtualization. However the disadvantages of paravirtualization are:

- Operating system modification
- Complex driver architecture
- Capability is limited by vendors

*Pickled VM*s are booted, initialized VM that can be suspended and its state stored on disk. In case of a load spike, VMs can be started up from the pickled state very quickly, adding replicated servers.

The VM can be classified as under:

- **System Virtual Machine:** Provides a platform for the execution of a complete operating system. Examples are VMware, Xen etc. System virtual machines are implemented by VMM or hypervisor. A VMM can run on the bare hardware i.e. native VM or on top of an OS (hosted VM).

- **Process Virtual Machine:** Provides a platform for the execution of a single program (process) like Linux process, Java VM, .NET VM etc.

5.2 Advantages of VMs

In the event of failure of a VM another identical VM having the replica of the failed VM running on different hardware can be utilized for uninterrupted computing to avoid down time. When one VM fails, another can take over. This is called primary-backup replication. Following are the main factors for the popularity of VMs (Table 5).

The advantages and disadvantages of Virtualization are shown in Table 6.

5.3 Virtualization Techniques

There are two major Virtualization techniques i.e.

Table 5. Factors for popularity of VMs

Server consolidation	Multiple OSs can be consolidated onto fewer *Severs* resulting to cost effectiveness and ease of administration.
Desktop Virtualization	Permits multiple OS to access native applications on a different platform like Windows, Mac, etc. Best option for improvement in functionality as well as cost effectiveness.
Testing and debugging	Enables developer to Test their applications in many operating system types and versions on a single machine.

Table 6. Pros and Cons of Virtualization

Advantage	Disadvantage
Power savings in cooling, floor space and Infrastructure	Licensing cost
Simplified disaster recovery, business continuity	Vulnerable to server failure
Increased server utilization in the average of 15% to 80%	A compromised virtualized hosts will affect guest machines
Faster deployment of IT infrastructure	Addition of guest server will require their own administration measures
Lower operating costs	The initial cost can be high
Improved protection of critical business data	

Table 7.

Process Virtualization	System Virtualization
✓ Virtualization Software runs above the OS ✓ Hardware provides user level instruction such as Application Binary Interface (a low level interface between the program and OS) /OS libraries (API). Example of process Virtualization includes Sun Java Virtual machine, Microsoft's .Net or even a binary translator like HP ARIES and Transmeta **Crusoe** (Crusoe, a family of x86 compatible microprocessors developed by Transmeta Corporation, Santa Clara, California, USA) (Dinkar Sitaram, Geetha Manjunath (2012))	✓ The Software is in between the host machine and guest machine (VM) ✓ The primary objectives are to provide virtualized hardware resources to guest OS/Applications enabling elasticity in hardware without affecting the VM (Dinkar Sitaram, Geetha Manjunath (2012))

- Process Virtualization
- System Virtualization

6. CASE STUDY

6.1 VMware

VMware is the leader in server and desktop virtualization. VMware plays at every level of Cloud Computing i.e. such as IaaS (vSphare and vCenter suits), PaaS (based on Cloud Foundry) and SaaS (via the VMware Horizon Application Manager).

Following is the virtualization software developed by VMware:

1. VMware view
2. VMware Thin App
3. VMware Workstation
4. VMware vSphere
5. VMware vCenter Server
6. VMware studio
7. VMware vFabric Product Family
8. VMware vCenter Operations
9. Management suite
10. VMware Go

The market share of the three Virtualization software vendors is shown in Table 8.

Table 8.

Vendor	Market Share
VMware	80.1%
Microsoft	15.1%
Citrix XenServer	4.1%

[Source: https://www.VMware.com]

6.2 Free Virtualization Software from VMware

1. **VMware Player:** VMware Player runs existing VMs, but cannot create a new VM. It has many other limitations like the *inability to stretch VMs*, *limited OS support* etc.
2. **VMware Server:** Suitable for small business environments. Capable of *Creating* and *Runing* VMs. Suitable for low-end server applications. Have similar options as workstation while implementation.
3. **VMware Workstation:** Allows users to Create, Run VMs as well as to import VMs including the capability of virtualizing a physical machine. It consists of features to create unlimited *Snapshots, Creating movie tutorials*, etc.
4. **VMware Academic Alliance:** Free online program through which the educational institutions can get unlimited licenses for classroom use, currently available in the USA.

6.3 VMware Workstation

VMware Workstation permits users to run multiple x86-based OS like Windows, Linux and Netware and their applications simultaneously. VMware Workstation is beneficial for school/college/university.

6.3.1 Benefits to College/University

1. **Teach Multiple Operating Systems:** Student can create multiple VM's and install different types of OS on a single host computer. Multiple VMs can run simultaneously on a single networked host (for example, a client and a server or two servers). Students will be having the option to load Windows / Linux based operating system as per their requirement.

The disadvantage to this option is the initial cost of purchasing the software, and also it would be hard to Setup and Administer the individual VMs.

2. **Easy Maintenance and Testing:** VM provides an easy way to recover deleted or corrupted OS (Operating System)s. Just copy the two files from previous VM i.e. Virtual Machine Configuration File (*.vmx*) and the Virtual Machine Disk Image File (*.vmdk*) is sufficient to recover corrupted OSs.

3. **Run Multiple Versions of Software:** Teachers can teach more than one application software by using two different VMs such as Office 2007 while previewing Office 2003.

4. **Isolate OS From the Local Network and Host Computer:** For programming and networking, run services and write software which might normally interfere with the host computer or the local network. This is beneficial so that students may not interfere with public or campus networks.

6.4 VMware Platform

VMware platform makes it possible to run an unmodified OS as a user-level application. The VMware can be used to run multiple unmodified OSs simultaneously on the same machine by running each OS (Windows, Linux) as VMs.

Currently, VMware supports the following guest OS:

- Windows 95/98/2000/NT
- FreeBSD
- Solaris
- Novell Netware
- DOS
- Linux.

All of these OS runs unmodified. Theoretically, any OS that can run on an x86 architecture as a guest OS.

For Host OSs, VMware currently supports Windows Vista, XP, 2000/NT and Linux (Ishtiaq Ali and Natarajan Meghanathan, 2011). Some of them are free and some of them are trial versions.

In order to build a customized appliance, it is essential to install VMware workstation. The following table shows the minimum Hardware configuration required to install VMware Workstation on a Host (Server) machine.

6.5 Default VM System File Location in the Hard Disk

Whenever a VM is created systematically, the VMware Workstation will prompt the user to give a name for the newly created VM and a directory for the VM files.

Table 9. Hardware configuration of Host for VMware Workstation

Hardware Resources	Minimum Requirement
RAM	• 1 GB RAM • 2+ GB recommended for Windows Vista / Windows 7 and Server 2008 / 2012 virtual machines
Processor	• 3.0 GHz P4, recommended 2.4+ GHz dual-core CPU or higher
Hard Disk	• Separate hard drive (80 GB+) for the VMs

Table 10. Files created by VMware Workstation

Extension	File Name	Description
.log	<vmname>.log or VMware.log	• Keeps a log of key VMware Workstation activity. • Useful for troubleshooting. • Reside in the directory which holds the configuration (.vmx) file of the VM.
.nvram	<vmname>.nvram or nvram	Stores the state of the VMs BIOS.
.vmdk	<vmname>.vmdk	• VM disk file, storing the contents of the VMs hard disk drive. • Grows to a maximum size of 2GB. • The contents are VMs data. • However the size of a .vmdk file varies on the guest OS.
.vmsd	<vmname>.vmsd	This is a Virtual Machine Snapshot Database. It is a centralized file for storing information and metadata about snapshots.
.vmsn	<vmname>-Snapshot.vmsn	This is the snapshot state file, which stores the running state of a virtual machine at the time when take that snapshot.
.vmss	<vmname>.vmss	Stores the status of a suspended VM.
.vmtm	<vmname>.vmtm	Configuration file storing Team data.
.vmx	<vmname>.vmx	Stores the settings chosen in the new VM setting editor.
.vmxf	<vmname>.vmxf	• Supplementary configuration file for VMs running in a team. • This file remains even if the VM is removed from the team.

[Source: http://www.VMware.com/support/ws5/doc/ws_learning_files_in_a_vm.html]

The Default directory for VM files is derived from the name of the guest OS. For shared VMs, the default directory for VM files is located in the shared VMs directory. Shared VM files must reside in the shared VMs directory.

6.6 Virtual Machines Directory

VMware Workstation stores standard VMs in the VMs directory. The default place of the VMs directory depends on the host OS.

Table 11. Default Virtual Machines Directory

Name of Host OS	Default VM Location
Windows XP Windows Server 2003/2008	C:\Documents and Settings\username\My Documents\My Virtual Machines Here, *username* is the name of the currently logged in user.
Windows Vista/7/8	C:\Users\ username \Documents\Virtual Machines, Here, *username* is the name of the currently logged in user.
Linux	homedir/vmware Here, *homedir* is the home directory of the currently logged in user.

6.7 VMs Shared Directory

Table 12 describes the host OS and the default location of shared VMs.

6.8 Selecting the Number of Processors for VM

While selecting custom configuration, the *New Virtual Machine wizard* will ask the user the number of processors for the VM to be created. However, multiple virtual processors can be allocated to a newly created VM if and only if the host machine have two or more logical processors. Single-processor hosts that have Hyper-threading Technology or dual-core CPUs are considered to have two logical processors. Host having two CPUs is considered to have at least two logical processors, regardless of whether they are dual-core or *Hyper-threading* enabled.

For Windows VM multiple virtual processors is not beneficial because of running mostly office and Internet productivity applications, so the default single virtual processor is best.

However, adding additional processors may likely to degrade the overall performance of the VM and the Host. Assigning all processors on Host to the VMs results enormously poor performance.

Table 12. Default Shared Virtual Machines Directory

Name of Host OS	Default Shared VMs Directory
Windows XP Windows Server 2003/2008	C:\Documents and Settings\All Users\Documents\Shared Virtual Machines
Windows Vista/7/8	C:\Users\Public\ Documents\Shared Virtual Machines
Linux	/var/lib/vmware/Shared VMs

Table 13. Processors in Virtual Machine

Types of Computing	No. of Processors
Desktop Applications	1
Server OS	2
Video encoding, modelling, and scientific applications.	4

6.9 VM I/O Controller Selection

During custom configuration, the *New Virtual Machine wizard* will ask to select the I/O controller type for the VM. An IDE controller will be installed for workstation and a SCSI controller for the VM.

However, SATA controllers also supported for some guest OS. The IDE controller is always ATAPI. For the SCSI controller, user can choose Bus Logic, LSI Logic, or LSI Logic SAS. If users are creating a remote virtual machine on an ESX host, then select a VMware Paravirtual SCSI (PVSCSI) adapter. PVSCSI adapters are high-performance storage adapters that can provide greater throughput and lower CPU utilization. PVSCSI is suitable for SAN environments. PVSCSI adapters are not suited for DAS environments. The LSI Logic adapter has improved performance and works better with generic SCSI devices. The LSI Logic adapter is also supported by ESX Server 2.0 and higher version (VMware, Inc, 2013).

6.10 Allocating Disk Space Limitation for a VM

When a new VM is created the *New Virtual Machine wizard* prompts user to set the size of virtual disk and specify whether to split the disk into multiple virtual disk (.vmdk) files. .vmdk file stores the contents of the VM in the hard disk. One can set a size between 0.001GB and 8TB for a virtual disk file (VMware, Inc, 2013). There are also options to store a virtual disk as a single .vmdk file or split it into multiple .vmdk files.

For custom configurations, user can allocate all disk space immediately rather than allow the disk space to gradually grow to the maximum amount. However, allocating all the disk space immediately might provide better performance, but it is a time-consuming operation for the user. If user allocate all the disk space immediately, then the shrink disk feature cannot use.

6.11 Disk Size Compatibility

The maximum size of a .vmdk file is 8TBs. However, the virtual disk size depends on hardware version, bus type, and controller type.

The controller type of the VM is defined in the **.vmx** file and the **scsi0.virtualDev** determine the type.

7. UNDERSTANDING COMMON NETWORKING CONFIGURATIONS

There are three networking options in the workstation i.e.:

- Bridged
- Network address translation (NAT) and
- Host only networking

Table 14. Disk Size Compatibility

Workstation Version	Bus Type	Controller Type	Maximum Disk Size
10	IDE	ATAPI	**8192GB**
10	SCSI	Bus Logic	**2040GB**
10	SCSI	LSI Logic	**8192GB**
10	SCSI	LSI Logic SAS	**8192GB**
10	SCSI	Paravirtualized SCSI	**8192GB**
10	SATA	All	**8192GB**
9, 8, 7, 6.5	All	All	**2040GB**
6.0, 5	All	All	**950 GB**

Table 15. Controller Type Of VM

.vmx Parameter	Type of Controller
Blank	Bus Logic
lsilogic	LSI Logic
lsisas1068	LSI Logic SAS

Each VM has its own virtual network adapter called VMnet. Multiple network adapters are possible within a single Virtual Machine (VMs). There are various networking modes for VMs.

1. **Bridged Networking:** The VM acts like any other physical computer on the network. The VM network adapter has own IP address and physical address. By bridged networking VMs can communicate with other VMs and other physical computers on the network including the Internet. It is the most flexible configuration possible. When user installs Workstation on a Windows or Linux host operating system, a bridged network (VMnet0) is set up for the user.

2. **Network Address Translation (NAT) /Shared Networking:** VM 'shares' IP address with the host computer. Host computer acts like a router/firewall. The VM can access other computers on the network, including the Internet. Other computers cannot access the VM directly. It is a more secure configuration than bridged. It won't work if the VM is to be a server. During the installation of a Workstation on a Windows or Linux host OS; a NAT network (VMnet8) is set up for the user. When the *New Virtual Machine wizard* is used to create a new VM and select the Typical configuration type, the wizard configures the VM to use the default NAT network. User can have only one NAT network.

3. **Local/Host Only Networking:** VMs can communicate with only other VMs and the host Computer.

4. **Do Not Use a Network Connection:** No network connection is the most secure configuration. It is the best configuration when no interaction with other computers, including the host, is desired.

5. **Custom Network:** Select a specific virtual network for remote virtual machine only.

7.1 Virtual Networking Components

7.1.1 Virtual Switches

A virtual switch is similar to a physical switch which connects networking components together. Virtual switches also known as virtual networks. They are named as VMnet0, VMnet1, VMnet2, and so on.

7.1.2 VN Adapter

The VN (virtual network adapter) appears in the guest OS as an AMD PCNET PCI adapter or Intel Pro/1000 MT Server Adapter. In Windows Vista / 7 / 8 guest OS;

Table 15. Default Virtual Network Switches

Type of Network	Name of Switch
Bridged	VMnet0
NAT	VMnet8
Host-Only	VMnet1

it is an Intel Pro/1000 MT Server Adapter. In Workstation 6.0 and higher version VMs can have up to 10 VN adapters.

7.1.3 DHCP Virtual Server

The virtual DHCP server provides IP addresses to VMs in configurations that are not bridged to an external network. For example, the virtual DHCP server assigns IP addresses to VMs in the host-only and NAT configurations.

7.1.4 NAT Device

The NAT device does the following:

- Passes network data between one or more VMs and the external network.
- Identifies incoming data packets intended for each VM.
- Sends incoming data packets to the correct destination

8. INSTALLING A GUEST OS WITH VMWARE WORKSTATION

In this section, demonstrate how to install guest OS using VMware Workstation. VMware Workstation is capable of managing several guest OS. However, VM player is given the option to customize the guest OS, according to the required configuration. The hosted architecture of VMware workstation allows virtualized I/O to co-exist with the existing host OS: VMApp, VMDriver and VMM. The VMApp application allows users to install guest OS. VMApp use VMDriver loaded with the host OS to establish the privileged VMM. This VMM directly runs on the hardware (Ishtiaq Ali and Natarajan Meghanathan, 2011).

The installation of VMware Workstation is similar to windows application software. After the installation of VMware workstation the system has to be restarted for the installation of network adapter on the host machine.

8.1 Installation Steps

Step 1: VMware workstation allows a user to install the guest OS using CD/DVD or ISO image. It is also important to insert the right optical media or image.

Step 2: After loading the VMware Workstation, select "New Virtual Machine" Option. Select "Typical" and Click "Next". This option will allow the user to accept the defaults or specify values for customizing the hardware.

Another option in this installation window is "Custom" if the user selects the "Custom" the user can specify the I/O adapter for SCSI.

Step 3: The next screen will be prompted with the option of installing the guest OS from the Installer disc or from the Installer disc image file (ISO).

Step 4: Type the user name and password. Clicking "Next" will prompt for the VM name and the location for the VM installation folder.

Step 5: Type the VM name, for example "Red Hat" and location for the VM installation folder. Clicking "Next" will prompt the user to specify the hard disk configuration.

Step 6: In this step, the user will specify the total disk capacity for the VM. VMware workstation is having a very interesting feature for keeping the guest VM in a single file or splitting the VM into 2 GB segments. Further, this feature allows to write VM on a disk, making it convenient to move the VM to different location/computer. The VM image can be distributed for Computer Networks or Network Security classes with all the required software installed on it. The students can load the VM image on their machine using the VM player.

Step 7: This step will show the selected configuration for the VM. The user has the option to make any changes by clicking on the "Customize Hardware" link. This step of installation also gives the user the option to change the memory requirement of the guest VM. User can change the network configuration by selecting the "Network Adapter" option from the list. The user can also change their virtual network adapter and add additional virtual network adapters. The VM should be powered off before adding or removing a network adapter.

The user can set the following options under the device section:

- **Connected:** Used to Connect/Disconnect the virtual network adapter while the VM is running.
- **Connect at Power On:** Automatically connects the virtual network adapter to the VM when powered. The user can change the following options in the Network connection when the VM is powered On / Off.

○ **Bridged:** With bridged networking, the VM appears as an additional computer on the same physical Ethernet network. The VM can use any services (file servers, printers, and gateways) available on the network to which it is bridged. Similarly, any physical host or other VM configured with bridged networking can use the resources of that VM.

○ **Replicate Physical Network Connection State:** If the user selects a bridged network and the VM is installed on a laptop or other portable device, this option automatically, renew the IP address of the VM as user migrates from network (wired to wireless or vice verse).

○ **NAT (Network Address Translation):** used to connect to the Internet or other TCP/IP network using the host computer's dial-up connection if the user cannot / do not want to give the VM an IP address for the external network. A separate private network is set up on the **Host**. The VM obtains an address on that network from the VMware virtual DHCP server.

○ **Host-only:** The VM is connected to the host OS on a virtual private network not visible to the outside host. Multiple VMs could be configured with host-only networking on the same host and on the same network.

○ **Custom:** "Custom" option is used to choose a virtual switch from the drop-down menu. This connects the VMs adapter to that switch. All VMs running on the same host computer and connected to the same virtual switch are on the same virtual network.

Step 8: Click on "Finish" to start the installation of the guest OS. This process will take 20-30 minutes, depending on the host system configuration and speed.

8.2 Navigation Between Guest OS and Host OS

Clicking inside a VM will make the VM active. If the user wants to interact with the host OS; the user should hold the *Ctrl+Alt* keys to release the mouse to the host OS.
Another navigation tool is the VMware tool for VMs/ Guest OS.
VMware tool provides several features:

- Shared folders.
- Drag and drop feature between Host and Guest OS.
- Time synchronization.
- Automatic grabbing and releasing of the mouse cursor
- Copying, pasting between Guest and Host.

8.3 Converting Physical Host Machine to Virtual Machine Using VMware VCenter

VMware also provides free VMware Vcenter Converter to convert physically installed operating system to a VM. It can convert Microsoft Windows and Linux based physical machines to virtual machines. This free software can be downloaded from http://www.vmware.com/products/converter/ with installation and conversion instructions.

8.4 VMware GSX, ESX and ESXi Hypervisor Architecture

The Figure below shows the VMware 3rd Generation Hypervisors architectures.

8.4.1 VMware GSX (VMware Server)

Introduced in the year 2001, VMware Server installs like an application and runs on the host OS. Resource management depends on the OS (Operating System).

8.4.2 VMware ESX Architecture

In ESX architecture, the virtualization kernel (VM kernel) is augmented by the Console Operating System (COS) or service console. The function of this management partition (COS) is providing an interface with the host. Various VMware® management agents are running in the COS, along with other infrastructure service agents like name service, time service, logging, and so on. Many customers install third party software for hardware monitoring, systems management, individual administrative users log to run configuration and diagnostic commands and scripts.

8.4.3 Architecture of VMware ESXi

VMware® ESXi is the next-generation hypervisor; provide a new establishment for virtual infrastructure. This new architecture function individually from any general-purpose operating system, providing improved security, increased reliability, and simplified management. The compact architecture enables it to be embedded in physical servers. Due to its compact architecture ESXi require few patches, consumes less physical hardware resources. Hence ESXi has more physical CPUs, RAMs and disk space for VMs. It has easy to install, streamlined deployment and configuration setup. VMware allows those modules that are digitally signed by them. The arbitrary code prevents from running on the ESXi host that improves the security and stability of the system.

Figure 4. VMware 3ʳᵈ Generation Hypervisors architectures

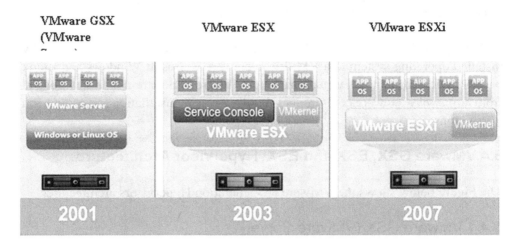

ESXi supports the complete VMware Infrastructure 3 suite of products such as:

- VMware Virtual Machine File System
- Virtual SMP,
- Virtual Center
- VMotion
- VMware Distributed Resource Scheduler
- VMware High Availability
- VMware Update Manager and
- VMware Consolidated Backup

8.4.4 Components of ESXi

The VMware ESXi architecture consists of the underlying operating system, called the VM kernel, and processes that run on top of it. The VM kernel provides services to the VMs, including management applications. VM kernel controls all hardware devices on the server, and manages the resources of the applications. The main processes that run on top of VMkernel are (VMware, Inc., 2011):

- **Direct Console User Interface (DCUI):** The low-level configuration and management interface, accessible through the console of the server, used mainly for initial basic configuration.
- The VMM provides the execution environment for a VM, as a process known as VMX. Each running VM has its own VMM and VMX process.

- Several agents used to enable high-level VMware Infrastructure management from remote applications.
- **The Common Information Model (CIM) System:** The CIM interface enables hardware-level management from remote applications via a set of APIs.

8.4.5 Management

The functionality of various agents in the ESX architecture is provided via APIs in the ESXi architecture. It allows an "agentless" approach for system management and hardware monitoring.

VMware ESXi has remote command line interface tools called vSphere Client which is the combination of VMware vSphere® Command-Line Interface (vSphere vCLI) and VMware vSphere® PowerCLI (vSphere PowerCLI) to provide commands for configuration, diagnostics and troubleshooting. A local version of **"esxcli"** known as the "ESXi Shell is accessible directly from the host's local shell for low level diagnostics and configuration.

CIM Broker: ESXi Common Information Model (CIM) runs on VMkernel. CIM is an open standard framework of monitoring hardware resources consisting of a CIM object manager, popularly known as CIM broker. CIM provides a mechanism for management, access to device drivers and underlying hardware. The CIM broker takes the all the information from the CIM provider and present it to the outside world using standard API's as shown in Figure 6.

Figure 5. VMware ESX and ESXi Management

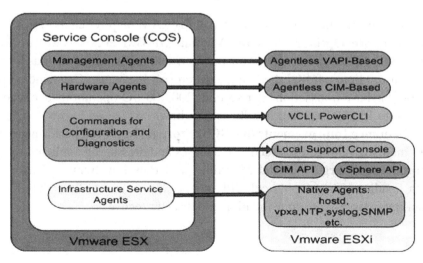

Figure 6. Architecture of CIM Broker

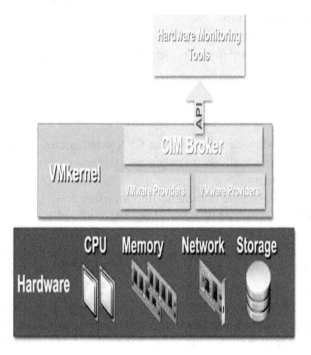

VMware ESX and ESXi are the most widely deployed hypervisors. VMware ESXi is a bare-metal Virtualization.

8.4.6 Key Features of VMware ESX and VMware ESXi

- **64-bit Architecture**: Support for up to 1TB RAM on physical hosts.
- **Performance Optimizations for Virtualized Workloads**: VMware ESX and ESXi 4.0 supports various business-critical applications such as Oracle Database, Microsoft SQL Server, and Microsoft Exchange. Can handle up to 8,900 database transactions per second, 200,000 I/O operations per second, and up to 16,000 Exchange mailboxes per host.
- **Performance Improvements for iSCSI Storage**: Improved performance for I/O-intensive applications such as databases and messaging applications.
- **Support for Larger Virtual Machines and Powerful Server Hardware**: Can handle up to 64 physical CPU cores, 256 virtual CPUs, 1TB RAM. Facilitates large-scale consolidation and disaster recovery.

- **Support for Eight-Way Virtual SMP**: Enables a single VM to use up to eight physical processors, simultaneously, virtualization of the most CPU-intensive applications such as Databases, ERP and CRM.
- **VMware VMsafe™:** Helps in protecting virtualized workloads in physical machine with a set of security API's. Enables third-party security products to gain the same visibility to identify and eliminates malware, viruses, Trojans and key-loggers.
- **VMDirectPath for VMs:** Enhance CPU efficiency for applications that require frequent access to I/O devices by directly giving access of the hardware devices to the VMs.
- **Improved Power Management:** Improve energy efficiency with dynamic voltage and frequency scaling. Supports Intel SpeedStep® and AMD PowerNow.

8.5 Resources Required for ESXi

Table 16 shows the resources required for various ESXi versions.
VMware vSphere 6.0 contains new features mentioned:

- Support up to 128 vCPUs and 4TB RAM.
- ESXi Hostes will support up to 480 pCPU, 12 TB RAM, 64 TB datastores, 1000 VMs, and 32 serial ports.
- vMotion Enhancements
- Network IO Control

Steps for Installing VMware ESXi 5.1.0 Update 1 in VMware Workstation 9

- Open VMware Workstation 10 and Click on "Create a New Virtual Machine"
- Choose Custom and click next.
- Select Workstation 6.5-7.x and click Next

Table 16. Resource requirements of ESXi

Resources Required	ESX1	ESX 2.X	ESXi 3.X	ESXi 4.X	ESXi 5.0	ESXi 5.1
Number of vCPUs	1	2	4	8	32	64
GB RAM per VM	2GB	3.6GB	64GB	256GB	1TB	1TB
Network I/O(Gb/Sec)	.5Gb	.9GB	9GB	30GB	>36Gb	>36GB
Storage I/O Ops/Sec	<5K	7K	100K	300K	1,000K	1,000K
CPU Cores/ESXi host	4	8	96	128	160	160

- Choose "Installer disc image file (iso):" and browse the ISO file location and select it. Click Next
- Type the name and location for the VM and click Next.
- Select the processor configuration and click Next
- Specify the amount of memory for the VM and click Next.
- Select the network connection type and click Next.
- Select the I/O controller for the VM (in most cases the recommended) and click Next.
- Select Disk to create a new virtual disk, click Next.
- Select the type of Virtual disk and click Next
- Specify Disk Capacity and Click Next
- Specify the Disk File and click Next
- Check the VM settings and mark the box below power on this VM after creation and click Finish
- Click with the mouse in the VM Screen and press Enter
- Press Enter to Install
- Press F11 to Accept and Continue
- Press Enter to Continue
- Selecting a keyboard layout and press Enter to Continue
- Default root password is blank press Enter to continue
- Enable Hardware Virtualization features in the BIOS and press Enter to continue
- Press F11 to Install
- After Installation, Press Enter to Reboot.
- Press F2 to customize the system.
- To continue with the default Root password as blank, press Enter
- Press Enter to configure a new Root Password
- Enter the new Password (twice for confirmation), and press Enter
- Select Configure Management Network and press Enter
- Go to IP Configuration and press Enter.
- Enter the right IP Address, Subnet Mask and Default Gateway and press Enter and then Esc to exit the Configure Management Network settings.
- Press Y (Yes) to confirm.
- Open the web site http://entered-ip-address (DNS).
- Press Continue to this website (not recommended).
- Download vSphere Client and install.
- Set for the ESXi server and Login.
- Check the box Install this certificate and do not display any security warnings for "192.1683.1.50" and click on the ignore button.

8.6 Launching the vSphere Client Page

- Inventory →work with ESXi host
- Roles →define user categories
- System Logs →review, save ESXi log files

8.7 Different ESXi Host Roles

The following are the roles of ESXi host

- **Default:** No access – no rights on ESXi host
- **Read –Only:** Look but cannot modify
- **Administrator:** Full control of local ESXi host.

9. HYPER-V

Hyper-V is a commercial hypervisor from Microsoft. Hyper-V runs on any OS supported by the hardware platform (*, 2014). Partitioning is used by Hyper-V for isolation of VMs. A Hyper-V partition is a logical unit of isolation in which each guest OS runs. At least one parent partition of the host computer must have an instance of Windows Server (2008, 2008 R2, or 2012) for running Hyper-V VMM. The Virtualization stack has direct access to the hardware devices running in the parent partition. The child partitions / guest OS are created by Hyper-V as per requirements of the hypercall API (Hyper-V, http://en.wikipedia.org/wiki/Hyper-V).

The following are the salient features of Microsoft Windows Server 2008 R2 Hyper-V:

- Maximum 4(four) vCPUs per VM.
- Up to 64 logical processors on hardware
- 1 TB of physical memory.
- 64 GB of RAM per VM.
- 512 vCPUs per host.
- Supports 384 active VMs.
- Hyper-V maximum cluster size of 16 nodes.
- Maximum of 1000 cluster VMs.

The following table shows the specifications for Hyper-V guest OS:

- 32 bits (x86) OS such as Windows 9x, XP, Vista (requiring patch), Windows 200x except Windows 2008 (self), Linux, Solaris and Unix (SOLARIS not supported)
- 64 bits (x86) OSs (Windows, SuSE Linux. Red Hat and other Linux should have Xen expansions)
- 32 bit and 64 bit OS can run concurrently
- Up to 4 virtual processors per VM
- Up to 31 GB memory for running up to 128 VMs, 1 GB reserved for Hyper-V server Parent Partition.

Child partitions have a virtual view of the resources; any request to the virtual devices is redirected via the VMBus to the devices in the parent partition. The VMBus manages the requests. If the devices in the parent partition are also virtual devices, then the request will be further redirected to the owner of the physical device. Parent partitions run a Virtualization Service Provider (VSP), which connects to the VMBus and handle device access requests from child partitions. Child partition virtual devices run a Virtualization Service Client (VSC), which redirect the request to VSPs in the parent partition via the VMBus. This entire process is transparent to the guest OS.

Another Hyper-V Virtualization feature is Enlightened I/O. Enlightened I/O enables virtualization of:

- Storage
- Networking and
- Graphics Subsystems
- Specialized Virtualization-aware implementation of high level communication protocols

Enlightened I/O takes the advantage of VMBus bypassing the device emulation layer. The only requirement is the guest OS must support Enlightened I/O of Hyper-V. Currently Enlightened I/O is supported by the following OS:

- Windows Vista/7
- Windows Server 2008/2008 R2
- Red Hat Enterprise Linux
- SUSE Linux

Upcoming Hyper-V with Server 2012 R2 has enhanced the virtualization technology further. Following section briefs the features of Server 2012 R2 Hyper-V.

Figure 7. Hyper-V architecture

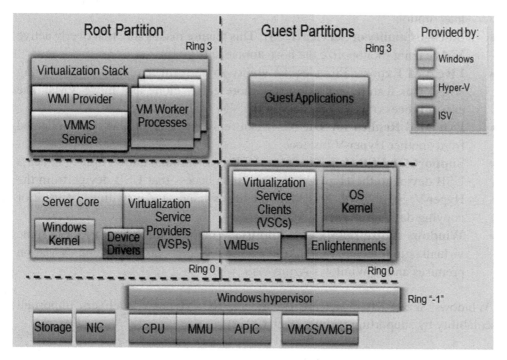

9.1 Features of Server 2012 R2 Hyper-V (Otey, M. (2013, June 03))

- **Generation 2 VMs:** Generation-2 virtual machines (VMs) leave all the legacy VM baggage behind. There are no BIOS and no legacy devices. The new VMs are *Unified Extensible Firmware Interface* (UEFI) based. They can boot without virtual SCSI or network adapters. The new Generation 2 VMs can run on Windows 8/ Windows Server 2012 64-bit OSs.
- **Full Remote Desktop Support:** Supports full remote-desktop capabilities even without network. It performs this by adding the Remote Desktop support into the Hyper-V management console. The connection to the VM is through over the VMBus interface.
- **Automatic Activation of VMs:** New Hyper-V makes the guest VM automatic activation hassle free.
- **Faster live Migration:** New Hyper-V achieves two times faster live migration by compressing VM memory. Further the live migration is also benefited by high performance on high speed network.

- **Online VHDX Resize:** The size of VHDX file can be resized without user interruption.
- **Storage Quality of Service (QoS):** This feature makes sure that overly active VMs cannot monopolize the host storage subsystems.
- **Live VM Export:** Provides the ability to perform live exports of running VMs. This feature can help users more easily clone and move VMs. The export process takes a snapshot of the VM's current state.
- **Extended Replica for DR:** User can replicate a target VM that replicated from another Hyper-V instance.
- **Support for USB Pass-Through:** USB pass-through allows user to attach a USB device to the Hyper-V host and then access that USB device from the Hyper-V guest VMs. This functionality is handy for installing software or copying data into Hyper-V VMs.
- **Windows Azure IaaS Compatibility:** Windows Azure IaaS uses the same virtualization technology like Windows Server 2012 running VMs on premises and in Windows Azure IaaS.

"Windows Server 2012 Release Candidate (RC) Hyper-V" delivers important scalability by supporting (Edwin Yuen (2012)):

- 320 logical processors per Host.
- 4 TB of physical memory per Host.
- 2,048 virtual CPUs per Host.
- 64 virtual CPUs per VM.
- 1TB of memory per VM.
- 1024 active VMs.
- Maximum 64 cluster nodes.
- Maximum of 8000 cluster VMs.

Microsoft declared a **Windows Server 2016 Hyper-V** host will support 24TB of RAM and up to 512 physical (host) logical processor support, and up to 16TB virtual memory support and 240 virtual CPUs per Virtual Machine.

9.2 Major Feature Differences vSphere and Hyper-V

Table 17 shows the different features of vSphere and Hyper-V.

Table 17. vSphere and Hyper-V features

System	Resource	vSphere (5.1)	Hyper-V
Host	Logical Processor (cores)	160	320
	Physical Memory	2TB	4TB
	Virtual CPU Per Host	2048	2048
VM	Virtual CPU Per VM	64	64
	Memory Per VM	1TB	1TB
	Active VM Per Host	512	1024
Cluster	Maximum Nodes	32	64
	Maximum VMs	3,000	8,000
Capability	Virtual Fiber Channel	Yes	Yes
	Maximum Virtual Disk Size	2TB VMDK	64TB VHDX
	Dynamic Memory	Yes	Yes
	Quality of Service	Yes	Yes
	Data Center Bridging (DCB)	Yes	Yes
	Storage Encryption	No	Yes
	IPsec Task Offload	No	Yes
	VM Live Migration	Yes	Yes

10. OPEN SOURCE VMMS

Xen is an open source hypervisor, which originated in 2003 as a Cambridge University research project. Xen runs on Linux platform, originally supported by XenSource Inc, which was acquired by Citrix Inc in 2007 (*, 2014).

Xen supports both paravirtualization and hardware-assistant full virtualization. The name comes from neXt gENeration virtualization. Initially created by University of Cambridge Computer Laboratory as a part of huge public distributed computing utility project called XenoServers, Xen is powering lots of the largest cloud deployments presently. Xen is used in different commercial and open source applications.

Xen hypervisor is developed collaboratively by the Xen community and engineers from more than 50 (fifty) innovative datacenter solution vendors. Xen is licensed under the General Public License (GPL).

10.1 XEN Architecture

Since the Xen hypervisor directly runs on the hardware, making it capable of handling CPUs, Memory and Interrupts. Xen hypervisior is the first program which runs after the bootloader. Above the Xen hypervisor lots of VMs run with a variety of applications on various OS called a "domain" or "guest". A special domain management and control (Xen DM&C), called a dom0 guest (domain 0) is the base machine contains the drivers for the devices in the system. The user of Dom0 is a system administrator has the following privileges (Multi Data Palembang, 2008):

- Create, delete or manage any DomU VM
- Higher privilege to access hardware

Xen hypervisor has the privilege to access physical I/O devices and also interact with other VMs running simultaneously on the system (Domain U: PV and HVM Guests). However, the Xen virtualization environment should be running in Domain 0 before starting any VM. The *Network Backend Driver* and the *Block Backend Driver* must be active in Domain 0 to handle network and local disk requests from *Domain U PV* and *HVM* Guests. The Network Backend Driver communicates directly with the physical networking hardware to route all VMs requests coming from the Domain U guests. Based upon the Domain U request, the Block Backend Driver communicates with the local disk to read /write data (Multi Data Palembang, 2008).

There are two drivers for a Domain U PV Guest to access network and disk, i.e. PV Network Driver and PV Block Driver respectively. Instead a special Qemu-DM daemon is started for each HVM Guest in Domain 0 for networking and disk access request. Every Domain U HVM Guest has Xen Virtual Firmware including standard start-up instructions of an OS for normal boot-up as shown in Figure 8.

In Xen 3.3 and higher versions the tool, Stub-dm have been developed with a new feature to eliminate the need for running Qemu in every Domain U HVM Guest. Figure 9 explains the various "domain" of Xen.

10.1.1 Domain Management and Control

Open Source Community are classified a series of Linux daemons are known as Domain Management and Control. For overall management of virtualization environment. The Domain Management and Control services must exist within the

Figure 8. Qemu- DM

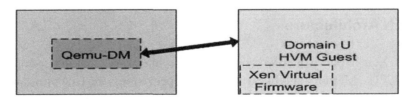

Figure 9. Xen architecture

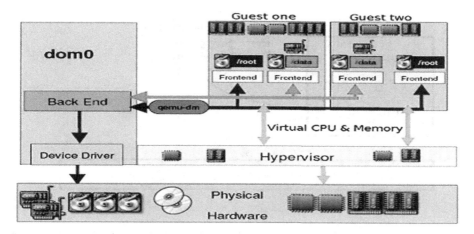

Domain 0 of the VM. The diagrams below show the daemons outside the Domain 0 diagram for a clearer understanding of the architecture (Protti, 2009).

10.1.2 Xend

Xend daemon, a python application is the system manager for Xen environment. It controls the libxenctrl library to make requests of the Xen hypervisor (Xen, 2009). Xm is a Xen command line tool which accepts user input and passes to Xend via XML RPC interface.

10.1.3 Libxenctrl

The C library Libxenctrl is an interface for Xen hypervisor via Domain 0. A special driver inside Domain 0, privcmd sends the request to the hypervisor as shown in Figure 10.

10.1.4 Interaction between Domain 0 and Domain U

Event channel is the communication interface exists between Domain 0 and the Domain U PV Guest via asynchronous inter-domain interrupts within the Xen hypervisor. PV Block Backend Driver access the local system memory blocks from Domain U PV guest shared memory by raising an interrupt in Domain 0 for the Xen hypervisor.

Figure 10. Xen Library

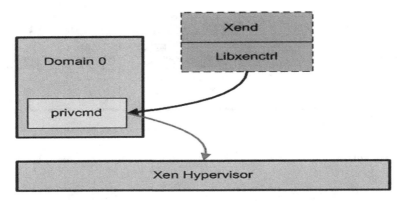

Figure 11 illustrates the event channel as a direct link between Domain 0 and Domain U PV Guest. Domain 0 and Domain U PV Guest smoothly share information across local memory by executing interrupts through the event channel for the Xen hypervisor.

10.1.5 Xen PCI Passthru

PCI Passthru is a new feature designed in Xen Hypervisor for improvement I/O performance and minimizes I/O virtualization overhead on the Dom 0 Guest. In this method the Domain U Guest allows to direct access the physical hardware without using the Domain 0 for hardware access. Domain U Guest is privileged to communicate directly to a specific hardware device via Xen PCI Passthru feature of Xen hypervisor (Xen, 2009). Figure 12 shows how this feature works.

Figure 11. Event channel between Domain 0 and Domain U PV Guest

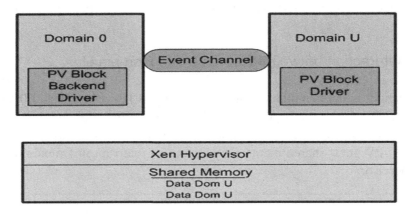

Figure 12. Xen I/O Performance

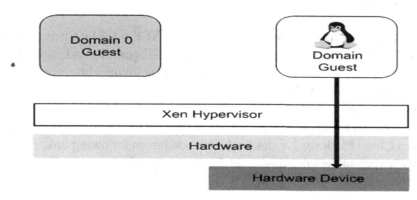

10.1.6 Xen PCI Passthrough Applications

- Playing video game not available on Linux.
- Multi-seat gaming on a single machine.
- Using a device without Linux support.
- Replace dual boot.
- Testing Software or Hardware driver.

The key characteristics of Xen architecture are shown in Table 18.

Table 18. Xen Characteristics

Small system file and Interface	Xen approximately 1 MB in size. Use microkernel design with a small footprint and limited interface to the guest. Robust and secure than other hypervisors.
Driver Isolation	The device driver is isolated in Xen by running the copy of the driver independently in a VM instead of running it from the host. In case of driver crash/compromised the driver is rebooted from Domain 0 which contain the drivers of all the hardware and related tools. Xen special domain called "domain 0" contains drivers for the hardware as well as the tool stack to control the VMs.
Toolstacks	Front-ends available for Xen and the implications here
Guest types	Xen is capable of running fully virtualized (HVM) guests, or paravirtualized (PV) guests. Every domain guest is isolated from other domain guests so that they cannot access each other's memory or networking connections.

11. XEN CLOUD PLATFORM (XCP)

Xen announced Xen Cloud Platform (XCP) in 2010. XCP is led by Citrix Systems. The goal of XCP is to provide a tool for automatic configuration and maintenance of cloud deployment. XCP is an open source software solution with complete APIs for Cloud service Providers. XCP will enable various open source projects such as Eucalyptus, converter, OpenNebula, OpenXenCenter, Xen VNC Proxy, and Nimbus to leverage the Xen hypervisor with new APIs focused on cloud computing (Lars Kurth). Xen Cloud Platform 1.6 can be downloaded from following link:

https://www.xenproject.org/downloads/xen-cloud-platform-archives/xen-cloud-platform-16.html

Figure 13 shows the development of the history of development of Xen in the cloud.

Salient features of Xen are:

- Xen hypervisor can be scaled up to 4,095 host CPUs with 5Tb of RAM
- Using Paravirtualization the hypervisor is capable of supporting up to 512 VCPUs with 512Gb RAM per MVs
- Hardware Virtualization (HVM) supports up to 128 VCPUs with 512 GB RAM per VMs.

Figure 13. XCP History of Development

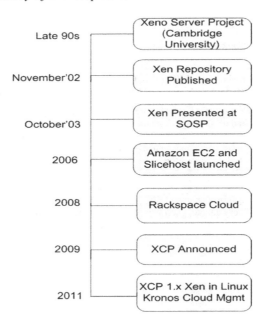

XCP includes the Xen Hypervisor (Fanatical, 2014) and enterprise ready Xen API Toolstack having the following functionality:

- Pool of host system management functionalities
- Advanced storage management functionalities
- Multi-tenancy supports
- Supporting SLA for guaranteed pay-per-use policies for cloud users and more
- Integrated Network and disk functionality such as Open vSwitch.

XenServer

The commercial distribution of Citrix XCP is XenServer.

XCP Flavors

XCP is available in the following two flavors:

- **XCP ISO:** The installation of XCP ISO is similar to XenServer. XCP ISO also has the same drivers like XenServer.
- **XCP-XAPI (Xen management API) Packages:** XCP-XAPI are XCP packages which are delivered in Linux distributions (currently with Debian and Ubuntu 12.04 LTS or newer) and are installed via the user's host Operating System package manager.

The features of XCP-ISO and XCP-XAPI packages are compared in Table 19.

Table 19. XCP-ISO and XCP-XAPI packages

XCP ISO	XCP-XAPI Packages
Complex application packages	Simple user configurable Linux packages
CentOS 5.x based Dom0	Most of the components are available with the distribution
Managed by XAPI	Managed by XAPI
Supports most of XenServer features	With limited features
Supports majority of the storage repository types	Limited set of shared SR types
Works with supplied CentOS Dom 0 only	Supports Debian/Ubuntu host OS. In future Fedora is likely to support.
Customization is difficult	Simple
Difficult to build from source	Easy

12. SYSTEM REQUIREMENTS FOR RED HAT ENTERPRISE LINUX 5

Red Hat Enterprise Linux 5 has Xen hypervisors, which supports both Full virtualization and Para Virtualization.

Minimum system requirements for installing Xen hypervisor on RHEL 5 are as follows:

- 6 GB hard disk space.
- 2 GB of physical memory (RAM).

12.1 Additional System Requirements for Guest OS

Additional hard disk space is required for the guest OS.

- Minimum one Processor core/thread for each virtualized CPU (vCPU, allocated to a VM) and one for the hypervisor.
- 2 GB of RAM for hypervisor (Xen) plus additional RAM for guests.

Table 20 shows the Full Virtualization and Para Virtualization resource requirements:

12.2 Installing Virtualization Packages

The Virtualization packages are available in Red Hat Enterprise Linux DVD. There are two options for installing Virtualization packages:

- During the installation of RHEL
- Using the yum command (after installation).
- **YUM (Yellow dog Updater, Modified)** is based on YUP (Yellow dog Updater). Yellow Dog is a version of Linux for the Power Architecture hardware. YUP, and higher version of YUM, were developed by the Linux community to maintain an RPM (Red Hat Package Manager) based system.

Table 20.

Full Virtualization	Para Virtualization
Intel VT extensions/*AMD processor* with the AMD-V extensions/*Intel Itanium* processor	• Red Hat Enterprise Linux 5 • Installation tree over the network using the NFS / FTP / HTTP protocols.

Installing the Xen Hypervisor with Yum

Write the command in a terminal window in RHEL5 as shown below

[root@server]# yum install Xen kernel-xen virt-manager

Press Y (yes) for installing the packages.

Recommended Virtualization Packages

- **Python-virtinst**: *Virt-install* command is used to create VMs.
- **Libvirt**: *Libvirt* API library is used for interacting with hypervisors using the **xm** virtualization framework. virsh command line tool manages and controls the VMs.
- **libvirt-Python**: The libvirt-python package contains a module that permits applications written in the Python programming language to use the interface supplied by the libvirt API.
- **virt-Manager**: Virt-manager (Virtual Machine Manager) is a graphical tool for administering VMs. The virt-manager uses libvirt library as management API.

Check the Xen kernel details using the following command.

[root@server]# uname –r

2.6.18-8.el5xen

12.3 Disk Space and Virtual Memory Requirement for VM

Table 21 shows the minimum virtual memory and disk space requirement of different OS.

12.4 Creating a VM Using Virt-Manager

Run virt-manager command in a terminal window as root as shown below

    [root@server]# virt-manager

- Click the Connect button and the main virt-manager window appears.
- The *virt-manager* window allows user to create a new virtual machine. Click the New button to create a new guest.
- The Create a new virtual system window appears which provides a summary of the information in order to create a virtual machine.
- Click Forward.
- The Choosing a virtualization method window appears. Choose between Para-virtualized or Fully virtualized.

Table 21. Virtual memory and disk space requirement of different OS.

Operating System	Minimum RAM	Maximum RAM	Disk Space
Windows Server 2008 32 bit/64 bit	512 MB; recommended 2 GB or more.	32GB	10 GB, recommended 40 GB or more.
Windows Vista 32 bit	512 MB; recommended 768 MB or more.	32GB	16 GB
Windows 2003	128 MB; recommended 256 MB or more.	32GB	2 GB
Windows XP SP2/3	128 MB; recommended 256 MB or more.	32GB	1.5 GB
Windows 2000 SP4	128 MB; recommended 256 MB or more	32GB	2 GB
Red Hat Enterprise Linux 3.6	64 MB	32GB	1.5 GB
Red Hat Enterprise Linux 4.5,4.6,4.7	256 MB	16 GB	800 MB
Red Hat Enterprise Linux 5.0,5.1,5.2	512 MB	16 GB	800 MB

(With the help of Intel® Processor Identification Utility check whether Virtualization Technology is being supported or not. It is an open source Windows based software download from following link:

https://downloadcenter.intel.com/download/7838/Intel-Processor-Identification-Utility-Windows-Version)

- Choose a Virtualization type and click Forward
- The next step is to choose the media for the installation of the guest OS.
  - Choose HTTP, FTP or NFS network protocol for para-virtualized installation. However, this is possible only Linux platform. Windows does not support para virtualization.
  - DVDs, CD-ROM or bootable images of OS such as .iso or .img files are required for fully virtualized guest OS installation. User can install Linux, Windows or any other OS on VM.
- After selecting proper installation media click Forward.
- The Assigning storage space window displays. Choose LVM disk based machines or image based for the guest storage.

The default location of the image based machine is:
/var/lib/xen/images/<machine name>

- Define the storage in hard disk for the VM and click the Forward button.
- Allocate the memory and CPU window displays

Choose the appropriate values for the virtualized CPUs and RAM. These values are crucial for the performance of the Hosts and VMs.

Most VMs require at least 512 MB of RAM to work responsively. Running too many VMs will overload the RAM, ultimately degrading system performance and responsiveness. Hence, restrict the number of VMs as per the permissible limit of the Host's RAMs.

Do not assign more virtual CPU (vCPU)s than physical processors. Over allocation of vCPU negatively affect the VM performance due to processor context switching overheads.

- **Ready to begin** the installation window presents a summary of all configuration information entered. Check the parameters entered and use the Back button to make changes, *if necessary*. Once user satisfied, click the Finish button to start the installation process.
- A VNC window pops up showing the beginning of the installation of the guest OS.

12.5 Starting a Guest VM

After a VM is created, users can view the VM in a graphical window by executing the *xm* command. This is applicable for RHEL 5, however in higher version the VM can be displayed by clicking the *open* button.

[root@server]# xm create –c <guestname>

The guestname is the configuration file for booting the domain. The **-c** option displays the running VM in a pop up window.

12.6 Xen Limitations

The Xen RPM package consists of Xen-enabled host and guest OS and hypervisor. Xen is a VMM capable of securely running multiple OS in their own Sandboxed domains (an environment created for running untested/unreliable program). Each Sandboxed domain is limited to 16 GB RAM.

However, the machine may have up to 64GB total. In other words, the hardware may have 64GB of RAM, if the user configures Dom0 to use only 16 GB of RAM and create 3 (three) DomU using only 16 GB of RAM each. This type of configuration uses all 64 GB of RAM with limited support for x86 kernels.

Table 22 shows the limitation of Full Virtualization and Para Virtualization

Table 22.

Full Virtualization [Maximum]	Para Virtualization [Maximum]
• 16 GB **RAM/Guest** for x86 guests. • 4 (four) virtualized (emulated) IDE **Devices/Guest**. • Limit 254 para-virtualized block **Devices/Host**. • 254 block devices using the para-virtualized **Drivers/Guest**. • 15 network **Devices/Guest**. • 15 virtualized SCSI **Devices/Guest**.	• 16 GB **RAM/Guest** for x86 Guests. • 168 GB **RAM/Guest** for x86_64 **guests**. • 254 **Devices/Guest**. • 15 network **Devices/Guest**

13. INTRODUCTION TO KVM

KVM is open source software. Kernel-based Virtual Machine (KVM) was designed to run on-top of a bare-metal Linux machine with CPU supporting virtualization extensions such as Intel VMX / AMD SVM. The features of KVM are:

- Supporting for 'nested KVM'.
- Graphical user interface tool similar to VMware/VirtualBox.
- Command line interface.
- Consist of a loadable kernel module (kvm.ko) for providing the core virtualization infrastructure.
- Processor specific module kvm-intel.ko or kvm-amd.ko for Intel and AMD processor respectively (MediaWiki.org, 2014).

The GUI tool used for the management of VM in KVM is known as virt-manager developed by Red Hat. GUI for KVM comes with a number of supporting tools including virt-install, virt-clone, virt-image and virt-viewer, which are used to *clone, install and view* VMs respectively (http://geek4support.com/, 2014), (Red Hat, Inc., 2014).

13.1 Libvirt and the Libvirt Tools

An essential part of the KVM configuration on Red Hat Enterprise Linux Server is libvirt. Libvirt interface communicates and manages KVM hypervisor and other virtualization solutions running on Linux (Protti, 2009). The advantage of the libvirt API includes the library for different management programs (such as virsh, virt-viewer, virt-manager) and the libvirtd daemon for handling library calls, managing virtual guest and controlling hypervisors (Red Hat, Inc., 2014). On Red Hat Enterprise Linux, the VMM graphical tool and the *virsh* command provide the main management interfaces that use libvirt. Figure 14 shows how libvirt integrates in Virtualization on Red Hat Enterprise Linux.

As shown in Figure 14, Libvirt is a hypervisor-independent virtualization API for a range of OS. Libvirt API manages VM, Virtual networks and storage. However, it does not support multi node management features such as load balancing.

Virsh

Before using *virsh* command libvirtd daemon needs to be started. *virsh* is a command line for libvirt (Red Hat, Inc., 2014). The *virsh* is built on the libvirt management API and operates as an alternate to the graphical management tool virt-manager. The *virsh* command is ideal for virtualization administration. *virsh* command can be used in read only mode by unprivileged users.

Virt-Viewer

This tool can be used to connect to the VM's console with RDP, VNC, SPICE.

Virt-Manager

The *virt-manager* is a management tool for managing virtualized guests. The administration function of a *virt-manager* includes the following (Linuxtopia, 2014):

Figure 14. Libvirt Architecture

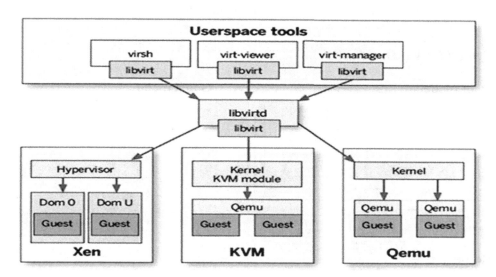

- Creating, configuring and migration of virtualized guest.
- View virtualized guests, host statistics, device information and performance graphs.
- Management of local and remote hypervisors

Qemu

Qemu is like a user space process, which communicates via /dev/kvm.

The qemu-img command is used to *create, inspect* image information, convert raw to vmdk image and formatting various file systems of KVM.

Virtio

The virtio drivers operate with the hypervisor. All Linux guests have *virtio* drivers integrated and windows VMs have *virtio* drivers that can be installed. Since *virtio* drivers are running in a virtualized environment, hence no emulation.

13.2 KVM Architecture

KVM is developed by implementing Linux kernel module with increased VMM functionalities. Linux system has two modes of execution, i.e. user and kernel mode, also known as unprivileged and privileged mode. The default mode is user mode. It changes to the kernel mode once it needs some kind of services from the kernel like request for writing to hard disk.

Whereas implementing the KVM, the developers included a third mode for process, known as guest mode as shown in Figure 15.

Figure 15. KVM Guest mode

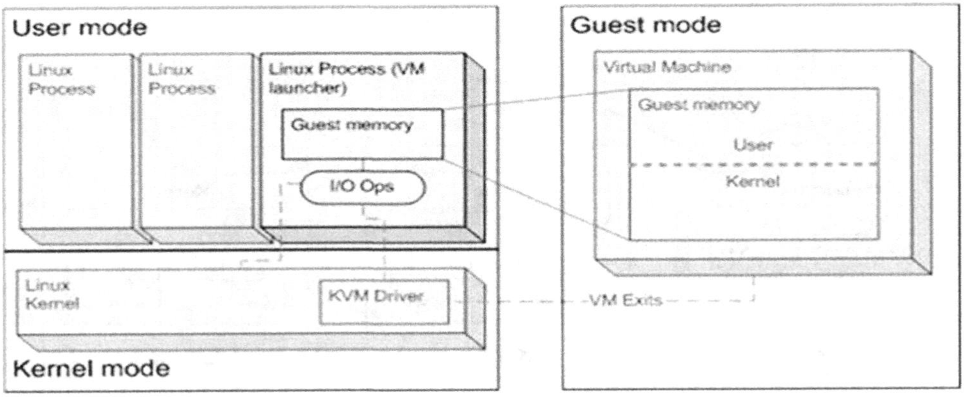

Guest mode of KVM has two common modes:

- User mode also known as guest-user and
- kernel mode also known as the guest-kernel.

In user mode, the Linux process performs I/O on behalf of a guest.

In the KVM every guest VM is executed as a simple Linux process. Each process is ready to run multiple applications acting as a virtual OS. Every VM is scheduled by the standard Linux scheduler. Quick Emulator (QEMU) handles all the I/O request of guest VM in KVM.

Every VM has its own virtual memory isolated from other VMs. The Physical memory of guests is actually the virtual memory provided to their OSs by KVM hypervisor.

13.3 Installation KVM

The following are the hardware resources required to install KVM on Red Hat Enterprise Linux Server

- 64-bit version of Red Hat Enterprise Linux.
- CPU supporting virtualization technology (Intel-VT / AMD-V).
- 2 GB of RAM plus additional RAM for VMs.
- 6 GB disk space for the host, plus the required disk space for each VM.

The easiest way to install KVM is by selecting the Virtualization host package while installing the Red Hat Enterprise Linux Server. Alternatively, add the required packages once the installation is completed by using YUM command.

[root@Server1~]# yum -y install qemu-kvm libvirt virt-manager virt-viewer bridge-utils

An essential part of the KVM configuration on Red Hat Enterprise Linux Server is libvirt. Libvirt is a generic interface for KVM hypervisor for managing KVM and other virtualization solutions running on Linux platform. *libvirt* provides the library for different management function. qemu-kvm package enables kvm on Red

Table 23.

User Mode / Guest-User	Kernel Mode / Guest-Kernel
Executes only Non-I/O guest code	Executes I/O or other special instructions

Hat Enterprise Linux. The virt-viewer displays the console of the VM and the *virsh* command provides the main management interfaces that use libvirt.

13.3.1 Creating a VM Using KVM Hypervisor

Step 1: Launch virt-manager command in terminal window Or Click on Application →System Tools →Virtual Machine Manager

Step 2: Click on Create a New Virtual Machine button (the leftmost button on the toolbar) for starting the process of creating a new VM. Enter the name of VM and select proper installation media.

Step 3: On the next screen of the installation verifies that the option Use CDROM or DVD is selected. If the DVD was found in the disc drive, then see the name of the disc in a drop-down list. Also select the OS type and version in this window.

Step 4: When asked for the amount of memory and number of CPUs, just accept the suggested default. Virtual Machine Manager detects the hardware that is on board, and it will suggest the optimal amount of RAM and virtual CPUs for the hardware.

Step 5: On the next screen, specify what kind of storage to be used. By default, the installer proposes a disk image file with a default size. Verify that after creating this image file, the system has enough disk space remaining in the system.

Step 6: On the last screen, just click Finish to start the installation.

14. VIRTUALBOX

VirtualBox is modular and flexible by design suitable for running on x86 and AMD64/Intel64 processor. VirtualBox is suitable for enterprise as well as home use. It was originally developed by Innotek GmbH and later on sold to Sun Microsystems. In January 2010 Sun Microsystems was purchased by Oracle Corporation, which now makes VirtualBox an Oracle product. VirtualBox is a "hosted" hypervisor. VirtualBox is freely available as Open Source Software under the terms of the GNU General Public License (GPL) version 2 ("Oracle VM VirtualBox," n. d.). VirtualBox uses software virtualization to run VMs. The following OS is currently supported by VirtualBox ("Oracle VM VirtualBox," n.d.):

14.1 VirtualBox Features

- **Fully Paravirtualized:** It provides device drivers which will improve the performance of virtualized input/output, mouse, networking and video.

Table 24.

Host OS	Guest OS
• Windows • Linux • Macintosh • Solaris	• Windows (NT 4.0, 2000, XP, Server 2003, Vista, Windows 7, Windows 8, Windows 10) • DOS/Windows 3.x • Linux (2.4, 2.6, 3.x and 4.x) • Solaris and OpenSolaris • OS/2 • OpenBSD

- **Shared Folder Support:** Provides easily exchange data between a guest OS and the host OS. Shared folders from the host OS are shown as a mapped network drive in guest OSs.
- **Virtual USB Controllers:** VirtualBox provides users with USB controllers which allow users to connect any type of USB devices to the virtual machines without the need to install device- specific drivers on the host OS.
- **Broad Virtual Network Driver Support:** VirtualBox can emulate many different legacy Ethernet cards and many different types of Intel Pro/1000 chipset for maximum OS compatibility.
- **Remote Desktop Protocol:** VirtualBox is different from other virtualization software. VirtualBox completely supports the standard Remote Desktop Protocol. VirtualBox allows a virtual machine to act as a Remote Desktop Protocol server, which will allow users to run the virtual machine remotely on a thin client that simply shows Remote Desktop Protocol data.
- **USB Over RDP:** With this feature a virtual machine which acts as a Remote Desktop Protocol server is able to access USB devices that are connected to the Remote Desktop Protocol client. With this method a server can virtualize a lot of thin clients that simply need to show Remote Desktop Protocol data and have USB devices plugged in.
- **Sound Driver Support:** VirtualBox can emulate Intel AC'97 and SoundBlaster 16.
- **Hardware Virtualization Support:** VirtualBox supports maximum of 16 vCPUs per VM with 16GB of RAM for each VM, and 32 virtual cores per host OS.
- **3D Support:** VirtualBox supports accelerated 2D graphics and experimental 3D graphics support for guest OSs. VirtualBox is able to allocate up to 128MB of virtualized video RAM.
- **Seamless Desktop Mode:** Windows applications from guest OS can easily be displayed on host OS without showing the entire guest OS desktop. For instance, Microsoft Windows applications can run on Linux OS without showing the entire Microsoft Windows user interface.

- **Support for Competing Virtual Disk Formats:** VirtualBox supports both VMware and Microsoft virtual disk formats.
- **VM Teleportation:** VirtualBox supports live migration between VirtualBox hosts.
- **Experimental Extensible Firmware Interface (EFI) Support:** In VirtualBox Mac OS X can be installed on a standard PC for running VirtualBox unmodified.

14.2 Architecture of Oracle VM VirtualBox

In VirtualBox hypervisor is implemented as a Ring 0 kernel service. The kernel contains a device driver called vboxsrv. The function of vboxsrv is as follows ("Oracle VM VirtualBox architecture - Getting Started with Oracle VM VirtualBox," n. d.):

- Allocating physical memory for the guest VM.
- Saving and restoring the guest process when a host interruption occurs.
- Turning control over to the guest OS to begin execution.
- Deciding when the VT-x /AMD-V events need to be handled.

When a guest VM is started from the VirtualBox GUI, the VBoxSVC process starts automatically in the background.

VBoxSVC

VBoxSVC is the first client process that starts automatically and keeps running in the background. VBoxSVC takes care of activities / tasks such as maintaining the guest VM state and bookkeeping. With the help of COM/XPCOM, it provides communication between different VirtualBox components.

StartVM

When a guest VM starts, startvm process is started automatically. The startvm starts with the following options ("Oracle VM VirtualBox architecture - Getting Started with Oracle VM VirtualBox," n.d.):

- With option.
- With no option.

The following are a few important components of VirtualBox:

Table 25.

With Option	With No Option
• Loads actual hypervisor with the help of VMM library. • Runs the VM. • Provides input/output for the guest VM.	• Plays the role of the VirtualBox manager. • Display the VMs and their settings. • Communicating the settings and the state changes to the VBoxSVC process.

- **IPRT:** This portable library is invoked whenever VirtualBox accesses host OS features. With the help of IPRT library the cross-platform portability is maintained.
- **VMM**: This is a vital part of the hypervisor.
- **REM (Recompiled Execution Monitor):** This provides software emulation of CPU instructions.
- **EM (Execution Manager):** Manages and controls the execution of guest VM code.
- **HWACCM (Hardware Acceleration Manager):** This provides support for VT-x and AMD-V.
- **PGM (Page Manager):** The guest VM paging activity is taken care by this component.
- **TM (Time Manager):** This component handles timers and all the aspects of time inside guests.
- **CFGM (Configuration Manager):** Provides the settings relating to guest VM and all emulated devices stored in a tree structure.
- **SSM (Saved State Manager):** This component saves and loads the VM state.
- **Main:** This API is used by all the client processes because client processes cannot access the hypervisor directly.

Oracle VirtualBox can be downloaded from following link: https://www.virtualbox.org/

VirtualBox platform packages are listed in Table 26.

Table 26.

VirtualBox Package	Supported OS
VirtualBox **5.1.8**	Windows x86/amd64
	OS X amd64
	Linux
	Solaris amd64

The following link gives an overview of supported guest operating system in Oracle VirtualBox.

https://www.virtualbox.org/wiki/Guest_OSes

14.3 Steps for Creating VM on Oracle VirtualBox

Open Oracle VM VirtualBox Manager and follow the following steps

Step 1: Click on New button from top left corner of the Oracle VM VirtualBox Manager or Click Machine menu and select New option or use keyboard shortcut key Ctrl+N

Step 2: Choose a name for the new VM and select the type of OS and version.

Step 3: Select the amount of memory (RAM) in MB to be allocated to the VM

Step 4: Add a virtual hard drive to the new machine / create a new hard drive file / select one from the list / from another location using folder icon.

Step 5: Choose the type of file that would like to use for the new virtual hard drive. Oracle VirtualBox has the following file types:

  ◦ VDI (VirtualBox Disk Image)
  ◦ VHD (Virtual Hard Disk)
  ◦ VMDK (Virtual Machine Disk)

Step 6: Choose whether new virtual hard drive file should grow as it is used (dynamically allocated) or it should be created at maximum size (fixed size).

Step 7: Type the name of the new virtual hard drive, file or click on the folder icon to select a different folder to create the file. Select the size of the virtual hard drive in megabytes.

Step 8: Now virtual machine will ready for installation. Simply click Start button from top tool bar or right click on the VM name and click on Start.

Step 9: Select a virtual optical disk file or a physical optical drive containing a disk to start new VM / select an image file using folder icon.

15. VIRTUAL MACHINE MIGRATION

The process of transferring the entire VM from one physical machine to another physical machine is called VM migration. The parameter which determines the effectiveness of migration are:

● **Down Time:** Time for which services of the VMs are not available to the user.

- **Total Migration Time:** Time between the process of migrations of VMs initiated at the source and the time when the migrated VM gets a consistent state at the destination.

The techniques of migration of VM are of two types i.e. Off-line migration and Live VM migration.

1. Off-line VM migration process pause the VM and transfer all the states of the VM to the destination host then finally resume the VM in the new host. The Off-line VM migration procedure is very simple, but it takes long (Soni & Kalra, 2013, p. xx).
2. Live VM migration, the state of the VM is transferred with minimum interruption from the host. The advantage of live VM migration is invisible downtime. However, smooth live migration requires fast network connectivity between the host (Soni & Kalra, 2013, p. xx).

The parameters for evaluation of the performance of live migration are shown in Table 27.
Live migration is completed in the following two steps:

1. Pre-copy migration.
2. Post-copy migration.

1. **Pre-Copy Migration:** It is an iterative method of the live migration. In the first round all memory pages and CPU states are transferred to the destination VM. Since VM is still running the instance of the source VM, so during the transmission some memory pages are modified. These modified pages are called dirty page.

Set of dirty pages is called writable working set (WWS) are transferred from the source VM to the destination VM page by page. During this step the VM will be

Table 27.

Parameter	Remark
Preparation	Resources are reserved for the destination to perform various operations.
Downtime	Time during which the VM is suspended in the source host.
Resume	Instantiation of the VM on the destination.
Total time	Time to completion of all the above mentioned activities.

active at both the source and destination. This process is repeated until the size of WWS is reduced to 1MB. When the size of WWS is reduced to 1 MB then the VM on the source are stopped and all the memory pages and CPU states are transferred to the destination VM. Now, the migrated VM is ready to start at the destination.

2. **Post-Copy Migration:** Post copy migration takes place in two steps (Kaur & Rani, 2015, p. xx):

    Step 1: The VM to be migrated is transferred to the destination.

    Step 2: All the working / active memory pages of the VM, vCPU states and virtual devices are transferred to destination host. This approach reduces the down time, but increase the total migration time.

The Pre-copy approach is more reliable than the Post-copy. Since in pre-copy approach, source node keeps the updated copy of all memory pages and CPU states, so in the case of destination failure VM can be recovered. This approach is also useful if the dirty page transfer rate is larger than the dirty page growth rate.

15.1 Advantages of VM Migration

Table 28 highlights the advantages of VM migration (Kaur & Rani, 2015, p. xx).

Live migration VM images and migration base line in RedHat KVM 3.2, VMware vSphere 5.1, Microsoft Hyper-V 2012 and Citrix XenServer 6.1 (Hu et al., 2013, p. xx). The VM image format varies from the hypervisor to the hypervisor. Each virtualization supports its own image format as shown in Table 29.

Table 28. Advantages of VM migration

Parameter	Advantages	Remarks
Load balancing	• Reduces the difference of resource usage across physical machines in the cluster. • Prevents overloading of physical machines.	System load is balanced by migrating VMs from overloaded physical machine to under-loaded physical machine.
Server Consolidation	• Reduces server sprawl/ slump in data centers. • A VM packing heuristic algorithm is used to pack as many VMs as possible to a physical machine. • Reduces power consumption by turning off unused/under- utilized physical machines.	Reduces overall operational costs.
Hotspot & Coldspot Migration (Posted & Rouse, 2012)	The physical machine having resource usages beyond the threshold limit (**Hotspot**) is transferred to **Coldspot** (under-utilized physical machine).	Hotspot are reconfigured / reallocate to **Coldspot** for effective utilization of physical machine / data center infrastructure.

Table 29. Table VM image Specification

Hypervisor	Memory Migration Media	Memory Migration Image	Storage Migration Media	Storage Migration Image
KVM	NFS	QCOW2	EXT4	QCOW2
VMware	NFS	VMDK	VMFS	VMDK
Hyper-V	iSCSI	VHD	NTFS	VHD
Xen Server	NFS	VHD	EXT3	LVM

15.2 Hypervisor Live Migration Command Interface

Each hypervisor has its own command API for live migration. Table 30 shows virtualization live migration command line interface.

15.3 Comparison of Different Live Migration Techniques (Soni & Kalra, 2013)

A comparison of different live migration techniques is shown in Table 31.

Table 30. Table Live Migration Command API

Hypervisor	API or Command Interface
KVM	ssh + virsh
VMware	Java web service SDK
Hyper-V	telnet + powershell
Xen Server	ssh + xe

Table 31. Comparisons live migration techniques

VM Migration Techniques	Concept	Pros	Cons
Stop and Copy approach	Stop the source VM and copy all the pages to the destination, and then start execution of that VM.	Simplicity	More downtime
Pre Copy Approach	Transfer VM's memory pages, then processor states are transferred to the destination	1. Downtime is very less. 2. Migration is completely transparent to the Application, OS and Remote clients.	Duplicate transmission overhead.

continued on following page

Table 31. Continued

VM Migration Techniques		Concept	Pros	Cons
Adaptive Rate Limiting approach		Used in WWS (writable working set) and OS migration built on top of the Xen hypervisor.	Service downtime as low as 60 milliseconds.	More total migration time.
Improved Pre Copy Approach				
Memory Compression Techniques	1. Adaptive memory compression approach	Memory compression based VM migration (MECOM) first used memory compression technique.	1. Provides stable and fast VM migration. 2. Reduces the downtime and total migration time.	The Compression process establishes extra overhead.
	2. Delta Compression	This technique implemented as a modification to the KVM hypervisor.	1. Downtime is reduced. 2. Increases migration throughput.	The Compression process established additional overhead.
Frequently updated pages of memory.	1. Page bitmap	Frequently updated pages into the page bitmap and those pages can only be transmitted in the last round of the iteration process.	Reduces 34% of data transfer and 32.5% of total migration time.	Not suitable for wide area live VM migration.
	2. Time series prediction technique	Frequently updated dirty pages in the past and future period were identified and transmitted them in the last round of iteration.	1. Less number of iterations. 2. Less downtime and migration time. 3. Fewer pages transferred.	Useful for high dirty pages iteration.
	3. Detecting memory update patterns	Detecting memory update patterns and terminating migration.	Provides minimum downtime and impact on end to end application performance.	Useful for memory intensive applications.
Post Copy Approach		Initially, VM's migration execution states and accordingly all memory pages are transferred only once during the whole migration process.	1. Each memory page is transferred at least once. 2. Baseline total migration time is achieved.	Downtime is very high in comparison to pre copy.
Other Approaches				
Recovering system and CPU scheduling		A novel approach based on recovering system and CPU scheduling.	Reduces the downtime and migration time in comparison to pre copy algorithm.	The reliability of the approach in complex environments is doubtful.
CR/TR-Motion (Check recovery/ Trace Replay)		Transfers execution trace file in iterations.	1. Provides transparent VM migration. 2. Downtime and total migration time are slightly reduced.	CR/TR Motion is effective when log replay rate is larger than the log growth rate.

16. COMPARISONS OF HYPERVISORS

Table 32 shows the comparison of Hypervisors discussed above.

Table 32. Xen, KVM, vSphere and Hyper-V features

Features	XEN	KVM	vSphere	Hyper-V
Base OS	Linux+QEMU	Linux+QEMU	Vmkernel(Linux-based)	Windows Server
Latest Release Version(2016)	4.4	2.6.32-279	5.0	2012 R2
Architecture	Hosted	Bare-Metal	Bare-Metal	Bare-Metal
Supported Virtualization Technologies	Para-Virtualization, Full Virtualization, Hardware Assisted Virtualization.	Para-Virtualization, Full Virtualization, Hardware Assisted Virtualization.	Full Virtualization, Hardware Assisted Virtualization.	Para-Virtualization, Hardware Assisted Virtualization.
CPU Scheduling features	SEDF (Simple Earliest Deadline First)	Linux schedulers (Completely Fair Queuing Scheduler, round-robin, fair queuing, proportionally fair scheduling, maximum throughput, weighted fair queuing)	Proportional Share-based Algorithm, Relaxed Co-Scheduling, Distributed Locking with Scheduler Cell	Control with VM reserve, VM limit, relative weight
Memory Address Translation Mechanism	Direct Pagetable (PV mode), Shadow Page table (HVM mode), Hardware-Assisted Pagetable	Shadow page table, Hardware-Assisted Pagetable	Emulated TLB, Shadow Page table, Hardware Assisted Pagetable (nested page table)	Shadow Pagetable, Hardware-Assisted Pagetable (Second Level Address Translation)
Network Management Features	FIFO-based scheduling	FIFO-base scheduling	Priority-based NetIOC (Network I/O Control), TCP segmentation offload, netqueue, distributed virtual switch	TCP offload, large send offload, VM queue

continued on following page

Table 32. Continued

Features	XEN	KVM	vSphere	Hyper-V
SMP Scheduling Features	Work-Nonconserve, Work-Conserve	SMP-Aware Scheduling	CPU Topology-aware Load Balancing	CPU Topology-based Scheduling
Disk Management Features	No-op, anticipatory, deadline, completely fair queue (CFQ)	No-op, anticipatory, deadline, completely fair queue (CFQ)	Latency-aware Priority-based scheduler, storage DRS	Fixed disks, pass through disks, dynamic disks
Virtual CPUs per VM	16	64	32	64
IPv6	No	Yes	No	Yes
Source code model	Open Source (GPLv2)	Open Source (GPLv2)	Proprietary	Proprietary
Virtualization live migration command API	ssh + xe	ssh + virsh	Java web service SDK	telnet+powershell
Memory migration media	NFS	NFS	NFS	iSCSI
Memory migration image	VHD	QCOW2	VMDK	VHD
Storage migration media	EXT3	EXT4	VMFS	NTFS
Storage Migration image	LVM	QCOW2	VMDK	VHD

CONCLUSION

In this chapter the authors discussed the Virtualization technology in details. Mostly used hypervisiors such as Xen, KVM, Hyper-V are discussed. Finally, a comparative study on the hypervisior are presented. Since the open source software are having lots of scope in the Cloud and the emerging Internet of Things (IoT), we focused more on open source hypervisior.

REFERENCES

Adair, R. J., Bayles, R. U., Comeau, L. W., & Creasy, R. J. (1966). A Virtual Machine System for the 360/40. IBM Corporation Cambridge Scientific Center Report No. 320-2007.

Adeshiyan, T., Attanasio, C. R., Farr, E. M., Harper, R. E., Pelleg, D., Schulz, C., & Tomek, L. A. et al. (2009, July). Using virtualization for high availability and disaster recovery. *IBM Journal of Research and Development, 53*(4), 1–11. doi:10.1147/ JRD.2009.5429062

Armbrust, M., Fox, A., Griffith, R., Joseph, A. D., Katz, R., Konwinski, A., & Zaharia, M. et al. (2009). A view of cloud computing. *Communications of the ACM, 53*(4), 50–58. doi:10.1145/1721654.1721672

Betonio, D. (2011, April 18). 12 excellent cloud computing operating systems. *Tripwiremagazine.com*. Retrieved October 17, 2016, from http://www. tripwiremagazine.com/2011/04/12-excellent-cloud-computing-operating-systems. html

Centos. (n. d.). Red Hat Enterprise Linux 5.4. Retrieved from http://www.centos. org/docs/5/html/5.4/Release_Notes/ index.html#id444217

Chubachi, Y., Shinagawa, T., & Kato, K. (2010). Hypervisor-based prevention of persistent rootkits. *Proceedings of the 2010 ACM Symposium on Applied Computing*, New York, NY, USA (pp. 214-220). doi:10.1145/1774088.1774131

Deka, G. C. (2014). Cost-Benefit Analysis of Datacenter Consolidation Using Virtualization. *IT Professional, 16*(6), 54–62. doi:10.1109/MITP.2014.89

Deka, G. C., & Das, P. K. (2014). An Overview on the Virtualization Technology. Handbook of Research on Cloud Infrastructures for Big Data Analytics, 289. doi:10.4018/978-1-4666-5864-6.ch012

Department of State Federal Data Center Consolidation Initiative Plan (DOS FDCCI Plan), Document Release: 3.0 for Public Distribution. (2011, September 30).

Fanatical, R. (2014, January 27). XCP overview. Retrieved October 17, 2016, from http://wiki.xen.org/wiki/XCP_Overview#What_is_XCP.3F

Flexiant.com. (2014, February 12). Hypervisor comparison | KVM, Xen, VMware, Hyper-V. Retrieved October 18, 2016, from Hosting Providers, https://www.flexiant. com/2014/02/12/hypervisor-comparison-kvm-xen-vmware-hyper-v/

Geek4support.com. (2014, August 29). KVM and Virtualization. Retrieved from http://geek4support.com/?p=598

Gmb, H. P. I. (1999). NEW! Parallels desktop 12 for Mac. Retrieved October 16, 2016, from http://www.parallels.com/

Goldberg, R. P. (1974). Survey of Virtual Machines Research. *Computer, 7*(6), 34–45.

Hu, W., Hicks, A., Zhang, L., Dow, E. M., Soni, V., & Jiang, H. … Matthews, J. N. (2013). A quantitative study of virtual machine live migration. *Proceedings of the 2013 ACM Cloud and Autonomic Computing Conference CAC '13.* doi:10.1145/2494621.2494622

Hyper-V. (2016). In Wikipedia. Retrieved from http://en.wikipedia.org/wiki/Hyper-V

Ishtiaq Ali1 and Natarajan Meghanathan. (2011, 01). Virtual machines and networks –installation, performance, study, advantages and virtualization options. Retrieved from http://airccse.org/journal/nsa/0111jnsa01.pdf

Jayaraman, A., & Rayapudi, P. (2012), Comparative study of Virtual Machine Software Packages with real operating system [Master's Thesis]. School of Computing, Blekinge Institute of Technology, Karlskrona, Sweden.

Kaur, P., & Rani, A. (2015). Virtual Machine Migration in Cloud Computing. *International Journal of Grid and Distributed Computing*, 8(5), 337–342. doi:10.14257/ijgdc.2015.8.5.33

Khanna, G., Beaty, K., Kar, G., & Kochut, A. (2006). Application Performance Management Virtualized Server Environments. *Proceedings of the 10th IEEE/ IFIP Network Operations and Management Symposium NOMS '06* (pp. 373-381).

Kirkland, J., Carmichael, D., Tinker, C. L., & Tinker, G. L. (2006). *Linux Troubleshooting for System Administrators and Power Users* (1st ed.). Prentice Hall.

Kurth, L. (n. d.). Xen cloud platform at build a cloud a day at scale 10x. Retrieved from http://www.slideshare.net/xen_com_mgr/xen-cloud-platform-at-build-a-cloud-day-at-scale-10x

MediaWiki.org. (2014). Kernel based Virtual Machine. Retrieved from http://www. linux-kvm.org/page/Main_Page

Mell, P., & Grance, T. (n. d.). "Cloud Computing" by National Institute of Standards and Technology. Retrieved from www.csrc.nist.gov

Multi Data Palembang. (2008, February 13). Xen architecture overview. Retrieved from http://repository.mdp.ac.id/ebook/library-sw-hw/linux-1/cloud/xen/docs/XenArchitecture_Q12008

Otey, M. (2013, June 03). Top 10 Windows Server 2012 R2 Hyper-V New Features. Retrieved October 25, 2016, from http://windowsitpro.com/hyper-v/top-10-windows-server-2012-r2-hyper-v-new-features

Packtpub.com. (n. d.). VirtualBox architecture- Getting Started with Oracle VM VirtualBox. Retrieved from https://www.packtpub.com/mapt/book/ Virtualization+and+Cloud /9781782177821/1/ch01lvl1sec14/Oracle+VM+Virt ualBox+architecture

Pedram, M., & Hwang, I. (2010). Power and Performance Modeling in a Virtualized Server System. *Proceedings of the 2010 39th International Conference on Parallel Processing Workshops (ICPPW)* (pp. 520-526).

Posted, & Kurth, L. (2013). VS16: Video spotlight with Xen project's Lars Kurth. Retrieved October 16, 2016, from http://www.xen.org

Protti, D. J. (2009, October 1). Linux KVM as a Learning Tool. *Linux Journal*, 186.

Red Hat, Inc. (2014). A Complete Virtualization Solution for Servers and Desktops. Retrieved from http://www.redhat.com/en/technologies/virtualization

Rosenblum, M., & Garfinkel, T. (2005, May). Virtual machine monitors: Current technology and future trends. *Computer*, *38*(5), 39–47. doi:10.1109/MC.2005.176

Rouse, M. (2012, February). What is hot spot/cold spot? - definition from WhatIs. Com. Retrieved October 19, 2016, from http://searchdatacenter.techtarget.com/ definition/Hot-spot-cold-spot

Sarathy, V., Narayan, P., & Mikkilineni, R. " Next generation cloud computing architecture", 19th IEEE international workshop on enabling technology: infrastructure for collaborative enterprise (WETICE), pp. 48-53,2012.

http://searchservervirtualization.techtarget.com/tip/Virtual-memory-management-techniques-A-beginners-guide

Semnanian, A.A., Pham, J., Englert, B., & Wu, X. (2011). Virtualization Technology and its Impact on Computer Hardware Architecture. *Proceedings of the 2011 Eighth International Conference on Information Technology: New Generations (ITNG)* (pp. 719-724).

Sitaram, D., & Manjunath, G. (2012). Moving to the Cloud. In Syngress (Ch. 9, p. 352).

Soni, G., & Kalra, M. (2013). Comparative Study of Live Virtual Machine Migration Techniques in Cloud. *International Journal of Computers and Applications*, *84*(14), 19–25. doi:10.5120/14643-2919

Soto-Navarro, R. (2012). Presenting Linux kvm. Retrieved from www.flux.org/ slides/linux-kvm-presentation-flux.org.pdf

Uhlig, R., Neiger, G., Rodgers, D., Santoni, A. L., Martins, F. C. M., Anderson, A. V., & Smith, L. et al. (2005, May). Intel Virtualization technology. *Computer*, *38*(5), 48–56. doi:10.1109/MC.2005.163

VirtualBox. (n. d.). Retrieved October 16, 2016, from https://www.virtualbox.org/

VirtualBox. (n. d.). Retrieved October 23, 2016, from https://www.virtualbox.org/

Visionsolutions.com. (2016). Business continuity & disaster recover software, vision solutions. Retrieved October 17, 2016, from http://www.visionsolutions.com/Company/About-Vision-Solutions.aspx

VMware. (2016, October 13). VMware Virtualization for desktop & server, application, public & hybrid clouds. Retrieved October 16, 2016, from http://www.vmware.com

VMware.com. (n. d.). Knowledge Base. Retrieved from http://kb.vmware.com/selfservice/microsites/search.do?language=en_US&cmd=displayKC&externalId=1003882

VMware, Inc. (2007). Understanding full Virtualization, Paravirtualization, and Hardware assist. Retrieved from http://www.vmware.com/files/pdf/VMware_paravirtualization.pdf

VMware, Inc. (2011). VmWare ESXi™ 5.0 Operations Guide Technical (white paper). Retrieved from https://www.vmware.com/files/pdf/techpaper/vSphere-5-ESXi-Operations-Guide.pdf

VMware, Inc. (2013). Using vmware workstation. Retrieved from www.vmware.com/pdf/desktop/ws10-using.pdf

VMWare, Inc2006). Double-Take Replication in the VMware Environment. Retrieved from http://www.vmware.com/pdf/vmware_doubletake.pdf

Weltzin, C., & Delgado, S. (2009). Using Virtualization to reduce the cost of test. *Proceedings of AUTOTESTCON '09* (pp. 439-442).

Wikipedia. (n. d.). x86 Virtualization. Retrieved from https://en.wikipedia.org/wiki/X86_virtualization

Wind, S. (2011). Open source cloud computing management platform. Proceedings of the IEEE conference on open system (ICOS '11) (pp. 175-179).

Xen. (2009, December). How does Xen work? Retrieved from http://www-archive.xenproject.org/files/Marketing/HowDoesXenWork.pdf

Xen. (2009, December). How does Xen work? Retrieved from http://www-archive. xenproject.org/files/Marketing/HowDoesXenWork.pdf

Xen® Hypervisor The open source standard for hardware Virtualization, http:// www-archive .xenproject.org/products/xenhyp.html

Xenproject.org. (n. d.a). Xen Cloud Platform 1.6. Retrieved from http://www. xenproject.org/downloads/xen-cloud-platform-archives/xen-cloud-platform-16.html

Xenproject.org. (n. d.b). Why Xen Project? Retrieved from http://www.xenproject. org/users/why-the-xen-project.html

Yuen, E. (2012). Independent Third Party Assessments of Hyper-V. *Technet. com*. Retrieved from http://blogs.technet.com/b/server-cloud/archive/2012/07/09/ independent-third-party-assessments-of-hyper-v.aspx

KEY TERMS AND DEFINITIONS

Bus Logic: Bus Logic adapters have parallel interfaces.

Customized Appliances: Is a user defined virtualized environment created by a user. A software appliance generally includes a customized and optimized operating system and the software application packaged within it.

Domain U HVM Guests: All fully virtualized machines running on a Xen hypervisor are referred to as Domain U HVM Guests.

Domain U PV Guests: All paravirtualized VMs running on a Xen hypervisor are referred to as Domain U PV Guests.

Host Machine or Host Computer: Physical Machine/Computer in which the Virtual Machine Monitor (VMM) or Hypervisor software is installed (Microsoft Virtual PC, Oracle Virtual Box or VMware etc.). It is physical machine.

Hyper-Threading: Hyper-Threading is a technology used by some Intel microprocessors that allows a single microprocessor to act like two separate processors to the operating system and the application programs that use it. It is a feature of Intel's IA-32 processor architecture.

KVM: Kernel-based Virtual Machine (KVM) is a kernel module that was originally developed by an Israeli organization called Qumranet to provide native virtualization technology for Linux-based platforms; essentially turning the kernel into a Tier-1 hypervisor. The founders of Qumranet were focused on using KVM as the foundation for a centralized virtual desktop solution (commonly referred to as VDI) for Windows clients. It has since been ported to multiple other platforms and architectures other than 32/64-bit x86 (NextStep4it, 2014). It got initially adopted into the upstream Linux kernel as of 2.6.20 (back in 2007). KVM uses QEMU for I/O hardware emulation. QEMU could be a user-space emulator which will emulate a range of guest processors on host processors with good performance (Protti, 2009).

Libvirt: Libvirt is free software available under the GNU Lesser General Public License. The libvirt project aims to provide a long term stable C API. The libvirt Open Source project currently supports Xen, QEmu, KVM, LXC, OpenVZ, VirtualBox, OpenNebula, and VMware ESX. The Red Hat Enterprise Linux 6 libvirt package supports Xen on Red Hat Enterprise Linux 5 and KVM on Red Hat Enterprise Linux 5 and Red Hat Enterprise Linux 6.

LSI Logic: LSI Logic adapters have parallel interfaces. The LSI Logic SAS adapter has a serial interface. The LSI Logic adapter has improved performance and works better with generic SCSI devices. The LSI Logic adapter is also supported by ESX Server 2.0 and higher.

Quick Emulator (QEMU): QEMU is a virtualization emulator that enables complete virtualization of the PC environment, including disks, graphic adapters, BIOS, PCI bus, USB and network devices. Any I/O requests by a guest OS are routed to the user mode to be emulated by the QEMU.

Sandbox: A sandbox is a security mechanism for isolating running programs specifically untested/untrusted programs or code.

Snapshot: A partial copy of a VM at a particular moment in time. Allows to 'go back' to the VM at that particular state. Some programs allow saving multiple snapshots. Snapshot just like a system restore in Windows Operating System.

Types of Hypervisor: Mainly there are two types of hypervisor i.e. Type 1 and 2. Xen is a Type-1 hypervisor. A Type-1 hypervisor runs directly up on the hardware with a separated layer from the host OS. Type-2 hypervisor runs together with the host OS. Due to the isolation from the host OS, the security, performance and scalability features in Type-1 are more enhanced than Type-2. Xen currently supports IA32, IA32 PAE, IA64, and AMD64 architectures. Indeed, multiple VMs can run in parallel on a single host with Xen.

Virtual Appliances: A minimal virtual machine image that contains the software appliance designed to run in a virtualized environment.

Virtual Disk: One or more files that reside on the host computer that make up the VM's hard disk.

Virtual Machine (VM) or Guest OS: A VM is a computing environment similar to physical machines. VM uses the physical resources of the host computer on which it runs. VMs have virtual devices. For example, install an operating system in a VM in the same way that on a physical computer. The User must have a CD-ROM, DVD, or ISO image that contains the installation files from an operating system vendor. The operating system that runs in virtual machine monitor or hypervisor on the host computer is known as a Virtual Machine (VM). It includes primarily of a configuration file and one or more virtual hard drive files. It is logical in nature.

Virtual Machine Monitor (VMM): The Virtualization software used for system Virtualization is known as a Virtual Machine Monitor (VMM) also known as hypervisors.

Virtual Network: The network configuration used by the VM. There are various options available: bridged, host only, NAT. VMs behave like just another computer on the network.

Chapter 3
Fog Computing and Virtualization

Siddhartha Duggirala
Bharat Petroleum Corporation Limited, India

ABSTRACT

The essence of Cloud computing is moving out the processing from the local systems to remote systems. Cloud is an umbrella of physical/virtual services/resources easily accessible over the internet. With more companies adopting cloud either fully through public cloud or Hybrid model, the challenges in maintaining a cloud capable infrastructure is also increasing. About 42% of CTOs say that security is their main concern for moving into cloud. Another problem which is mainly problem with infrastructure is the connectivity issue. The datacenter could be considered as the backbone of cloud computing architecture. As the processing power and storage capabilities of the end devices like mobile phones, routers, sensor hubs improve we can increasing leverage these resources to improve your quality and reliability of services.

INTRODUCTION

Cloud computing has completely transformed how businesses function and handle their IT infrastructures. By consolidating all the available resources and providing software defined resources based on the demand has been an efficiency driver. The main reasons the cloud computing really took of are the resource utilisation, efficiency, on demand resource delivery and financial benefits associated with them.

Up until the recent years the processing power, storage available at the end points like user PCS, embedded devices room mobile phones are limited. So, it made

DOI: 10.4018/978-1-5225-2785-5.ch003

logical sense to move the burden of processing and storage to the cloud. An effective example of this is Chromebook from Google or any one of the plethora of cloud services we use every day. The only big disadvantage of these services or products is that they are completely network dependent. Heavy usage of network bandwidth and latency expectations place higher demands on the network infrastructure. This sometimes reduces the quality of experiences for the end users and in extreme cases can even be fatal.

Right now in 2017, there are about 2 devices connected to internet per every human on Earth and the number of devices estimated to be connected to internet is estimated to be 50 billion by 2020. These include the mobile phones, smart routers, home automation hubs, smart industrial machines, sensors smart vehicles (Hou, Li, Chen et al., 2016) and the whole gamut of smart devices. To give an idea of how much needs to be pushed through the Internet due to these devices, Boeing flight generate about 1 TB of data or even more for one hour of operation, the weather sensors generate about 500gb of data per day. Our mobile phone sensors are capable of generating more than 500mb of logs per data and that multiplied by number of smart phones is staggering amount of data. This along with the increasing rich media usage in the Internet will be a huge challenge for the next generation networks.

As the processing power and storage capabilities of the end devices like mobile phones, routers, sensor hubs improve we can increasing leverage these resources to improve your quality and reliability of services. Processing or even caching the data near wherever it is generated or utilised frequently not only of loads of the burden on the networks but also improves the decision making capabilities for commercial or industrial instalments, quality of experience for personal usage.

Handling this new generation of requirements of volume, variety and velocity in IOT data requires us to evaluate the tools and technologies. For effective implementation of these use cases places the following requirements on the infrastructure:

1. **Minimise Latency:** Milliseconds, even microseconds matter when you are trying to prevent a failure at a nuclear power station, or preventing of some calamity or to make a buyable impression on a customer. Analyzing data and gaining actionable insights are near as the device itself makes all the difference between a cascading system failure and averting disaster.
2. **Optimising Network Utilisation:** Data generated by the sensors is huge. And not all the data generated is useful. It is not even practical to transport this vast amount of data to centralised processing stations/Data centre nor is it necessary.

3. **Security and Privacy:** Data needs to be protected both in transit and at rest. This requires efficient encryption, monitoring and automated response in case of any breach (Stojmenovic & Wen, 2014).

4. **Reliability:** As more and more intelligent systems are deployed, their effect on the safety of citizens and critical infrastructure cannot be undermined.

5. **Durability:** As the devices themselves can be deployed across wide area of environment conditions. The devices themselves need to be durable and made rugged to work efficiently in harsh environments likes railways, deep oceans, utility field substations and vehicles (Hou, Li, Chen et al., 2016).

6. **Geographic Distribution and Mobility:** The Fog devices should be dispersed geographically as to provide the storage and processing resources to the sensors/actuators producing and acting based on the decisions made. The sensors themselves can be highly mobile. The fog environment should be able to provide consistent resources even in this highly dynamic scenarios. This is especially the case with Wireless sensor area networks, Personal body area networks, Vehicular area network (MANET/VANET).

7. **Interoperability**: The fog devices are intended to be connected to all sorts of devices. Many of these devices have proprietary communication protocols and are not based on IP. In these cases, the fog nodes should be able to communicate and even translate them to IP protocols incase the data needs to be pushed to cloud.

FOG COMPUTING

In simple terms, Fog computing (Yi, Li, & Li, 2015) or Edge computing extends the cloud to be closer to the things that produce, act on and consume data. The devices at the edge are called fog nodes can be deployed anywhere with network connectivity, alongside the railway track, traffic controllers, parking meters, or anywhere else. Any device with sufficient network, storage and computing resources can be a Fog nodes. For example, network switches, embedded servers, CCTV cameras, industrial controllers.

Analyzing data close to where it is collected/generated minuses network latency and offloads gigabytes of less valuable data from the core network, keeping the critical, sensitive data inside the network.

Cisco coined the term Fog computing and defined it as an extension of cloud computing paradigm from the core of network to the edge of network, a highly virtualized platform providing computation, storage (Wu & Sun, 2013) and networking services between end devices and tradition cloud servers. In other work authors defined "Fog computing as a scenario where a huge number of heterogeneous ubiquitous and decentralized devices communicate and potentially cooperate among themselves and with the network to perform storage and processing tasks without any third-party intervention. These tasks can be basic network functions or sophisticated, novel services and applications that run in a virtualized environments. Users leasing a part of their devices to host these services get incentives for doing so,". Although the exact definition of Fog computing is still being constructed it is essential to separate this from related technologies.

Similar concepts such as Mobile cloud computing and Mobile Edge computing overlap with Fog computing. In Mobile Edge computing (Hu, Patel, Sabella et al., 2015), cloud server running at the edge of the mobile network performs specifics tasks that cannot be accomplished with traditional network infrastructure. While Mobile Cloud computing refers to infrastructure in which data storage and processing occurs outside the mobile devices. MCC pushes the data and computation to the cloud making it feasible for the non-smartphone users to use mobile applications and services. Fog computing is a more generalized platform with virtual resources and application aware processing.

Applications of Fog computing is as diverse as IoT and Cloud computing itself. What IoT and Fog computing have in common is to monitor and analyse real-time data from network connected things and acting on them. Machine-to-machine coordination or human-machine interaction can be a part of this action. Unlimited possibilities,

As we have seen in earlier sections, the following scenarios make a good case for Fog computing:

1. Data is generated from thousands or millions of things/sensors distributed geographically.
2. Data is collected at the extreme edges of the infrastructure: factory floors, warehouses, roadways, etc.
3. The time taken to analyse, take a decision and act on the data is in range of milliseconds.

Difference between Fog computing and Cloud computing:

The core difference comes in the way resources are organized. In cloud computing the resources are centralized whereas in Fog computing the resources are scattered and available possibly nearer the client. Cloud service providers are generally single tiered organizations whereas the fog ecosystem as such is multi-tiered. Fog computing supports dynamic, mobility better than cloud computing as the resources allocated are near-by the usage itself. Due to the service locality and geographic distribution

Figure 1. Fog platform high level architecture

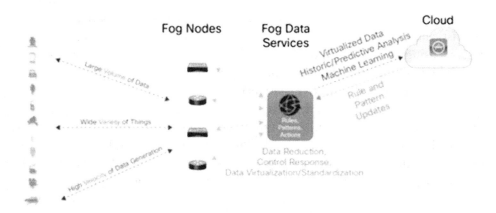

Figure 2. Cloud computing vs. Fog Computing

Requirement	Cloud Computing	Fog Computing
Latency	High	Low
Delay Jitter	High	Very low
Location of server nodes	Within the internet	At the edge of the local network
Distance between the client and the server.	Multiple hops	One hop
Security	Undefined	Can be defined
Attack on data enroute	High probability	Very low probability
Location awareness	No	Yes
Geographical distribution.	Centralized	Distributed
Number of server nodes	Few	Very large
Support for mobility	Limited	Supported
Real time interactions	Supported	Supported
Type of last mile connectivity.	Leased line	Wireless

of resources the latency in transmission of data is highly reduced. This mode of processing has an added benefit of adhering to local security and privacy norms. The differences are highlighted in the succeeding table (Figure 2).

If you look at the financial side of implementing fog computing, a study at Wikibon found that cloud-only infrastructure is costlier to maintain as compared to Cloud with Fog/Edge computing infrastructure. One of the main reasons for this is the average life cycle of a cloud server is a measly 2 years. In proper Fog computing infrastructure the servers' life time is upto 8 years. This would make a huge difference for companies small and large in both short term and long term technology infrastructures.

As we have already seen the major demerit with cloud computing is latency (Bonomi, Milito, Zhu et al., 2012). Latency in feeding the data into the system to analyzing it and producing tangible insights. These insights in many cases help in making split-second decisions. Some data is valuable at the moment it is recorded. For example, a pressure gauge going critical in a manufacturing plant, or a security breach at a critical site or Complex event processing. Fog computing helps in analysing at the sources and give results with-in milliseconds range. And the insights are fed to visualisation tools to communicate and coordinate with other systems, the data is then sent to cloud for archiving, aggregation and further batch analysis can be done at the cloud level. As shown in Figure 3. As we move on to transactional analytics and Historical analysis cloud become the ideal choice to do run the analyses.

Another advantage in analyzing the data near the source is all the data generated need to be fed into cloud system. The data generated will have a lot of noise or unnecessary data which doesn't provide us with any significant insight. So, pushing the data just wastes precious network bandwidth and cloud storage.

Data thinning removes this unnecessary data and strips away all the noise just leaving us with only the data that really matters. For example, a driverless car might generate Petabytes of image data a year of bumpers or speed breakers or any line it crosses and that generated data in entirety is so useful. A Boeing jet generates 2.5TB data per 1 hour of flight operation. An oil drill sensors generate more than 10 GB of data per second.

Figure 3. Processing latency from Fog computing to Cloud computing

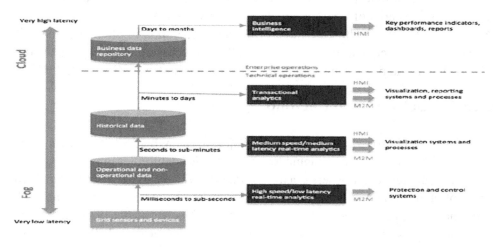

As the minimalist principle states "More is not always better." The processing of the data at the fog nodes not only reduce the time to insight but they in-turn help in making emergency responses more efficient.

Application Scenarios Healthcare Monitoring

One of important ways the Fog computing might help in Health care is to take conservative snap decisions and escalate the risky situations for deep analysis which can further help in reducing the risk of false negatives. One such effective implementation is for alerting doctor of cardiac arrests (Stantchev, Barnawi, Ghulam et al., 2015).

Earlier notification systems required users to wear unfriendly chest straps and needed extensive monitoring. Not to mention expensive and often obstructive to the normal flow of life of patients. The implementations based on wearable solved this problem. They are relatively cheap and are used friendly. Data is pushed to the cloud or remote servers from these devices for analysis. On the software side, many implementations based on statistical models do not have required positive detention. Rates. To eliminate these errors sophisticated neural network based techniques were employed. Although these techniques provided with high levels of detection rates, they are slow. The simple statistical model scored points in this regard. In addition with the latency of networks to push the data to cloud for processing they couldn't provide analysis within required time frame. To circumvent these problems one can look at processing primary analysis nearer to the patient and push the processed data to the cloud for further analysis. Through this a quick response can be given in a way to avert a possible emergency or handle it in a more efficient manner.

These analyses also come under the broad class of Mobile Big Data analytics use cases. Fog computing provides elastic resources to large scale systems without the latency concerns of cloud computing (Buyya, Yeo, Venugopal et al., 2009). As explained in the health care monitoring case, federation of cloud and fog will take care of data acquisition, aggregation and pre-processing, reducing bandwidth overload and data processing. Bonomi, et al. (Bonomi, Milito, Zhu et al., 2012).

Content Delivery and Caching

Traditional caching or content delivery techniques are heavily server dependent. Even they provide a sense of geo-graphic locality for multi-datacenter implementations. Delivering content to end-users is a not-optimally efficient. What a particular client or set of client want and network level statistics are only available at a local level. This knowledge can be leveraged to optimise the web performance. Since fog nodes lie in the vicinity of the user it can gather statistics and usage knowledge to optimise the user experience. And this reduces the requirement of bandwidth as the data most required will most probably in the vicinity of the user itself. J. Zhu, et al. consider web optimisation from this new perspective in the context of fog computing (Zhu, Chan, Prabhu et al., 2013).

Software Defined Networking

In broadest terms, the network is connection between various servers and storage clusters inside as well as outside a datacenter. This is the fundamental contributor to QoS and delivery performance of applications. Businesses creating their cloud environments should have a keener look at their whole infrastructure mainly the network which glues every component together. Many of the large enterprises work in distributed geographical locations, while the applications that are pre-dominantly media based, time-sensitive. This puts pressure on QoS (Quality of Service) for applications delivered over the network. (Nunes, Mendonca, Nguyen et al., 2014).

Networking has traditionally been completely about hardware. With almost all the major functions are hardcoded in the hardware making it difficult and expensive to upgrade firmware. With the sophistication of software, these functionalities are slowly moved into the software layer, this is called network function virtualization (Martins, Ahmed, Raiciu et al., 2014). Software defined networking is a complete reproduction of physical network at software level, while being more flexible and can be customised according to the application's requirements. The applications can run exactly the same as if they are run on physical network. (Barroso, Clidaras, & Hölzle, 2013).

A protocol is a set of rules governing communications. Networking protocols lay down the format of message, how they will be identified and what actions need to be taken.

Figure 4. Network packet

8 Bytes	6 bytes	6 Bytes	2 Bytes	0-1500 Bytes	0-46 Bytes	4 Bytes
Preamble	Destination Address	Source Address	Frame Length	Data	Pad	Checksum

Figure 5. Virtual Network

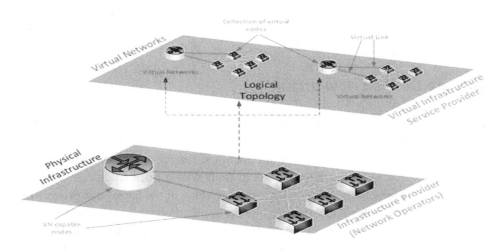

NETWORK FUNCTION VIRTUALIZATION

If Overlay networks gives the capability of creating network tunnels per flow. The next logical step is offload the functions of hardware based networking services like Firewalls, Load Balancers and provide them as a service on the tunnel. This is Network Function Virtualization. Network function Virtualization proposes to virtualise entire classes of network node functions in to building blocks using virtualization. The popular functions for this are firewalls and IDS/IPS systems from companies like PLUMgrid or Embrane (Wu & Sun, 2013).

Network Function Virtualization runs on x86 platforms, instead of having its own hardware appliance.

The NFV architecture has the following three important components:

1. **Virtualized Network Function:** Software implementation of network functions.
2. **Network Function Virtualization Infrastructure:** The combination of software+ hardware on which VNFs are deployed.
3. Network Function virtualization management and Orchestration architecture.

Instead of buying huge, expensive IDS for handling the whole network, one can simply buy specific functions to be deployed.

Software Defined Networking

SDN simply is about making datacenter networking infrastructure pooled and automated resource which can be configured and maintained through software and can seamlessly extend across public/private cloud boundaries. How will this help? Centralized control of networking infrastructure, optimum utilisation of existing physical network, workload optimisation to name a few benefits.

The key of computing trends driving the need of network programmability and a new network paradigm include: changing traffic patterns of applications, big-data computations, consumerisation of IT (Jain & Paul, 2013).

SDN starts with abstracting applications form underlying physical networks. Then it provides consistent platform to specify and enforce policy across all clouds. And finally it provides with a standards based mechanism for automatic deployment of networks while being extensible (Barroso, Clidaras, & Hölzle, 2013).

By separating the control plane from the data plane, SDN makes it possible to build programmable network. It relies on network switches which can be programmed through an SDN controller. Unlike the Overlay networks and NFVs which work on top of physical networks, SDN changes the physical network itself. SDN is implemented on network switches unlike other network virtualization (Jain, & Paul, 2013) techniques. BigSwitch and Pica8 are two notable names selling SDN products. This reduces the necessity to buy black proprietary box switches which are expensive. Instead one can easily buy a cheap white box switches and install SDN controller.

Few characteristics of SDN architecture are: Network control is directly programmable, agile as it is easy for the network manager to enforce changes in

Figure 6. Software Defined Networking architecture

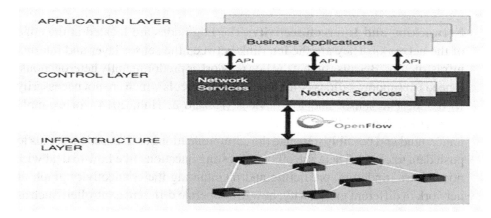

Figure 7. Control and Forwarding element separation within a router

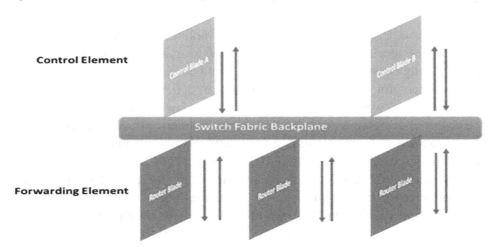

policies efficiently and quickly, software based SDN controllers centrally manage the network, the networking resources can be configured programmatically.

RESEARCH CHALLENGES IN FOG COMPUTING

The fog computing is slowly clutching its way into mainstream. There are still several issues that needs to be tackled. The Fog layer should be interoperable and fault resilient. To achieve this goal in a non-compromising way we need to work on security protocols which don't flood the Fog or create any bottleneck. As the emphasis on standardisation evolves, surely certain challenges will be tackled. we will identify issues and research challenges in implementing and realising full potential of fog computing.

4. **Networking and Interconnectivity:** The Fog nodes are located at the edge of the networks. They are the interlink between the sensor layer and internet infrastructure. Because of that the Fog network is predominantly heterogenous. It needs to support various communication protocols which are not necessarily IP based. The sensor and IoT devices (Aazam & Huh, 2014) for example support ZigBee, MQTT and various other protocols. The fog nodes need to understand and possibly translate the communications to IP based protocols to push data to cloud. There are other interesting questions like how to deal with node churn, updating, predicting and maintaining the connectivity graph of network in different granularity; how to cooperate different controllers such as

constantly connected controller (at the edge infrastructures) or intermittently connected controller (at the end devices) and where to place controllers in fog network.

5. **Quality of Service:** Four important metrics for QoS in Fog networks are connectivity, reliability, bandwidth and latency. Bandwidth refers to the amount of network bandwidth and storage bandwidth at the individual nodes. The reliability and latency requirements are especially critical for use cases control systems.

6. **Interfacing and Programming Model:** A unified interfacing and programming model is required to ease the porting of applications to fog computing platform. It would be difficult for each application developer to orchestrate heterogenous, dynamic resources to build compatible applications on diverse platforms. And the applications should be aware of the platform level optimisations.

7. **Security and Privacy:** The main advantage of Fog computing is the data locality. This reduces the effect of privacy leakage. However, machine to machine authentication and authorization, user client access control and enforcement of policies is a challenge. This can be rectified using privacy preserving techniques and end-to-end encryption of data. However, this needs more to be done (Stojmenovic & Wen, 2014).

8. **Provisioning and Resource Management:** The challenges lie in the mobility of end node since metrics such as bandwidth, storage, computation and latency will be changed dynamically. Resource discovery and sharing Resource discovery and sharing is critical for application performance in fog. The dynamic provisioning of resources and application aware hardware provisioning also is one interesting challenge.

9. **Accounting, Billing and Monitoring:** Sustainable business model with sufficient incentives and benefits for the fog services providers and users to make Fog computing viable. How are the incentives decided and how the pricing polices are set is going to one challenge for widespread adoption of Fog computing. And how the pricing policies are enforced. Research directions looks at the similar pricing models of cloud computing (Buyya, Yeo, Venugopal et al., 2009). However, they pose additional challenges on Fog computing platforms.

CONCLUSION

Fog computing will help businesses be more agile and efficient in their operations, help in decluttering and reduces information overload at the higher decision making levels. Fog computing is an extension to the cloud bringing the virtual resources called fog nodes nearby the data generation and consumption. It's application areas are as vast as IoT deployment, 5G network deployment, SDN, Personal Area network, Plant management. Cisco IoX platform is pioneer in this domain providing production level platform for the companies to introduce fog in their environments. The major research challenges include the deployment of fog nodes, International device communication protocols.

REFERENCES

Aazam, M., & Huh, E.N. (2014, August). Fog computing and smart gateway based communication for cloud of things. *Proceedings of the 2014 International Conference on Future Internet of Things and Cloud (FiCloud)* (pp. 464-470). IEEE.

Barroso, L. A., Clidaras, J., & Hölzle, U. (2013). The datacenter as a computer: An introduction to the design of warehouse-scale machines. *Synthesis lectures on computer architecture*, *8*(3), 1-154.

Bonomi, F., Milito, R., Zhu, J., & Addepalli, S. (2012, August). Fog computing and its role in the internet of things. *Proceedings of the first edition of the MCC workshop on Mobile cloud computing* (pp. 13-16). ACM. doi:10.1145/2342509.2342513

Buyya, R., Yeo, C. S., Venugopal, S., Broberg, J., & Brandic, I. (2009). Cloud computing and emerging IT platforms: Vision, hype, and reality for delivering computing as the 5th utility. *Future Generation Computer Systems*, *25*(6), 599–616. doi:10.1016/j.future.2008.12.001

Hou, X., Li, Y., Chen, M., Wu, D., Jin, D., & Chen, S. (2016). Vehicular fog computing: A viewpoint of vehicles as the infrastructures. *IEEE Transactions on Vehicular Technology*, *65*(6), 3860–3873. doi:10.1109/TVT.2016.2532863

Hu, Y. C., Patel, M., Sabella, D., Sprecher, N., & Young, V. (2015). Mobile edge computing—A key technology towards 5G (no. 11). ETSI White Paper.

Jain, R., & Paul, S. (2013). Network virtualization and software defined networking for cloud computing: A survey. *IEEE Communications Magazine*, *51*(11), 24–31. doi:10.1109/MCOM.2013.6658648

Martins, J., Ahmed, M., Raiciu, C., Olteanu, V., Honda, M., Bifulco, R., & Huici, F. (2014, April). ClickOS and the art of network function virtualization. *Proceedings of the 11th USENIX Conference on Networked Systems Design and Implementation* (pp. 459-473). USENIX Association.

Nunes, B. A. A., Mendonca, M., Nguyen, X. N., Obraczka, K., & Turletti, T. (2014). A survey of software-defined networking: Past, present, and future of programmable networks. *IEEE Communications Surveys and Tutorials*, *16*(3), 1617–1634. doi:10.1109/SURV.2014.012214.00180

Stantchev, V., Barnawi, A., Ghulam, S., Schubert, J., & Tamm, G. (2015). Smart items, fog and cloud computing as enablers of servitization in healthcare. *Sensors & Transducers*, *185*(2), 121.

Stojmenovic, I., & Wen, S. (2014, September). The fog computing paradigm: Scenarios and security issues. *Proceedings of the 2014 Federated Conference on Computer Science and Information Systems (FedCSIS)* (pp. 1-8). IEEE. doi:10.1145/2757384.2757397

Wu, F., & Sun, G. (2013). *Software-defined storage. Report.* Minneapolis: University of Minnesota.

Yi, S., Li, C., & Li, Q. (2015, June). A survey of fog computing: concepts, applications and issues. *Proceedings of the 2015 Workshop on Mobile Big Data* (pp. 37-42). ACM.

Zhu, J., Chan, D. S., Prabhu, M. S., Natarajan, P., Hu, H., & Bonomi, F. (2013, March). Improving web sites performance using edge servers in fog computing architecture. *Proceedings of the 2013 IEEE 7th International Symposium on Service Oriented System Engineering (SOSE)* (pp. 320-323). IEEE.

ADDITIONAL READING

Feng, D. G., Zhang, M., Zhang, Y., & Xu, Z. (2011). Study on cloud computing security. *Journal of software*, *22*(1), 71-83.

Joshi, Y., & Kumar, P. (Eds.). (2012). *Energy efficient thermal management of data centers*. Springer Science & Business Media. doi:10.1007/978-1-4419-7124-1

Sotomayor, B., Montero, R. S., Llorente, I. M., & Foster, I. (2009). Virtual infrastructure management in private and hybrid clouds. *IEEE Internet Computing*, *13*(5), 14–22. doi:10.1109/MIC.2009.119

Wikibon.org. (n. d.). Cloud. Retrieved from http://wikibon.org/wiki/v/Cloud

Zhang, Q., Cheng, L., & Boutaba, R. (2010). Cloud computing: state-of-the-art and research challenges. *Journal of internet services and applications, 1*(1), 7-18.

KEY TERMS AND DEFINTIONS

DAS: Direct attached storage.
DR: Disaster recovery.
NAS: Network attached storage.
SAN: Storage Area Network.
TCO: Total Cost of Ownership.
VM: Virtual Machine.

Chapter 4
Virtual Supercomputer Using Volunteer Computing

Rajashree Shettar
R. V. College of Engineering, India

Vidya Niranjan
R. V. College of Engineering, India

V. Uday Kumar Reddy
CA Technologies, India

ABSTRACT

Invention of new computing techniques like cloud and grid computing has reduced the cost of computations by resource sharing. Yet, many applications have not moved completely into these new technologies mainly because of the unwillingness of the scientists to share the data over internet for security reasons. Applications such as Next Generation Sequencing (NGS) require high processing power to process and analyze genomic data of the order of petabytes. Cloud computing techniques to process this large datasets could be used which involves moving data to third party distributed system to reduce computing cost, but this might lead to security concerns. These issues are resolved by using a new distributed architecture for De novo assembly using volunteer computing paradigm. The cost of computation is reduced by around 90% by using volunteer computing and resource utilization is increased from 80% to 90%, it is secure as computation can be done locally within the organization and is scalable.

DOI: 10.4018/978-1-5225-2785-5.ch004

1. INTRODUCTION TO NEXT GENERATION SEQUENCING

Modern quantitative biology has changed the perspective of data rich genomic sequencing technology. Large scale genomic data analysis requires the need for a new computational framework supported by High Performance Computing. One such application is the Next Generation Sequencing (NGS), which deals with terabytes or petabytes of genome data requiring high computational power.

Next Generation Sequencing (NGS) (Wilson et al., 2002; Narzisi et al., 2011) is a technique of sequencing the exact order of nucleotides which form the basic building blocks of Deoxyribonucleic Acid (DNA). NGS with a market size of over 2.7 billion dollars has diverse uses in fields of biological sciences ranging from identification of diseases in human beings to invention of sequence for novel species. Traditionally sequencing was done by treating DNA chemically and identifying nucleotides using color codes, but this technique of sequencing is not suitable for organisms with just thousands of nucleotides. Earlier, the cost of producing base pair information stored as 'reads' was limited to wet laboratory techniques and was very expensive. Hence the rate of production of data was very slow, but new sequencing technologies combined with wet lab techniques and information technology started producing millions to billions of short 'reads' quickly. The traditional assembly tools used earlier was incapable to handle this huge data.

To overcome these problems a number of assembly technologies have been invented that uses computations performed by computer, also known as the *In silico* approach. These assemblers started with small datasets and were effective. As the size of 'reads' increased, the assemblers required either a single computer with very large amounts of memory and computing resources or the data to be sent to third party for execution such as cloud computing which might lead to security concerns. These constraints make the analysis of huge amount of genomic data a tedious task.

An alternate solution to Cloud and Hadoop is to use volunteer computing which is proposed and explained in this chapter. In particular emphasis is on recommending a solution to Next Generation Sequencing (NGS) which uses an open source grid middleware namely Berkeley Open Infrastructure for Network Computing (BOINC) designed to handle various applications that require high computational power, data storage or both. This will be a great enabler for bioinformatics scientists to create applications that use public computing resources.

1.1 Importance of Big Data and Cloud in Sequencing

Bioinformatics domain has brought in lot of challenges with respect to management of enormous amount of genomic data that is growing exponentially. Modern Biology has moved from wet lab computing techniques to big data analytics, cloud computing and open source techniques for analysis and inference of bioinformatics data.

From global perspective, Big Data is a recent trend which has attracted many researchers and scientist to work upon (Sharma et al., 2015). MapReduce with Hadoop, a programming model is one of the techniques to analyze big data. It provides a platform for data processing in parallel fashion (Seema et al., 2015). Big data analytics enables analyzing large data of size varying from Petabyte (PB) to Exabyte (EB) to extract hidden pattern and useful information from large datasets (Fisher et al., 2012).

Conventional database services suffer from performance issues when fed with large amount of data. Many machine learning techniques and data mining algorithms can be developed and integrated with MapReduce, a general purpose parallel programming model to improve efficiency of systems with large data. Hence, normally a large data is divided into smaller datasets and are assigned to different mapper nodes to work in parallel. The intermediate results from all these nodes are collected. At reduce nodes, computations of algorithms will be carried out to form the final result. Hadoop is an open source platform used for computation of large data developed by Apache foundation (White et al., 2009). Hadoop adopts Hadoop Distributed Files System (HDFS) for storage and MapReduce. Hadoop requires commodity hardware to work on large amount of data and hence the cost of buying special hardware is cut off (Singh et al., 2014).

Although many tools have been developed for parallelizing of genomic data using Hadoop and MapReduce programming model, most of the Bioinformatics applications are difficult to setup, use, configure and maintain using this technology. These applications are dependent on many software libraries (Nicolae, 2012). The implementation of this technology requires high level of programming expertise to parallelize Hadoop jobs and appropriate tools to enable visualization of the data on Hadoop platform for summarization of the results.

On the other hand, Cloud offers very huge amount of computing resources for processing of genomic data. The usage of cloud software poses some challenges in terms of transferring of large data over low-bandwidth. Other challenge that needs to be addressed is with respect to privacy and security issues of bioinformatics application data that is processed in the Cloud environment. The major challenge in Cloud computing technology for Bioinformatics applications is in transmitting of huge amount of genomic data over the internet which takes lot of time. The data transfer rate is highly dependent on the bandwidth available to push data to cloud and pull data from the cloud which normally takes lot of time.

Major inhibitor to adopt cloud computing technology in bioinformatics and life sciences sector is the privacy and security of genomic data and is a growing challenge especially in public cloud. The capabilities provided by most cloud infrastructure are very little on data, application and interoperability.

To overcome these problems a new solution called volunteer computing is proposed which addresses both security concerns and data transfer costs.

1.2 Concepts of Next Generation Sequencing

Next Generation Sequencing (NGS) is a technique of sequencing the exact order of nucleotides which form the basic building blocks of Deoxyribonucleic Acid (DNA). NGS offers low cost solution and generates high throughput with enormous amount of sequence data known as 'reads'. Traditionally, sequencing was done by treating DNA chemically and identifying nucleotides using color codes, making sequencing impossible for organisms with just thousands of nucleotides. DNA has to be split into small fragments to get accurate sequences. NGS produces thousands or millions of sequences by parallelizing the sequencing procedure. NGS randomly fragments DNA into various small fragments of nucleotides called as 'reads'.

De nova assembler, an assembler tool processes these 'reads' to produce the larger fragments of DNA called contigs. The contigs thus produced are larger sequences of DNA that are separated by gaps because of missing overlap information among contigs. The contigs are scaffold into larger contigs considering the ends of the contig and the gap information. These super contigs are mapped again to get mapped scaffold, which in turn is used to obtain DNA sequence. The size of these 'reads' data is enormous for higher organisms. The existing De novo assemblers require huge computing power to process these large datasets. Cloud computing techniques to process this large datasets could be used which involves moving the data to third party distributed system to reduce computing cost. This might lead to security concerns about sensitive data being exposed to outside world. Hence to resolve such type of issues, a new distributed architecture for De novo assembler has been proposed.

The new distributed architecture for De novo assembler uses volunteer computing paradigm, where various users called volunteers voluntarily donate their idle computing resources combining them leads to huge processing power that matches computing power of super computers. It uses Berkeley Open Infrastructure for Network Computing (BOINC) software as middleware to enable communication between volunteers and the server. The volunteers perform most of the processing. The architecture can be controlled to be limited to a particular institution or organization, hence overcoming the security concerns. The idle computer systems at various institutions or organizations could be made as volunteers avoiding the need of procurement of high end systems for the purpose of De novo assembly.

There is no need to procure extra hardware for De novo assembly in NGS, hence the computation cost has been reduced by around 90% and resource utilization of clients is increased to around 80% to 90%. The quality of the contigs generated is benchmarked based on its length using a measure called N50 (similar to weighted median). The N50 values using the new architecture are increased by 5% to 15% and maximum contig length is also increased by around 4%. The other achievement is the ability to scale for any size of 'reads' datasets as the number of clients can be increased or decreased easily as per need.

1.3 Traditional Methods of DNA Sequencing

DNA sequencing finds its application in many domains. DNA sequencing involves many steps from wet lab techniques to scaffolding software that produces the genome map from the set of contigs. Deoxyribonucleic acid (DNA) sequencing (Wilson et al., 2002) consists of finding the exact sequence of nucleotides in a given DNA sample. Order of the four bases has to be determined namely (A), (G), (C), and (T) in a DNA strand using appropriate technique.

The following section 1.3.1 and 1.3.2covers some of the traditional methods of DNA sequencing.

1.3.1 Sanger Sequencing

Sanger Sequencing uses radioactive chemical reaction to identify each and every base pair of the DNA to find out the exact base pair. The process uses four tubes with different gels, each of which is reacted to one of the (A), (T), (G), and (C) base pair only. These are then assembled together to get the complete DNA sequence.

The fragments of DNA are separated via gel electrophoresis and the sequences are read using a laser beam. But this method was suitable only for sequences of from 15 to about 200 nucleotides (Sanger, et al. 1977). Even with modifications and better techniques it was useful only for lengths up to 500 nucleotides.

1.3.2 Maxam-Gilbert Sequencing

Chemical procedure is used to sequence the DNA. The DNA molecule is partially broken at each repetition of a base (Maxam et al., 1977). Base position is determined based on length of the fragment. DNA is cleaved at Guanines, at Adenines, at Cytosines and at Thymines equally based on the reactions. Electrophoresis on a polyacrylamide gel is performed to determine the DNA sequence from pattern of radioactive bands. This technique is not scalable and it permits sequencing of 100 bases only from the point of labeling.

1.4 Modern Methods of DNA Sequencing

Traditional sequencing techniques discussed in the above section 1.3.1 and 1.3.2 were not suitable to sequence large sequences such as whole chromosomes. To enable sequencing of whole chromosomes, modern DNA sequencing techniques are used.

DNA sequencing is the process of using any method to find the correct order of nucleotides bases Adenine (A), Guanine (G), Cytosine (C) and Thymine (T) within a strand of DNA molecule (Wilson, et al. 2002). It can be used to sequence a small genome or the whole genome of any organism. Due to huge size of the DNA (usually contains of millions of base pairs) it is not possible to identify the sequence of all nucleotides at a single shot. Hence modern DNA techniques are used as discussed in section 1.4.1 and 1.4.2.

1.4.1 De Novo Sequencing

To enable sequencing of whole chromosomes, the most common method used is fragmentation of the chromosome into short DNA fragments or 'reads' (either by chemical or mechanical means). These DNA fragments are then preprocessed to filter some of the errors. These preprocessed DNA fragments are then individually sequenced to get small 'reads'. These 'reads' are assembled back to get long contigs. This sequencing technique is called as De novo meaning, "from the beginning" in Latin. This method does not use any predefined sequence and everything has to be assembled back from short 'reads' available. This process is best compared to get an exact order of words in a page that is shredded into small pieces. In this process some of the words may be missing or some words may be duplicated. The usual solution is to assemble the words to make a sentence as shown in figure 1 and assembling those sentences to get the whole page.

Figure 1. De novo sequencing example

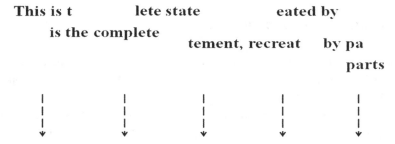

In reality, it is not always possible to construct back the whole DNA because of lack of overlaps between the 'reads'. Hence, effort is made to get longer sequences of fragments called as contigs. A contig refers to a set of overlapping DNA segments which represents consensus region of DNA. Larger contigs are usually preferred as they resemble more of the actual DNA. These contigs are assembled into scaffolds and usually represented in the form of a De Bruijn Graph (DBG) that has to be parsed through to get the required DNA sequence. A scaffold represents large but usually discontinuous region of DNA that comprises of sequence of contigs and the gaps between them. The gaps are caused because of lack of overlaps between contigs.

1.4.2 Next Generation Sequencing

The main objective for DNA sequencing is to reduce the computing cost of De novo assembler by avoiding procurement of expensive computers. It should also produce contigs that are accurate and cover the maximum set of 'reads' possible. The proposed method is to set up a volunteer computing grid system using BOINC as middleware between server and client. An assembly program uses distributed computing framework to enable assembly of large genomes datasets is executed in BOINC. The assembler uses additional clients to scale the DBG assembly algorithms to large datasets. The assembler used is Velvet software package (Zerbino et al., 2008) and the software is tweaked to enable the execution on both client and server to be able to assemble large datasets that was not feasible in normal Velvet.

The role of Velvet is to assemble short reads produced by the Next Generation Sequencing. Velvet uses De Bruijn Graph algorithm to assemble the sequences. Velvet software package eliminates errors and resolve the repeats in the sequence produced. Velvet software enables translation of huge data generated to into genome sequence.

The process starts with creation of DBG based on the overlap information found using hash functions and it simplifies the DBG to reduce the number of edges and nodes. After removal of errors the final DBG is scanned through to get the required DNA sequence.

Velvet works in four stages different stages: (1) hashing the 'reads' to form k-mers (2) graph construction (3) error correction (4) resolve repeats. Once these stages are completed they can be read to get maximum contigs using Velveth and Velvetg software applications. Velveth software package requires more resources to construct roadmaps (an intermediate form to store the overlap information) and this roadmaps are used by Velvetg to create a graph and give out the contigs that satisfy given length and coverage criteria.

Assembly algorithms uses graph based techniques to find the 'reads' with high probability of becoming neighbors. Graph based assembly techniques are usually classified into two sub classes namely (1) Overlap Layout Consensus (OLC)

(Pevzner et al., 2001; Miller et al., 2010) method (2) De Bruijn Graph method (DBG) (Compeau et al., 2011; Chikhi et al., 2015). Both these methods assemble the whole genome sequence by exploiting overlap information about 'reads' which conforms to Lander Waterman model (Lander et al., 1988). In terms of space and time complexity, OLC algorithms are preferable for low-coverage long 'reads' and DBG algorithms are better choice, since it offers higher coverage of short reads and enables larger genome assembly, further comparisons of the both can be found at (Li et al., 2012).

1.5 Applications of Next Generation Sequencing

The demand for fast, accurate, and cost effective DNA sequencing has given rise to Next Generation Sequencing (NGS) technology. NGS enables sequencing of huge amount of DNA in parallel using different methodologies. It overcomes the limitations of Sanger sequencing methods used for sequencing genome. NGS technique has led to development of many tools for sequencing each with its advantages and disadvantages.

1.6 Challenges in Next Generation Sequencing

Next Generation Sequencing (NGS) technology is increasingly becoming popular among the bioinformatics scientists. In this context handling of NGS data storage, retrieval and analysis has become a great challenge and it demands for the necessity to have high bandwidth, data processing speed, storage space and other computational facilities to process NGS data.

The challenges of Next Generation Sequencing with respect to De nova assembly are as mentioned below:

1. **Assembly of Small Reads Into a Larger Contig:** The assembly of small reads into larger contig often creates false alignment with high base calling errors and thereby creating ambiguity within the genome.
2. **Storage Problems with Intermediate Files:** There are many number of intermediate files generated during the process of assembly. And the location of these files plays an important role in selecting the correct files. When using middleware these locations are not identified properly. It has been resolved using fixed location in client and passed as parameter to a new shell and batch script to pass this location to the assembler.
3. **Debugging the Graph:** The reads are split iteratively into k-mers and graph is built. The reads are represented as nodes. Verifying the correctness of the

graph thus generated is a problem given the huge number of intermediate notations used.

4. **Debugging Middleware:** When setting up the application on the middleware, there can be problems to identify real cause of failure over the network as the error messages displayed can be generic in nature for any issues over network.

5. **Need for Template to Understand DNA Sequences:** To solve some of the serious health issues in animals including human beings and to study the reasons for extinction of animals there is a need for generation DNA template for particular species to study DNA.

The probability of generating correct DNA template is very high if the DNA is sequenced using huge amount of short read fragments. The De novo assembler tool proposed effectively processes huge amount of short 'reads' of genome data and generates contigs using parallel computing. The parallel computing environment uses volunteer computing concept that could be set up in laboratory at affordable cost. A desktop computer is to be designated as server that interacts with the clients. Server has to collect the results from clients and assimilate them and pass it back to user.

2. SYSTEM ARCHITECTURE OF DE NOVO ASSEMBLER

The De novo assembler proposed is designed using virtual computing techniques. The assembler contains two modules (a) the client module (b) the server module. Both these modules are communicated using BOINC middleware. BOINC middleware is installed in both client and server and it enables the client to donate their idle computing resources for execution of the assembler. Server stores the data and splits the data into various subsets. Clients search for the overlap information among the subset of 'reads' received from server to get the contig information. The server receives these results from different clients and assimilates them into a single file to be delivered to the user. The input files must be in proper format as specified with control parameters given by user. The 'reads' must be preprocessed to remove any errors in the files. The implementation of the middleware application software follows an iterative Software Development Life Cycle model (Victor et al., 2003; Pankaj et al., 2004).

Various parameters have been provided to the volunteer such that they can customize the level of details they can process, to resolve the error themselves. The input data is given in the form of FASTA or FASTQ file format. These are processed to find out the sequences present in those files and these sequences are stored in separate file. The overlap information is stored in the required graphical format in a different file called roadmaps.

2.1 Architecture of BOINC

Berkeley Open Infrastructure for Network Computing (BOINC) (Anderson, 2004) is an open source middleware designed for various applications that require high computational power, data storage or both such as Folding@home, SETI@home and Climateprediction (Stainforth et al., 2004), (Beberg et al., 2009). It helps the scientists to create applications that use public computing resources. It also enables the volunteers to support multiple projects at the same time and a way to manage their resources contribution. It is designed in such a way that it is not susceptible to a single node failure and is used for a wide range of applications.

Although there are many grid middleware architectures such as Condor (Litzkow et al., 1988), GLOBUS (Schopf et al., 2006), Computational Fluid Dynamic (CFD) (Lin et al., 2004), BOINC has been selected as the optimal solution for many scientific applications compared to other solutions as they use more client resources because of the local schedulers.

The input file (in FASTA or FASTQ format) is uploaded to server and the set of control parameters is assigned to the server. A valid file is sent to splitter sub module, which passes the same file to the sequencer module. This sequencer identifies the 'reads' as sequences and assigns a sequence number and sends this file back to splitter. The splitter splits this into multiple files with proper header, trailer and file name and stores them in a designated folder. The scheduler sub module in server selects one of the file generated by splitter and creates a work unit that contains the commands to be executed and selected input file. This work unit is received by client and is forwarded to hashing submodule after a set of basic validations. The hashing function passes the input file to create tree sub function. This function returns the splay tree created. Hashing is applied on the splay tree to check for the overlap information to return the roadmap file. This roadmap is used to create graph, which is done by create graph submodule and is passed to correct graph where any errors present are removed before exporting the graph to a graph file. Once the graph file is generated, it is parsed by a separate module which generates node information. This parsed node information is passed to next function for extending the nodes to form contigs. The client process all the files and gets the contigs from each file it received and this is communicated to the server. The system architecture of De novo assembler is depicted in figure 2.

When the server receives all the contigs files from the registered clients, all these contigs are stored in the designated folder. These contigs are passed to a server submodule, merger to scan through all the files, it merges the files based on the header information and generates a single contig file and stored in the designated location for the user.

Figure 2. System Architecture of De novo Assembler

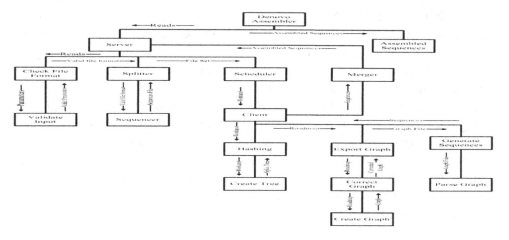

BOINC is scalable, fault tolerant and does high-performance task distribution (Desell et al., 2008). The other methods require more administration compared to BOINC for volunteer computing and have less check pointing mechanism. As explained in (Yao et al., 2009), BOINC has a scalable architecture which contains two independent components, server software component and client software components of the middleware. Each client downloads an application and part of the data to be processed. It computes the results for the data and results are sent back to server. These results are consolidated by the server and the solution is returned to the user. The general architecture of BOINC is as shown in figure 3.

Figure 3. BOINC Architecture

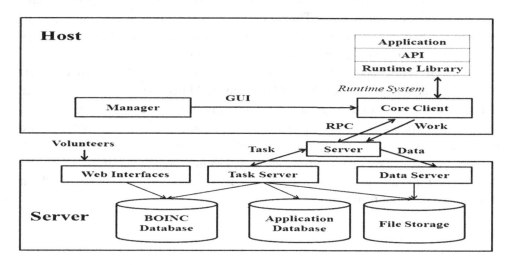

Server middleware software uses set of daemons to perform the various tasks of sever as shown in figure 3. A task server assigns works to the client, handles reports for completed tasks and also handles the remote procedure calls requested by the clients. Data server validates the upload, access of files and checks legitimacy of the files. There are many other daemons not shown in figure such as transition, validate, assimilator, file delete that assists the server in completion of its tasks. Any system that downloads the BOINC client middleware and connects to the project by registering on their page can contribute resources to projects. The web pages of the projects enable clients to select how their resources could be used.

The main goal of BOINC is to increase number of applications and increase the participation of clients in volunteer computing and retain the participating clients (Darch et al., 2010). Various methods have been employed such as inventions of 3G-Bridge to make BOINC compatible with EDGeS (Urbah et al., 2009) as explained in (Kacsuk, 2011). Increasing awareness about BOINC will have positive impact in participation as explained in (Toth et al., 2011).

3. VOLUNTEER COMPUTING CONCEPTS

Volunteer computing uses computer resources of people, who are willing to donate their computing resource (called as volunteers) to compute or store huge data (Anderson et al., 2006), (Paneque et al., 2011). There are many applications that need resources and there are many computers with idle resources. Many scientific applications started using these idle resources by convincing the owners of the resource to owe them, and to come up with a new way of computing called as volunteer computing.

In volunteer computing, clients register themselves to certain projects and download BOINC application. This application acts as middleware and runs in background in client machine. It downloads work unit from the server, performs some operations on the data in work unit and writes the result back to server.

Generally, Volunteer Computing adopts a parallel master-slave/master-worker computing model (Durrani et al., 2014) as depicted in figure 4. In this model, the master (server) breaks the huge task assigned to it into number of smaller tasks. It is the responsibility of the master to distribute the small tasks to the workers. The master gets the result from the workers which are assigned with smaller tasks by the master and workers perform the necessary computation. The master receives the results from various workers and verifies data results and then aggregates them to compute the final result.

Figure 4. Volunteer Computing Architecture

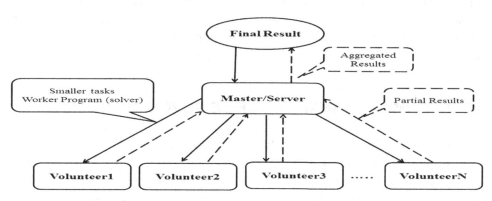

The middleware handles all the operations of the volunteer computing system. For a volunteer computing system to work successfully below given requirements have to be accomplished:

1. Huge task has to be divided into number of small tasks in an efficient manner.
2. To increase the throughput of the complete system, scheduling of tasks and resources has to be done in an efficient manner.
3. The resources available at the workers have to be managed in a robust manner by using an appropriate model for resource management.
4. Different projects are executed at the middleware and the volunteers need to trust the middleware.
5. Projects must use appropriate security policies to gain volunteers trust.

BOINC model consists of volunteers and projects. BOINC projects are applications requiring high computational power normally related to research work or work related to high throughput analysis. Each and every project is associated with its own BOINC server. Computer owners (Volunteers) contribute resources by executing the BOINC client software program on their computers and other computing devices.

Massive amount of processing power could be accumulated from heterogeneous devices located at geographically distant places using the BOINC architecture. BOINC a high performance parallel distributed computing platform, developed at Space Sciences Laboratory, University of California, Berkeley (Anderson, 2004).

Project specific code is executed at the workers. BOINC server has various server modules such as data server, scheduling server, database server, and BOINC daemon. The server has the responsibility of generating new work units and assigning it to the workers. The server reorganizes the scheduler's database access, generates results and identifies error conditions and validates the results. It acts as an assimilator to handle newly generated canonical results. The server is also responsible for cleanup operation which is taken care by purging the entries related to input files, output files, instance database and jobs that are no longer needed.

4. PERFORMANCE ANALYSIS OF DE NOVO ASSEMBLER

De novo assembler integrates many subtasks into a single task to effectively assemble the set of 'reads' into contigs. The De novo assembler has to be executed on cluster of desktops as opposed to a single machine. The main constraint for execution of complete volunteer computing system is the hardware and operating system configurations of the client machines which volunteer to donate resource. Since the architecture and the instruction set of each client is different from other client using different operating system and hardware components. The client systems that need to connect to a server and provide computing power should have Intel architecture with either Windows or Linux machines. Since the data is transferred using network, the clients should be connected to the server using some proper channel like high speed Internet or LAN supporting proper bandwidth power. Otherwise, the performance of the overall system will be degraded. The input data being processed should be made available in flat text files containing a sequence of 'reads'. The data should be free from errors and has to be in the required format. The functional requirements of the server include splitting the huge data amount of 'reads' into work units for different clients such that maximum accuracy could be achieved. The client receives the data from server and short reads from the work unit received from the server. The client searches for overlap information in the work unit it receives and creates a roadmap file. The client searches the roadmap file and creates a graph to store the information about k-mer overlaps among various nodes.

The graphs are scanned to get the all the possible contigs that have length greater than a certain threshold. The threshold is subjective and is decided by the user. All these contigs thus identified are sent back to the server in a contig file. Server receives all these files from different clients and merges them together to produce a single contig file to be used by the user for post processing.

The performance characteristics of the De novo assembler is measured by using various metric to evaluate the accuracy of the contigs generated and the metrics used are as listed below:

1. **N50:** N50 value is the benchmark used to determine the usefulness of the contigs. The N50 calculation for the project is based on the contigs length taken from the contig file. For example, the lengths of the contig is as shown

in the set L. L={23, 26, 33, 36, 44, 45, 47, 67, 69, 73, 80, 198} the elaborated list, L' will have 741 elements and the median is found for that elaborated list. The median of the original list is 46 whereas the N50 value for the same list i.e., the median of the elaborated list L` is 69. The larger N50 values means there are more contigs with larger lengths, hence is better than smaller N50 value.

2. **Length of Contigs:** This metric measures the length of the contigs generated by the assembler. The maximum length of the contigs generated can be found in log file. The higher the length of the contig, it gives more accuracy.

3. **Total Number of Contigs:** This metric measure the count of total number of contigs generated and this total count should be less as it occupies less space.

4. **Computation Time:** This metric gives the time required to process the reads file into contigs.

5. **No. of Nodes in Graph:** This metric is used to compare and find out if any nodes are missed while splitting of sequence files.

6. **Split Length:** The split length is user specified value used to divide the 'reads' for clients. The complete 'reads' dataset is divided into smaller files each having 'split length' and number of reads.

The dataset used for experiment contains 50,000 'reads' of human genome. This data set has been processed without any minimum coverage cutoff for various hash lengths. The coverage filters out contigs that are resulted from small number of 'reads'. The resultant contigs have the following statistics as mentioned in table 1.

The goal of this experiment is to select ideal hash length for further experiments, after these experiments the hash length of 23 was selected because it gives moderate values of every parameter.

The performance analysis for various metrics is discussed below. The following results are obtained by splitting the dataset into various lengths to identify the ideal

Table 1. Statistics for experimental dataset

Hash Length	N50 Value	Maximum Contig Length	Total Contigs
21	44	305	355815
23	73	757	206085
25	98	1152	163334
27	148	1806	135599
29	184	2209	121434
31	207	3123	109489

split length. After identification of ideal split length it is used in production for De novo assembly.

1. **N50:** The performance analysis results of N50 values for various split lengths ranging from 1000 to 25000 is shown in table 2. The maximum, minimum, average and median values obtained for various split length are shown in table 2. The values are also represented in the graph as shown in figure 5. The actual N50 value for the same data without split is 73.

Higher the N50 values, better the contigs. But the maximum contig value produced (for split length 100) is 103 and the mean and median for N50 values produces for the same split length is very far away from the maximum N50. Hence it is ignored as outlier and the optimum split length is identified using further parameters. Hence optimum split length for the dataset is 2500 as it has next highest value.

Table 2. N50 statistics for split length

	Split Length (In Number of Reads)								
	1000	2000	2500	3000	4000	5000	10000	20000	25000
Max	103	95	99	95	95	92	92	97	87
Average	80.5	82.71	83.55	84.24	86.08	86.4	89.8	93	86.5
Median	80	82	82.5	83	86	85.5	89	91	86.5

Figure 5. N50 statistics for various split lengths

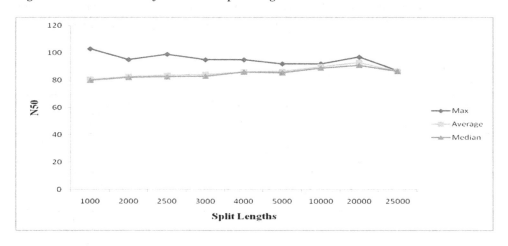

1. **Max Length:** The performance analysis results of maximum length values for various split lengths ranging from 1000 to 25000 is shown in table 3. The values are also represented in chart in figure 6. The actual maximum length value for the same data without split is 757.

   The maximum contig length identified (for split length 2500) is 1576. The average of the contigs length is also maximum (816.1) for split length 2500. Hence, the optimum split length for the dataset is 2500.

2. **Total Contigs Count:** The performance analysis results of contigs count for various split lengths ranging from 1000 to 25000 is shown in table 4. The actual contig count value for the same data without split is 206085.

Table 3. Maximum contig length for split length

	Split Length								
	1000	**2000**	**2500**	**3000**	**4000**	**5000**	**10000**	**20000**	**25000**
Max	826	1086	1576	1231	1007	901	1189	1137	790
Min	146	237	431	346	831	493	607	786	539
Average	294.42	526.17	816.1	698.23	755.85	676.8	696.2	904	664.5

Figure 6. Maximum contig length statistics for split length

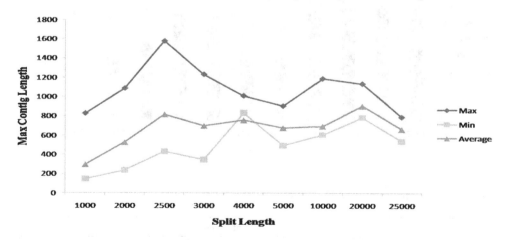

The contig count should be lesser such that the amount of storage required is less. But the number of contigs for various split length has been increased because of large number of small contigs with less coverage being produced by each client. The values are also represented in chart in figure 7.

3.   **Total Nodes Count:** The performance analysis results of node count for various split lengths ranging from 1000 to 25000 is shown in table 5. The actual node count for the same data without data split is 5470.

The total number of nodes has to be moderate because too many nodes may have nodes that are not properly simplified and node count too less may indicate missing

Table 4. Contig count for split lengths

	Split Length									
	1000	2000	02500	03000	04000	5000	10000	20000	25000	50000
Contig count	383031	356239	366842	366951	355764	348705	320153	326916	258339	206085

Figure 7. Contig count statistics for split length

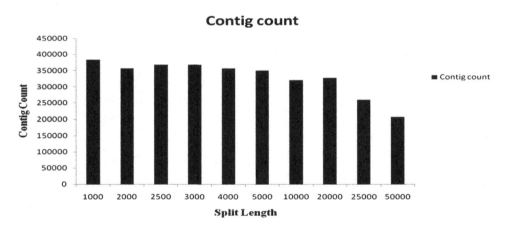

Table 5. Total node count for split length

	Split Length									
	1000	2000	2500	3000	4000	5000	10000	20000	25000	50000
Node count	5084	4691	4669	4788	4547	4464	4293	4716	5015	5470

of important information due to the use of parallel computing. The splits length of 2500 to 5000 is moderate for the given data set. The values are also represented in chart in figure 8.

4.1 Inference from the Result

From the result obtained the following inferences are made:

- The least values for N50 among various split data is also more than the actual N50 value for the actual data, which means the accuracy of the sequences generated by splitting the values into smaller datasets have increased.

- The mean, median and maximum values for N50 are constant for the split values around 1/10th of the actual data.

- The maximum contig length produced from different split values are greater than actual contigs length. The average of maximum contigs length produced by split lengths in mid-range is very close to actual value. Hence extreme split length such as 1000 and 25000 has to be avoided.

- The node count to be processed will be less by around 1000 for various split length compared to the actual number of nodes. Node code processed by each of the client is dependent on the split length alone. Hence the split length that produces moderate node count has to be selected.

- The total contig count is gradually increasing for every split length that produces more data sets from the actual dataset. This is because of large number of contigs with minimum coverage produced in each client.

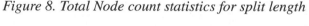

Figure 8. Total Node count statistics for split length

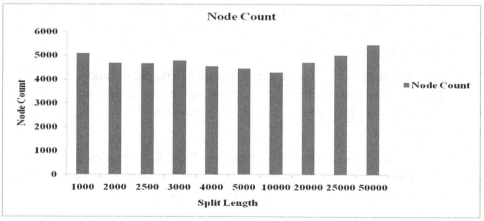

- The execution time is increased when compared to the actual computation time mainly because of the time added during network communication, splitter and merger programs.
- The cost for computation is reduced by around 90% because there is no need for procuring any additional hardware for De novo assembler.

5. RESEARCH DIRECTIONS IN NEXT GENERATION SEQUENCING

Next Generation Sequencing (NGS) enables a wide area of research applications with the aid of Bioinformatics tools. Some of the research directions in this area are as mentioned below:

1. To identify novel genetic alterations for molecular characterization of cancers, cancer progression, study of tumor complexity, heterogeneity and evolution.
2. Large scale Genome sequencing to expedite the characterization of both normal and tumor genomes.
3. Tool for Transcriptomes analysis with integration to Gene Ontology enrichment.
4. Metagenomics tool for bacterial diagnostics.

REFERENCES

Anderson, D. P. (2004). BOINC: A System for Public-Resource Computing and Storage. *Proceedings of the Fifth IEEE/ACM International Workshop on Grid Computing* (pp. 4-10). doi:10.1109/GRID.2004.14

Anderson, P. D., & Fedak, G. (2006). The computational and storage potential of volunteer computing. *Proceedings of Sixth IEEE International Symposium on Cluster Computing and the Grid* (pp. 73-80). doi:10.1109/CCGRID.2006.101

Beberg, L., A., Ensign, D. L., Guha Jayachandran, Khaliq, S., & Pande, V. S. (2009). Folding@home:Lessons from eight years of volunteer distributed computing. *Proceedings of the IEEE International Symposium on Parallel & Distributed Processing* (pp. 1-8).

Chikhi, R., Limasset, A., Jackman, S., Simpson, J. T., & Medvedev, P. (2015). On the representation of de Bruijn graphs. *Journal of Computational Biology*, 22(5), 336–352. doi:10.1089/cmb.2014.0160 PMID:25629448

Compeau, C. P. E., Pevzner, P. A., & Tesler, G. (2011). How to apply de Bruijn graphs to genome assembly. *Nature Biotechnology, 29*(11), 987–991. doi:10.1038/nbt.2023 PMID:22068540

(1926). Darch, Peter, & Carusi, A. (2010). Retaining volunteers in volunteer computing projects. *Philosophical Transactions of the Royal Society A: Mathematical, Physical and Engineering Sciences, 368*, 4177–4192.

Desell, T., Szymanski, B., & Varela, C. (2008). Asynchronous Genetic Search for Scientific Modeling on Large-Scale Heterogeneous Environments. *Proceedings of IEEE International Symposium on Parallel and Distributed Processing* (pp. 1-12). doi:10.1109/IPDPS.2008.4536169

Durrani, N. (2014). Volunteer computing: Requirements, challenges, and solutions. *Journal of Network and Computer Applications, 39*, 369–380. doi:10.1016/j.jnca.2013.07.006

Fisher, D., DeLine, R., Czerwinski, M., & Drucker, S. (2012). Interactions with big data analytics. *Interactions-Microsoft Research, 19*(3), 50–59. doi:10.1145/2168931.2168943

Kacsuk, P. (2011). How to make BOINC based desktop grids even more popular. *Proceedings of IEEE International Symposium on Parallel and Distributed Processing Workshops and Ph.D Forum* (pp. 1871-1877). doi:10.1109/IPDPS.2011.350

Lander, S. E., & Waterman, M. S. (1988). Genomic mapping by fingerprinting random clones: A mathematical analysis. *Genomics, 2*(3), 231–239. doi:10.1016/0888-7543(88)90007-9 PMID:3294162

Larman, C., & Basili, V. R. (2003). Iterative and incremental development: A brief history. *Computer, 36*(6), 47-56.

Li, Z., Chen, Y., Mu, D., Yuan, J., Shi, Y., Zhang, H., ... Yang, B.(2012). Comparison of the two major classes of assembly algorithms: Overlap–layout–consensus and de-bruijn-graph. *Briefings in Functional Genomics, 11*(1), 25-37.

Lin, X., Sun, X., Lu, X., Deng, Q., Li, M., . . . Chen, L. (2004). Recent Advances in CFD Grid Application Platform. *Proceedings of the 2004 IEEE International Conference on Services Computing* (pp. 588-591).

Litzkow, J., M., Livny, M., & Mutka, M. W. (n.d.). Condor-a hunter of idle workstations. *Proceedings of IEEE, 8th International Conference on Distributed Computing Systems* (pp. 104-111).

Maxam, M. A., & Gilbert, W. (1977). A new method for sequencing DNA. *Proceedings of the National Academy of Sciences of the United States of America, 74*(2), 560–564. doi:10.1073/pnas.74.2.560 PMID:265521

Miller, R. J., Koren, S., & Sutton, G. (2010). Assembly algorithms for next-generation sequencing data. *Genomics, 95*(6), 315–327. doi:10.1016/j.ygeno.2010.03.001 PMID:20211242

Narzisi, G., & Mishra, B. (2011). Comparing De Novo Genome Assembly: The Long and Short of It. *PLoS ONE, 6*(4), e19175. doi:10.1371/journal.pone.0019175 PMID:21559467

Nicolae, B. (2012). Bridging the gap between HPC and IaaS clouds.

Paneque, L., & Katrib, M. (2011). HAMLET: Heterogeneous Application Middleware Layer for Extensive Tasks. *Proceedings of CIBSE2011* (pp. 11-23).

Pankaj, J., Palit, A., & Kurien, P. (2004). *The time boxing process model for iterative software development.* In *Advances in Computers* (Vol. 6, pp. 67–103). .

Pevzner, P., Tang, H., & Waterman, M. S. (2001). An Eulerian path approach to DNA fragment assembly. *Proceedings of the National Academy of Sciences of the United States of America, 98*(17), 9748–9753. doi:10.1073/pnas.171285098 PMID:11504945

Sanger, F., Nicklen, S., & Coulson, A. R. (1977). DNA sequencing with chain-terminating inhibitors. *National Academy of Sciences, 74*(12), 5463-5467.

Schopf, M., J., Pearlman, L., Miller, N., Kesselman, C., Foster, I., . . . Chervenak, A. (2006). Monitoring the grid with the Globus Toolkit MDS4. *Proceedings of Conference Series in Journal of Physics, 46*(1), 521-525. doi:10.1088/1742-6596/46/1/072

Seema, M., & Jha, C. K. (2015). Handling big data efficiently by using MapReduce technique. *Proceedings on International Conference on Computational Intelligence & Communication Technology IEEE* (pp. 703-708).

Sharma, S., & Veenu, M. (2015). Technology and Trends to handle Big Data: Survey. *Proceedings of 2015 5th International Conference on Advanced Computing and Communication Technologies* (pp. 266-271). doi:10.1109/ACCT.2015.121

Singh, K., & Kaur, R. (2014). Hadoop: Addressing Challenges of Big Data. *Proceedings of International Conference on Advance Computing IEEE* (pp. 686-689).

Stainforth, D., Martin, A., Simpson, A., Christensen, C., Kettleborough, J., Aina, T., & Allen, M. (2004). Security principles for public resource modeling research. *Proceedings of 13th IEEE International Workshops in Enabling Technologies: Infrastructure for Collaborative Enterprises* (pp. 319-324).

Toth, D., Mayer, R., & Nichols, W. (2011). Increasing Participation in Volunteer Computing. *Proceedings of IEEE International Symposium on Parallel and Distributed Processing Workshops and Ph.D Forum* (pp. 1878-1882).

Urbah, E., Kacsuk, P., Farkas, Z., Fedak, G., Kecskemeti, G., Lodygensky, O., & Lovas, R. et al. (2009). Edges: Bridging egee to boinc and xtremweb. *Journal of Grid Computing*, 7(3), 335–354. doi:10.1007/s10723-009-9137-0

White, T. (2009). *Hadoop: The Definitive Guide. O'Reilly Media, Yahoo!* Press.

Wilson, J., & Hunt, T. (2002). Molecular Biology of the Cell, A Problems Approach (4th ed.). New York: Garland Science.

Yao, H., Zhao, L., Li, Y., & Yang, J. (2009). Using BOINC desktop grid for high performance memory detection. *Proceedings of 4th IEEE International Conference on Computer Science & Education* (pp. 1159-1162).

Zerbino, R. D., & Birney, E. (2008). Velvet: Algorithms for De novo short read assembly using de Bruijn graphs. *Genome Research*, 18(5), 821–829. doi:10.1101/gr.074492.107 PMID:18349386

KEY TERMS AND DEFINITIONS

Assembler: To reconstruct the original DNA sequence, assembler tool aligns and merges the fragments of DNA sequences.

BOINC (Berkeley Open Infrastructure for Network Computing): It is open source middleware software designed for applications that require high computational power, data storage or both. It helps the scientists to create applications that use public computing resources. BOINC is scalable and does high performance task distribution and exhibits fault tolerance.

Contig: The term contig means "contiguous". It represents DNA sequences which are overlapping. This sequence helps to reconstruct the original DNA sequence of a chromosome.

De Novo Assembler: Assembly of 'reads' into contigs is done using a reference genome or without any reference genome. The assembler tool that assembles the contigs without any reference is called as De novo assembler, the name is derived from Latin meaning 'from the beginning'.

DNA: Deoxyribonucleic acid (DNA) is a molecule involved in encoding of genetic instructions of living organisms.

N50: The N50 is a statistical measure representing a set of contig or scaffold lengths. It is used to benchmark the quality of contigs generated from the assembly process. Longer contigs have greater N50 value. For example, to calculate N50 value for a list, L of positive integers is as mentioned below: (a) Identical to the list L, create another list L'. The list L' contains 'n' copies of every element 'n' present in the list L. (b) The N50 of the list L is the median of L'. For Example: If the list, L = (2, 2, 2, 3, 3, 4, 4, 8, 8), then L'={2, 2, 2, 2, 2, 2, 3, 3, 3, 3, 3, 3, 4, 4, 4, 4, 4, 4, 4, 8, 8, 8, 8, 8, 8, 8, 8, 8, 8, 8, 8, 8, 8, 8, 8, 8}. The N50 value is 4 which is the median value from the list, L'. The median of the 36-element from the set L' is the average of the 18th smallest element, 4 and 19th smallest element, 4, N50 value is 4, whereas the median for the same list, L is 3.

Next Generation Sequencing: Next Generation Sequencing revolves around parallelizing the sequencing process and is a variant of DNA sequencing technologies which produces thousands or millions of sequences concurrently.

Nucleo-Bases: Bases or Nucleo-bases are found within nucleotides. Nucleo-bases are nitrogen containing biological compounds found in ucleotides i.e. the basic building blocks of DNA consists of four bases called Adenine (A), Thymine (T), Guanine (G), and Cytosine (C). They can form pairs called as Base Pairs (BP) to form the double helix structure of chromosome. Pairing is unique among these bases. In DNA, base (A) is always paired with a (T) using 2 bonds and (C) is paired with (G) using 3 bonds to have the double helical structure.

Read: A 'read' is short sequence of genome that can be read at a time. Based on the technology used the length of the reads ranges from 20 to 1000 base pairs. The 'reads' of many interesting species are already available and are freely downloadable from National Center for Biotechnology Information (NCBI) database.

Scaffold: A scaffold is also known as a "supercontig". One or more contigs bound together and oriented in forward direction separated by gaps represents a supercontig.

Volunteer Computing: To enable distributed computing volunteer computing makes use of computers volunteered or donated by the general public. This allows contribution of idle resources from people located anywhere in the world towards solving large parallel programs.

Work Unit: It indicates the computation to be performed by clients. It is specified using several parameters such as name, application to be performed by work unit and the input on which the computation has to be performed.

APPENDIX

De Bruijn Graph: It is a graph which is directed, consisting of 'm' symbols and it represents overlaps. The overlaps are identified from the sequences of symbols. The graph consists of m x n vertices. The graph is made up sequences of all possible length 'n' of the given symbols. In a sequence, each symbol may appear multiple times. The set, S of 'm' symbols is as shown in equation (1.1) and the set of vertices, 'V' is as shown in equation (1.2).

$$R = r_1, \ldots r_m \tag{1.1}$$

$$V = R_n = \{(r_1, \ldots r_1, r_1), (r_1, \ldots r_1, r_2), \ldots, (r_1, \ldots r_m), \ldots, (r_m, \ldots r_m, r_m)\} \tag{1.2}$$

If the symbols are shifted by one place to the left, to the end of this vertex a new symbol could be added thereby, the new symbol can have a directed edge to the earlier vertex.

Thus the set of arcs, E represented as directed edges is as shown in equation (1.3).

$$E = \{((v_1, v_2 \ldots v_n), (v_2, \ldots v_n, r_i)) : i = 1, \ldots m\} \tag{1.3}$$

For example, if $m = \{1, 0\}$ and $n = \{2\}$, then $R = \{1, 0\}$, there will be 4 vertices $V = 2^2 = 4 = \{11, 10, 01, 00\}$. The edges are represented using the graph as shown in figure 9. Similar such graph is constructed for 'reads' information and is used to generate the contigs.

Figure 9. Example of a De Bruijn Graph

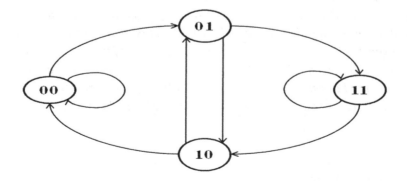

Chapter 5

Mobile Cloud Computing Integrating Cloud, Mobile Computing, and Networking Services Through Virtualization

Chitresh Verma
Amity University, India

Rajiv Pandey
Amity University, India

ABSTRACT

Mobile computing is a critical technology area which is actively integrated with field of cloud computing. It is broadly an application of virtualization technology at both ends of client server architecture. The mobile and cloud computing is a natural combination as mobile devices have limited computing and storage capacity, thus to reap the benefits of high end computing, cloud is the answer. Thus, amalgamation of mobile platform with cloud platform is inevitable. This chapter shall deliberate on the various aspects of mobile computing, mobile cloud computing and its relationship with virtualization technology. The detailed integration aspects and virtualization shall be signified through case study and suitable real time examples. The chapter shall envisage a case study, modeling the virtualization in the context of mobile cloud.

DOI: 10.4018/978-1-5225-2785-5.ch005

INTRODUCTION

The mobile cloud computing is established on cloud computing. It assimilates the cloud computing with mobile computing. This integration is accomplished using the virtualization technology. The chapter refers to the technologies involved in mobile cloud computing with a spotlight on the practical aspects and their industrial exploit. The role of virtualization in these aspects shall be highlighted. Along it the high level abstraction at virtualization level is demonstration with the implementation of mobile computing.

1. CLOUD COMPUTING

The term cloud computing refers to remote computation using the shared data storage and processing systems with the help of Internet based services. (Wang, C. et al., 2010) It acts as a basic framework for shared resource access for a variety of models like networking, storage and services. It requires the least amount of investment in managing and operating the resources. The decrease in operating cost is linked with remote and shared infrastructure in multiple parts of the world. The combined cost of operating the systems leads to lower cost of owning and operating the hardware and software systems. Also, the support system like UPS, power supply and other additional cost are significantly reduced in the cloud computing environment.

1.1 Working of Cloud Computing

Cloud computing is made up of two words where cloud related to internet with computing to data processing. It may be defined as the use of various information technology services including hardware related from remote locations using common interaction. These services have shared infrastructure to deliver high performance computation, storage and other solution to their clients.

1.2 Types of Cloud Computing

The cloud computing has been divided into four major services by the researcher. These major types of services are SaaS, PaaS, IaaS, and MBaaS. (Kavis, M. J., 2014)

- SaaS stands for software as a service which has all the functions built-in. These functions are only configuring as the user requirement by the expert of that respective service.

Figure 1. Different types of cloud computing illustrated in stacked relationship (Designed by author)

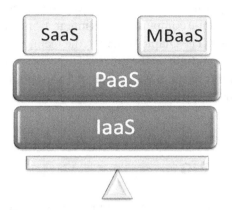

- PaaS stands for platform as a service where all requirements of the software development are available. The user can quickly build and deploy the application using these services.
- IaaS stands for infrastructure as a service where the basic hardware related services are offered. These services may be servers, storage, and networking.
- MBaaS stands for mobile backend as a service model where the server end business logic and hosting are offered as a service. The push notification and e payment are two popular examples of MBaaS. (Aliyev, A. et. al, 2016)

1.2.1 IaaS, PaaS, SaaS and MBaaS

1. Software as a Service (SaaS):
    The entire solution in the form of web application is available on the internet. The "pay-as-you-go" model is used for service charge by most of SaaS provider where the subscription is based on the amount of usage of the services. (Wohl, A., 2010)
2. Platform as a Service (PaaS)
    The Set of all required tools and library for running of a software application are provided in this service. PaaS helps in quick development and deployment of web applications without any issue of underlying infrastructure. (Buyya, R. et. al., 2011) In many cases it also provides the infrastructure for many SaaS application development.
3. Infrastructure as a Service (IaaS):
    It is a set of basic service and hardware for any software to run on. It includes the servers, operating systems and networking. (Mell, P. et. al., 2010) These

services are rented to the client in a shared manner. The shared services help in reducing the cost of operating them. It is also sometimes referred as public cloud. If the infrastructure has not shared them it is called a private cloud. There is also a combination of both infrastructures called hybrid cloud.

4. Mobile backend as a Service (MBaaS)

   It is also known as "Backend as a Service (BaaS)". It is a service where the entire data exchange and business logic requirement at the server end is offered as a ready to use. (Lane, K., 2015). The mobile application developers use these services as and when required to reduce the workload on the application. Many times, these services are consumed by using the APIs. The popular services in the MBaaS are "push notification", "authentication", "social networking" and "payment gateway".

1.3 Virtual Machines

The virtual machines (VMs) are a special type of software copies which run the entire operating system and installed application software set on virtual hardware. The virtual hardware is built using the virtualization technologies like the hypervisor. Main server virtualization hypervisor product providers are Hyper V from Microsoft, vSphere from VMware and XenServer from Citrix. (Fayyad-Kazan et al, 2013) All of these server products logical separate each virtual machine from each other. They also allow sharing same physical hardware among the different virtual machines or instances. It reduces cost and requirement for additional physical hardware. While it increases the use of physical hardware which would be idle in traditional systems.

Shared resource utilization is a major benefit of using virtual machines. The traditional system has low usage of physical hardware systems. The VMs allows maximum exploitation of physical hardware. The result is better cost per hardware return.

Special application software is used for management of the virtual machines. This software helps in creating, cloning, turn on/off and delete the virtual machines as per requirement of the clients. It provides tools and drivers for creating, installing and running various operating systems in a virtual environment. In general practice, a copy of the virtual machine is configured which is called golden image. This golden image is used for replicating the same machine for clients in a virtual environment.

1.4 Cloud Computing on VM

Virtual machines (VMs) had a critical role to play in cloud computing architecture. The cloud can extend their compute and storage capacity using the VM technology.

Virtual machine and cloud strategy

The virtual machine and cloud integration technique varies with each service provider. But some common fundamental are present in each service provider. Some of them are as follows:

1. Software defined data center (SDDC)

    It is a customer oriented service involving scale up and down of data center resources and solution using the virtualization technologies. It is similar to Infrastructure as a Service concept in service oriented architecture (SOA). All the components and its subcomponents like storage device can be altered as per customer requirements.

2. Different types of cloud solution

    There are three major types of cloud solution. These are discussed in detail in below points.

    a. Private cloud

    The private cloud does not have any shared infrastructure and sometimes entire infrastructure is in the client location itself. It supports both traditional enterprise application and modern micro services based applications.

    b. Public cloud

    It is based on shared infrastructure. The shared infrastructure is offered, which reduce cost of operating the system. It is also more widely used cloud type.

    c. Hybrid cloud

    It is adoption of IT infrastructure without isolating cloud infrastructure except certain functions. It uses the public cloud in non sensitive functions and private cloud in sensitive functions.

1.5 Advantages of Cloud Computing on VM

Cloud computing on virtual machines offers many advantages over the traditional systems. Some of these advantages are as follows:

1. Non disruptive storage for multiple machine and backups with cloning technology of virtual machines.
2. Quick reloaded of entire system with virtual systems performing faster reset than physical hardware.
3. In case of application failure, the application can rebuild using the golden image within minimal time and effort.

2. MOBILE CLOUD COMPUTING

Amalgamation of cloud computing, mobile computing and networking services forms the mobile cloud computing (MCC). It has multiple service providers involved like mobile network service provider. It aims to build better user experiences while keeping costs at a minimum. Therefore, it also creates new business areas for the service providers.

2.1 What is Mobile Cloud Computing?

Mobile cloud computing (MCC) is synchronized framework of systems on both mobile device and cloud to store and process the data to provide better user experience. The mobile device has limited storage and computational power. So, the function of data storage and computation actually shift to the cloud where larger storage and powerful computational power is available under mobile cloud computing. The mobile device acts as a thin client or web service based architecture for events and data exchange.

Mobile cloud computing can be defined as a unified interface of smart device with internet connectivity with cloud based servers and storage system to provide unconditional functions of storage and processing through predefined protocol to use.

2.2 Why Mobile Cloud Computing?

Smart device is bounded by their limited memory size, processing power and battery life. These limits are overcome with MCC.

Mobile cloud computing has many benefits over the traditional systems. Some of them are as follows:

1. Better harnessing of the infrastructure at both mobile and cloud end. The mobile device can perform minimal storage and process with most of it transferred to the cloud environment.
2. Low cost of high performance computation from the mobile devices with the help of cloud systems.
3. Dynamic performance on a mobile device based user plan for cloud computing. Thus, systems become cost effective for the end users and service providers.

2.3 Mobile Cloud Computing on VM

Virtual machines play a critical role in realization of mobile cloud computing. The resource hungry applications are transferred to the cloud using the virtual machine

(VM). The entire applications are encapsulated inside a virtual machine at mobile devices.

2.3.1 Advantage of Mobile Cloud Computing with Virtualization

The use of mobile cloud computing with virtual platform provides much discrete improvement over other techniques. (Dinh, H., 2013) Some of these advantages are as follows:

Figure 2. Reference architecture for mobile cloud computing (Designed by author)

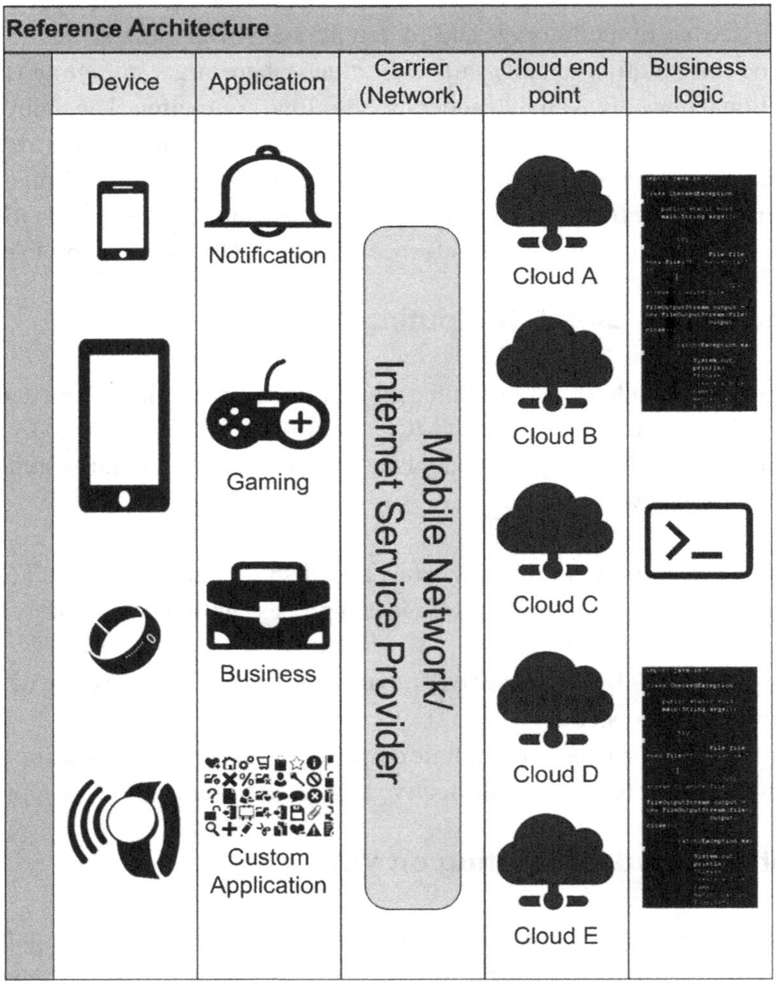

1. The battery lifetime of mobile device is improved in mobile cloud computing environment.
2. Improve the storage capacity and performance of applications by using cloud infrastructure. The user of mobile device can store large amount of data and perform computation on them.
3. The cloud based storage systems reduce the chances of data loss due to hardware failure. Disaster recovery system is easily employed in the cloud infrastructure due economy of scale.
4. Mobile cloud computing had opened doors for a highly secure method of data storage. Many frameworks like digital right management can be implemented in a more effective manner. The data provider can control flow of data in the mobile devices network. Moreover, the malicious data on a mobile device can be tracked and removed from the system.
5. Multiple mobile devices can be used for the same device with active synchronization of the devices with cloud systems.
6. Users can scale up and down resources in the cloud based on their requirements and budget.
7. Integration of different services is also possible. Even if these services involved different service providers.

3. UNDERSTANDING OF MOBILE CLOUD COMPUTING USING VIRTUALIZATION TECHNOLOGY

With exponential grow in the number of mobile devices and its computation obligation, the worth of mobile cloud computing is ascending also. It could be understood by analyzing the rapid escalation of more applications running on mobile devices alongside becoming more resources starving. Cloud based resource needs are also changing with different mobile devices. Scenario such resource scaling up/ down requires the virtualization technology. Further, it becomes important to understand and implementing the mobile cloud computing functions with virtualization technology.

The implementation of mobile cloud computing involves two end points. These end points are as follows:

1. Cloud systems end point
    The software and hardware present at cloud platform forms the cloud systems end point. These have high-end hardware which runs a complex set of software to process incoming requests from multiple devices.

2. Mobile device end point

    The mobile device has their own communication mechanism where they create a mobile device end point. This endpoint server serves as a destination for the response from cloud systems. It is also to be noted, these end point runs on virtual systems like Java virtual machine (JVM) in case of the Android platform.

3.1 Major Issues for VM in the Context of MCC

There are many issues related to VM usage in mobile cloud computing, which restricted accomplishment of complete potential. These issues are discussed in below section.

1. Architectural related constraint

    The architecture is a core element of any system. Reference architecture of mobile cloud computing is heterogeneous composition. The mobile device has a different architectural design with comparison to cloud systems architecture design. Thus the integration of both them is an issue for a developer.

2. Battery life concern of mobile devices

    The battery life is limited in any mobile device. It is considered a vital resource in them. The data exchange between device and cloud system required the battery consuming process like network calls. This reduces the normal battery life of mobile devices.

3. Virtual machine exchange in real-time:

    The applications running on the mobile device transfer to the cloud environment to release resources of mobile device. But this migration in real time is a big problem as the package, then transfers and unpackaged of the entire application at cloud end.

4. Security Issues:

    The security of data which is exchanged over the network is a big concern for application developers. The passive data thief is very much a possibility in the circumstances.

3.2 Mobile Computing with Android and Android Studio IDE

This section shall deliberate on the various aspects of mobile computing using Android mobile platform. Android platforms use the Java virtual machine, for its virtualization requirements. We shall have a brief introduction of Android mobile application development to better understand of level of abstraction in virtualization layer.

The Google has developed an integrated development environment (IDE) for android developers called Android Studio. It based on IntelliJ IDEA, which is also an IDE for Java developers. (Faustine, A. et. al., 2014) Setup of Android Studio is available for free on the Android Studio Website (URL: https://developer.android.com/studio/index.html). One can download it and install on his machine. Upon launch of the Android Studio, a welcome screen is shown as in figure 3.

The development of Android mobile application involves multiple steps. These steps are as follows:

1. Create an Android project
    Get started by choosing the "New Project" option from the menu bar. A list of options is displayed on the screen as shown in figure 4. Choose the appropriate option as per your requirements of the application. Name the project as "Demo Project". After completing all the obligatory details, progress bar is shown as in shown in figure 5.
2. Writing code in Android Studio
    The windows screen containing multiple panels to help in coding the Android application appears once the entire configuration is completed as shown in figure 6. Left side panel is used to navigate to file for coding the logic of the application and other tasks.

Figure 3. Welcome screen of Android Studio version 2.2.2(Captured by author)

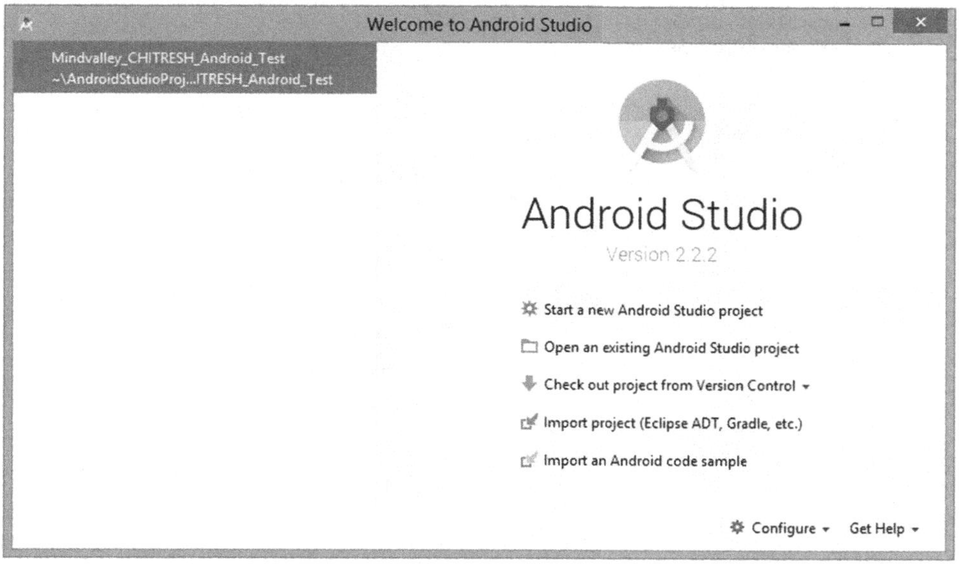

Figure 4. New Project dialog box having fields like "Application name"

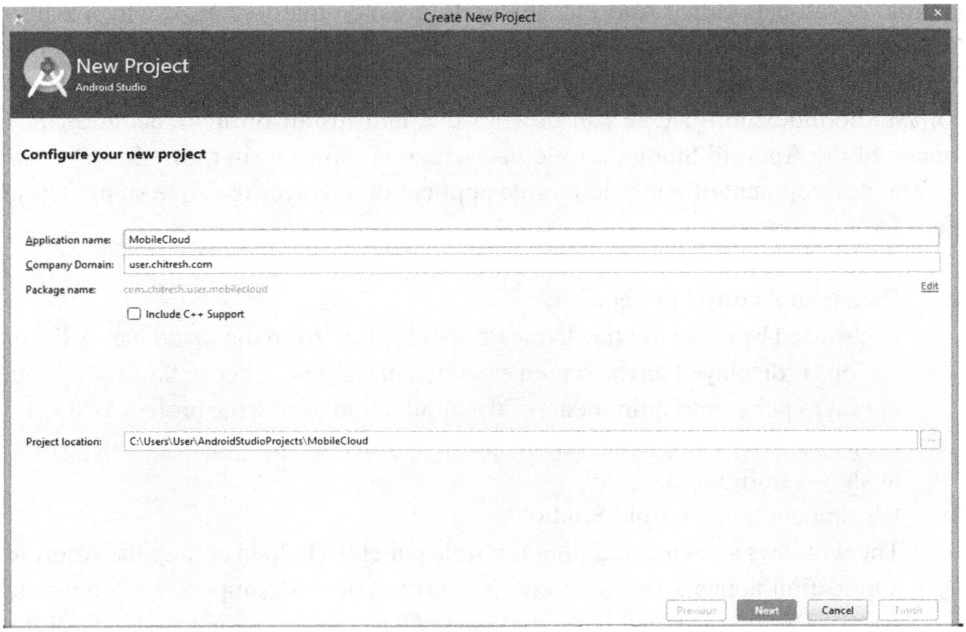

Figure 5. Progress bar for creating project dialog box (Captured by author)

Figure 6. Coding window on the Android Studio environment (Screenshot captured by author)

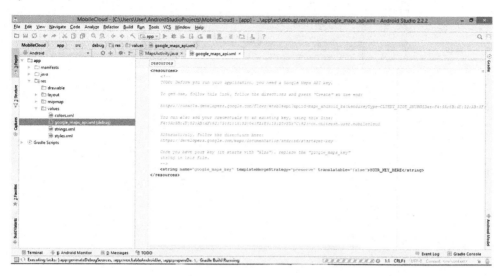

3.   Setup of the emulator device

For testing purpose, we need to setup an emulator device or USB debugging on real device. One can easily create emulator using already provide tools in Android Studio.

4.   Running the application on an emulator

Application can be tested on emulator or real device using the run at the top panel of Android Studio. Upon running the application, a dialog is pop ups for choosing the deployment target device as shown in figure 7. After launching the application, the developer can trace the logs in the bottom panel.

3.3 Quickblox: MBaaS Provider Using Virtualization Technology

Quickblox is an IT services company which also provides Mobile Backend as a Service (MBaaS). Their services include push notifications, video calling and messaging. (Ghule, K et. al.) These services are supported and maintained by infrastructure of Quickblox.

In order to use these services of QuickBlox, you have to follow certain steps. These steps have been discussed in the below sections.

Figure 7. Dialog asking for deployment target for running the Android application

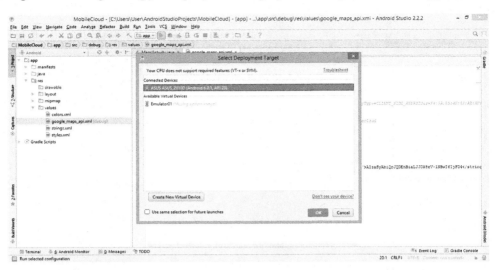

3.3.1 Understanding of QuickBlox and its Services

To make use of QuickBlox services certain prerequisite is vital. The tools which are obligatory are Java runtime environment (JRE), Android Studio and Maven. All of these tools can be easily downloaded from the Internet. After installing all the tools, open a browser and to browse GitHub repository using URL "https://github.com/ QuickBlox/quickblox-android-sdk-releases". This repository contains binary code for services of QuickBlox and their guidelines for integration of the latest version of QuickBlox with an Android project.

In order to use the services, software development kit (SDK) needs to be added in the android project. For this task, we need to include the SDK references to the android reference file and this reference file is build.gradle file. So, after including lines the file should seem like as follows:

```
repositories {
      maven {
          url "https://github.com/QuickBlox/quickblox-
android-sdk-releases/raw/master/"
      }
  }
```

We also need to add dependencies of SDK in build.gradle file. Dependencies can be added using the below mentioned lines.

```
dependencies {
    compile "com.quickblox:quickblox-android-sdk-core:2.5.1@aar"
    compile("com.quickblox:quickblox-android-sdk-chat:2.5.1@
aar") {
        transitive=true
    }
}
```

Now, you can use the SDK for your project. The services could reduce the workload of mobile device and perform its resource starving activities at the cloud end.

3.4 Android Application with Google Map: An Example of Integration of Cloud Computing and Mobile Computing

The Google Map is a library of Android framework provides by Google. (Singhal, M., 2012) It widely used in many applications for navigation, better visualization and situational awareness. The most popular applications like Uber, Instagram and Amazon are using this API for enhancing the user experience.

Certain prerequisites are required for building the application with Google Map.

1. Android Studio integrated development environment installed on developer system. We have already discussed it in detailed in section "Getting started with Mobile Computing: Android and Android Studio IDE".

Figure 8. Basic architecture of mobile cloud computing using Google API (Designed by author)

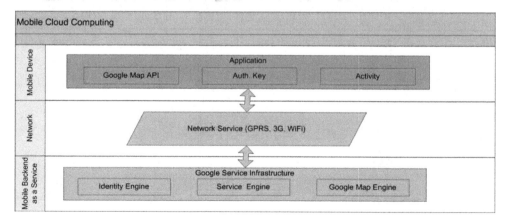

2.   A Mobile device for testing purpose is also required, which also configured with Android Studio including the debug drivers.

3.   Knowledge of the Java programming language, Android application lifecycle and its library files as part of Android development package.

The use of Google APIs requires a Google Account. These Google APIs can be browsed using the URL "https://console.developers.google.com/flows/enableapi?apiid=maps_android_backend&keyType=CLIENT_SIDE_ANDROID". Upon entering the URL, a login in the Google Account is required and after the successfully completing the login a window similar to figure 9 should appear on the screen.

The developer could generate the API key by filling up the necessary details in the credential form. API key is shown in a dialog box as shown in figure 10. This API key is consumed in file "AndroidManifest.xml". (Rani, C. R. et. al., 2012) The sample code of AndroidManifest is provided below.

```
<?xml version="1.0" encoding="utf-8"?>
<manifest xmlns:android="http://schemas.android.com/apk/res/
android"
     package="com.mobile.user.mobilecloud">
     <!--
          The ACCESS_COARSE/FINE_LOCATION permissions are not
```

Figure 9. Landing page of Google APIs after the login Google Account (Captured by author)

Figure 10. Dialog showing API key created by Google APIs (Screenshot captured by the author)

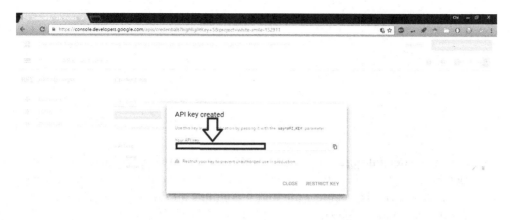

```
required to use
        Google Maps Android API v2, but you must specify
either coarse or fine
        location permissions for the 'MyLocation'
functionality.
    -->
    <uses-permission android:name="android.permission.ACCESS_
FINE_LOCATION" />
    <application
        android:allowBackup="true"
        android:icon="@mipmap/ic_map_launcher"
        android:label="@string/app_name"
        android:supportsRtl="true"
        android:theme="@style/AppTheme">
        <meta-data
          android:name="com.google.android.geo.API_KEY"
          android:value="@string/my_google_maps_key" />
        <activity
          android:name=".MyMapsActivity"
          android:label="@string/title_activity_my_maps">
```

```
        <intent-filter>
            <action android:name="android.intent.action.
MAIN" />
            <category android:name="android.intent.
category.LAUNCHER" />
        </intent-filter>
    </activity>
  </application>
</manifest>
```

For our understanding, the AndroidManifest sample code has permission parameters, Google APIs details and declaration of the activities. Further, the root tag of this XML file is manifest tag and it contains all the tags along the details. This XML file controls the flow of application and security aspects.

4. EXAMINING THE INDUSTRIAL OFFERINGS CONCERNING THE MOBILE CLOUD COMPUTING ON VMS

V2Soft is a cloud based IT service provider, including mobile backend services. (V2Soft, 2016) It offers a full range of service platforms to its customers. Some of these services are discussed in below points.

1. **Authentication and Authorization Services:** They are offering multi-layered security using multiple devices. It is available for enterprise level solutions.
2. **Updating and Monitoring Services:** Various kinds of update can perform using the services on any mobile device. It has the function of monitoring the device with remote lock mechanism for security breach.
3. **Cloud Business Logic Services:** The application can directly deploy on mobile devices without any business logics. These business logics can be kept at cloud infrastructure to reduce the resource depend on application on mobile end.
4. **Remote Installation of Mobile Application Services:** The application installation can be remotely achieved by using the mobile application services. It helps in better service delivery to any customer.

All of these services are supported by virtualization technologies under cloud based environment settings. It allows user to have the flexibility of using the services in different devices.

5. SUMMARY

The chapter deliberated on the mobile computing and cloud computing integration techniques and practical implementations. We had learned the mobile cloud computing concept and its advantages of using virtualization technologies. Further, we understand the aspect of mobile application using Android Studio. Brief overview of application development of Google Map to utilize the Google APIs is provided. It could be used as a template for other complex implementation of mobile backend services. Finally, we discussed the case study of a company offering in mobile cloud computing domain for understanding the industry aspects.

CONCLUSION

The reader could build a mobile application to maximize the benefits of VM technology on both mobile and cloud. The virtualization is the most important pillar of mobile computing, cloud computing and mobile cloud computing. The implementation of these computing technologies has become easier due to the virtualization technologies as shown in the chapter with little or no knowledge. This easiness can be linked to high level of abstraction at the virtualization layer.

FUTURE RESEARCH WORK AND DIRECTIONS

In future, the fog computing concept could be comprehended in the discussed technologies. The fog computing involves deployment of the local and middle level high end computational infrastructure. It is interesting to study the application development in such environment and the level of knowhow of virtualization required as in deliberated in this chapter.

ACKNOWLEDGMENT

We are grateful to our families for their moral support over the due course of chapter writing. We also feel like to acknowledge the contribution of all the people involved with their suggestion in improving this chapter eminence.

REFERENCES

Aliyev, A., & Samadov, R. (2016). *E-commerce payments with cloud service mbaas.* Doctoral dissertation.

Dinh, H. T., Lee, C., Niyato, D., & Wang, P. (2013). A survey of mobile cloud computing: architecture, applications, and approaches. *Wireless communications and mobile computing, 13*(18), 1587-1611.

Faustine, A., & Mvuma, A. N. (2014). Ubiquitous mobile sensing for water quality monitoring and reporting within lake victoria basin. *Wireless Sensor Network, 6*(12), 257–264. doi:10.4236/wsn.2014.612025

Fayyad-Kazan, H., Perneel, L., & Timmerman, M. (2013). Benchmarking the Performance of Microsoft Hyper-V server, VMware ESXi and Xen Hypervisors. *Journal of Emerging Trends in Computing and Information Sciences, 4*(12), 922–933.

Ghule, K., Tikone, N., Sonar, S., Ghate, B., & Sonone, S. (2015). *Android App With Integration Of Quickblox XAMPP Chatting, Google GCM And Client-Server Architecture.*

Kavis, M. J. (2014). *Architecting the cloud: Design decisions for cloud computing service models (SaaS, PaaS, AND IaaS).* John Wiley & Sons. doi:10.1002/9781118691779

Lane, K. (2015). *Overview of the backend as a service (BaaS) space.*

Limited, V. (n.d.). *About Us - V2Soft.* Retrieved December 29, 2016, from https://www.v2soft.com/about-us

Mell, P., & Grance, T. (2010). The NIST definition of cloud computing. *Communications of the ACM, 53*(6), 50.

Rani, C. R., Kumar, A. P., Adarsh, D., Mohan, K. K., & Kiran, K. V. (2012). *Location based services in Android.* International Journal Of Advances In Engineering & Technology.

Singhal, M., & Shukla, A. (2012). Implementation of location based services in android using GPS and web services. *IJCSI International Journal of Computer Science Issues, 9*(1), 237–242.

Wang, C., Wang, Q., Ren, K., & Lou, W. (2010, March). Privacy-preserving public auditing for data storage security in cloud computing. Proceedings of IEEE INFOCOM '10 (pp. 1-9). IEEE. doi:10.1109/INFCOM.2010.5462173

Wohl, A. (2010). Software as a Service (SaaS). In *The Next Wave of Technologies: Opportunities* from Chaos (pp. 97-113).

ADDITIONAL READING

Antonopoulos, N., & Gillam, L. (Eds.). (2010). *Cloud computing: Principles, systems and applications*. Springer Science & Business Media. doi:10.1007/978-1-84996-241-4

Barr, K., Bungale, P., Deasy, S., Gyuris, V., Hung, P., Newell, C., & Zoppis, B. et al. (2010). The VMware mobile virtualization platform: Is that a hypervisor in your pocket? *Operating Systems Review, 44*(4), 124–135. doi:10.1145/1899928.1899945

Bhaskar, R., & Shylaja, B. S. (2016). Knowledge based reduction technique for virtual machine provisioning in cloud computing. *International Journal of Computer Science and Information Security, 14*(7), 472.

Buyya, R., & Sukumar, K. (2011). *Platforms for building and deploying applications for cloud computing*. arXiv:1104.4379

Catteddu, D. (2010). Cloud Computing: benefits, risks and recommendations for information security. In Web Application Security (pp. 17-17). Springer Berlin Heidelberg. doi:10.1007/978-3-642-16120-9_9

Hayes, B. (2008). Cloud computing. *Communications of the ACM, 51*(7).

Forman, G. H., & Zahorjan, J. (1994). The challenges of mobile computing. *Computer, 27*(4), 38–47. doi:10.1109/2.274999

Furht, B., & Escalante, A. (2010). *Handbook of cloud computing* (Vol. 3). New York: Springer. doi:10.1007/978-1-4419-6524-0

Huerta-Canepa, G., & Lee, D. (2010, June). A virtual cloud computing provider for mobile devices. *Proceedings of the 1st ACM Workshop on Mobile Cloud Computing & Services: Social Networks and Beyond* (p. 6). ACM. doi:10.1145/1810931.1810937

Krutz, R. L., & Vines, R. D. (2010). *Cloud security: A comprehensive guide to secure cloud computing*. Wiley Publishing.

Kumar, K., & Lu, Y. H. (2010). Cloud computing for mobile users: Can offloading computation save energy? *Computer, 43*(4), 51–56. doi:10.1109/MC.2010.98

Marston, S., Li, Z., Bandyopadhyay, S., Zhang, J., & Ghalsasi, A. (2011). Cloud computing—The business perspective. *Decision Support Systems*, *51*(1), 176–189. doi:10.1016/j.dss.2010.12.006

Rittinghouse, J. W., & Ransome, J. F. (2016). *Cloud computing: implementation, management, and security*. CRC press.

Rogers, R., Lombardo, J., Mednieks, Z., & Meike, B. (2009). *Android application development: Programming with the Google SDK*. O'Reilly Media, Inc.

Satyanarayanan, M., Bahl, P., Caceres, R., & Davies, N. (2009). The case for vm-based cloudlets in mobile computing. *IEEE Pervasive Computing / IEEE Computer Society [and] IEEE Communications Society*, *8*(4), 14–23. doi:10.1109/MPRV.2009.82

Stojmenovic, I. (Ed.). (2003). *Handbook of wireless networks and mobile computing* (Vol. 27). John Wiley & Sons.

Velte, A. T., Velte, T. J., Elsenpeter, R. C., & Elsenpeter, R. C. (2010). *Cloud computing: a practical approach* (p. 44). New York: McGraw-Hill.

Zaki, Y., Zhao, L., Goerg, C., & Timm-Giel, A. (2011). LTE mobile network virtualization. *Mobile Networks and Applications*, *16*(4), 424–432. doi:10.1007/s11036-011-0321-7

KEY TERMS AND DEFINITIONS

Google APIs: They are collection of application programming interfaces which could be used by after login into Google account. It allows incorporation of Google developed libraries with any application.

JVM (Java Virtual Machine): It is a virtual machine which used in Java programming. It makes the Java platform independent. The Java byte code runs on this virtual machine.

VMware: VMware is a virtualization tools which widely used in data center. It could scale up and down services and its infrastructure. It supports both desktop & server platform for applications virtualization.

XenServer: It is special application software which is developed by Citrix Systems. It assists in creating and managing virtual machines (VMs). It uses open-source Project Xen Hypervisor for its many functions.

Chapter 6
OpenGL® API–Based Analysis of Large Datasets in a Cloud Environment

Wolfgang Mexner
Karlsruhe Institute of Technology (KIT), Germany

Matthias Bonn
Karlsruhe Institute of Technology (KIT), Germany

Andreas Kopmann
Karlsruhe Institute of Technology (KIT), Germany

Viktor Mauch
Karlsruhe Institute of Technology (KIT), Germany

Doris Ressmann
Karlsruhe Institute of Technology (KIT), Germany

Suren A. Chilingaryan
Karlsruhe Institute of Technology (KIT), Germany

Nicholas Tan Jerome
Karlsruhe Institute of Technology (KIT), Germany

Thomas van de Kamp
Karlsruhe Institute of Technology (KIT), Germany

Vincent Heuveline
Heidelberg University, Germany

Philipp Lösel
Heidelberg University, Germany

Sebastian Schmelzle
Technische Universität Darmstadt (TUD), Germany

Michael Heethoff
Technische Universität Darmstadt (TUD), Germany

DOI: 10.4018/978-1-5225-2785-5.ch006

ABSTRACT

Modern applications for analysing 2D/3D data require complex visual output features which are often based on the multi-platform OpenGL® API for rendering vector graphics. Instead of providing classical workstations, the provision of powerful virtual machines (VMs) with GPU support in a scientific cloud with direct access to high performance storage is an efficient and cost effective solution. However, the automatic deployment, operation and remote access of OpenGL® API-capable VMs with professional visualization applications is a non-trivial task. In this chapter the authors demonstrate the concept of such a flexible cloud-like analysis infrastructure within the framework of the project ASTOR. The authors present an Analysis-as-a-Service (AaaS) approach based on VMware™-ESX for on demand allocation of VMs with dedicated GPU cores and up to 256 GByte RAM per machine.

INTRODUCTION

Due to the ability of X-rays to penetrate materials, they are highly appropriate to visualize internal structures of opaque objects. Moreover, X-ray-computed tomography provides the opportunity to visualize internal structures of optically dense materials in 3D. The intensity of X-rays emitted by synchrotron light sources is several orders of magnitudes higher than from laboratory sources and provide brilliant and partially coherent radiation for fast imaging with synchrotron radiation (Cloetens, Bolle, Ludwig, Baruchel, & Schlenke, 2001). The application of synchrotron-based X-ray-micro-tomography for biological samples was the onset of a new era of morphological research on millimetre-sized animals like small arthropods (e.g. Heethoff & Norton, 2009; van de Kamp, Vagovič, Baumbach, & Riedel, 2011; Schmelzle, Norton, & Heethoff,2015). In recent years, new setups enabled unrivalled opportunities of high-throughput measurements, 3D/4D-tomographic imaging of dynamic systems, and even living organisms (dos Santos Rolo, 2014). Online data evaluation became possible by the usage of advanced graphic processors for scientific computing (Chilingaryan, Kopmann, Mirone, dos Santos Rolo, & Vogelgesang, 2011). These new technologies, however, result in large amounts of data: currently up to 100 GByte per volume summing up to 15 TByte/day. Technical limitations are reached regarding data acquisition, storage, and organization. Analysis of tomographic data is usually time-consuming and many analysis steps relies on commercial applications that provide visual output based on the OpenGL® API for Microsoft operating systems (Mauch et al., 2014). An example for frequently used commercial applications are AMIRA™ and VG Studio MAX™, which are costly and might not be available at all user's home institutions.

In order to simplify the access to efficient analysis tools the idea was born to analyse the tomographic datasets in a cloud environment. This environment is based on a computing centre that is located directly at the data producing synchrotron facility. A tailored analysis tool chain should be pre-installed, licensed products could be used more effectively and complex installation procedures of open source tools or custom developments are avoided. But such an approach faces several difficulties for a virtual instantiation:

- Possible lag of virtual machine desktops.
- Analysis software like Amira requires GPU support for the OpenGL® and DirectX API as well as NVIDIA® CUDA™ support.
- Interactive operation with 3D objects requires high frame rates.
- Users might have only small bandwidth.
- Very large VM RAM requirements for datasets in the magnitude of 50 to 100 GB.
- High speed network interconnect from the VM to the data storage for loading and saving such datasets in a few minutes.

In order to deal with the challenges presented by fast state-of-the art synchrotron X-ray imaging, partners from the University of Darmstadt, the University of Heidelberg and Karlsruhe Institute of Technology (KIT) established the project ASTOR ("Arthropod Structure revealed by ultra-fast Tomography and Online Reconstruction), which is funded by the German Federal Ministry of Education and Research. In this chapter an overview of ASTOR's cloud concept is given and different aspects are presented in detail.

ASTOR WORKFLOW, OVERVIEW

The requirements for the cloud concept are driven by the ASTOR workflow (Figure 1). The workflow starts in step 1 by submitting a proposal for tomographic experiments via the web portal for beam time proposals (Ressmann, Mexner, Vondrous, Kopmann & Mauch,2014). After acceptance of the proposal beam time is scheduled for the project. A number of micro tomography experiments (Figure 1, step 2) are performed by the users and supported by the on-site scientists of the facility.

Typically, a single tomographic scan is composed of about 2000 2D projections acquired over an angular range of 180° (see e.g. Schwermann et al., 2016 for details). After the experiment, 3D volumes are semi-automatically reconstructed from the 2D projections by a filtered back projection algorithm (Chilingaryan et al., 2011). The resulting tomographic volumes are transferred for further data analysis to the

Figure 1. The scientific analysis workflow

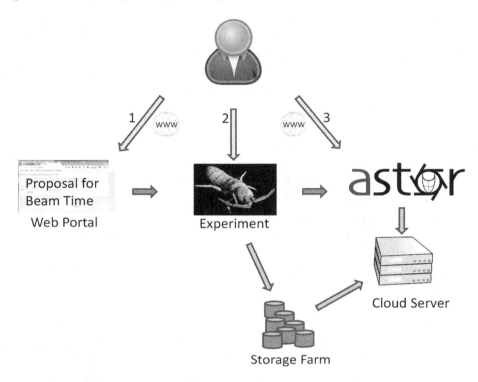

ASTOR portal (Figure 1, step 3). Depending on the scientific questions this may include different post-processing steps like image segmentation, surface generation, creation of interactive 3D models etc. (van de Kamp et al., 2014). A single dataset requires about 65 GB of disc space, comprising raw data and reconstructed tomogram. Post-processing adds approximately 35 GB, thus accumulating to 100 GB of storage space per sample.

Remote analysis of tomographic data via the ASTOR portal is realized by virtual machines, which are created and managed via a web browser, and then accessed by a viewer client. Furthermore, the portal allows browsing and management of all data acquired at the experiment.

ASTOR Cloud Concept and Analysis Environment

The architecture consists of three main parts (see Figure 2 for architecture layout):

Figure 2. The ASTOR Architecture

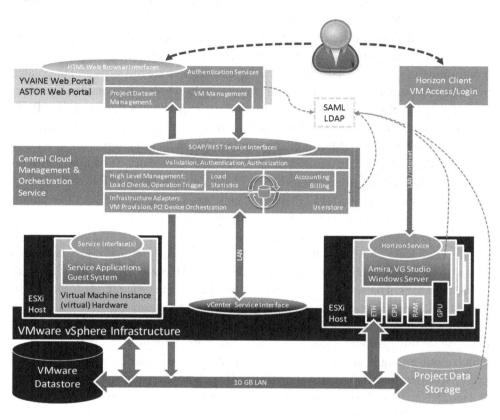

1.   The underlying data processing and virtualization infrastructure with network, datastores and the VMware vSphere™ environment,
2.   an abstraction middleware which encapsulates the virtualization system
3.   finally, two web-based management portals and the remote login client.

Besides these components, there is a central identity provider system based on Shibboleth/SAML and LDAP which is used by several systems and services at the research facility.

The virtualization infrastructure is a full-featured VMware vSphere solution including vCenter™ server and shared datastores using Network File Service (NFS) (VMware images) and Common Internet File System (CIFS) (project data storage, Lightweight Direct Access Protocols (LDAP) authenticated), connected by a high performance local 10 GBit Ethernet to the hypervisors. This layer also stores the prepared VM templates with preconfigured software and LDAP-enabled login. The following section "Hardware and Network Concept" covers this layer in more detail, including a description of the hardware components used. The motivation for using VMware and NVIDIA will also be addressed.

On top of the hardware and the virtualization infrastructure, there is an abstraction layer (the "Central Cloud Management and Orchestration Service" shown in Figure 2). It communicates with the vCenter server API, to orchestrate the VMs and templates by calling the numerous required vSphere functions. Its whole functionality is exposed by a simplified cloud-like API which hides the complexity of the vSphere API. It also implements some additional functions which are not included in vSphere, and integrates Shibboleth/SAML and LDAP based user authentication. This service is placed in the same Local Area Network (LAN) as the vCenter Server, but with no special bandwidth requirements. Its own API is accessible via SOAP over Hypertext Transfer Protocol Secure (HTTPS), so it can be exposed securely to the public internet, as was done in the present case study. The service is described in more detail in the section "Cloud Service".

The user layer comprises the third part of the architecture and consists of web portals which are connected to the cloud service SOAP endpoints and the datastore CIFS interfaces. The second component of the user layer is the remote login client. This standalone client connects directly to the guest system and enables the use of fully OpenGL accelerated software within the virtual machines. In a physical machine for tomographic applications, the users work with high-resolution displays which require a high bandwidth connection to the graphics card. DisplayPort 3.1 for example allows for a bandwidth of up to 30 GBit/s. The currently employed VMware Horizon™ remote desktop system however enables remote interactive graphic operations with high frame rates and high resolutions, even via a low bandwidth public internet connection. For use in ASTOR, Horizon View is configured for Teradici's PC-over-IP™ protocol, allowing a remote desktop connection with up to 2560x1600 pixels, multi monitor and OpenGL API support without noticeable image lag.

HARDWARE AND NETWORK CONCEPT

Server Infrastructure

The following cost-effective PC-based virtualisation server hardware consisting of VMware certified components has been selected:

- Supermicro™ X9DRi-LN4+ Board
- 350 GByte DDR3 RAM
- 2 Quad Core Intel® Xeon(4) CPU E5-2609

- 2 x NVIDIA® Grid-K2™ with 2 Kepler™ GPUs
- Dual Port Intel 82599 10 Gigabit SFI/S Controller

Two identical servers allow for a maximum of 8 virtual machines with dedicated GPU access. For the VM-Images and templates a RAID 5 Storage with 21 Terabyte has been attached via a private 10 Gigabit network (Figure 3). The same network connection has been used for the ESXi cluster communication.

To ensure full transmission speed, access to the virtual machines and to the dataset, storage has been handled via separate 10 GBit/s ports (Figure 3). Four thousand images (of about 10 Mbyte each) from a samba share (CIFS protocol) on the data storage could be read on a virtual machine with around 400 MByte/s.

In order to provide access to the virtual machines (VMs) a previously existing VPN-Server was initially employed as a secure-access gateway. An alternative option would have been the previously mentioned "VMWare View connection server", which would have generally simplified and enhanced access to the VMs from the user point-of-view by eliminating the VPN requirements, but it was nonetheless considered beneficial during the test-phase of the project, that additional remote-

Figure 3. Astor Hardware and Network Layout

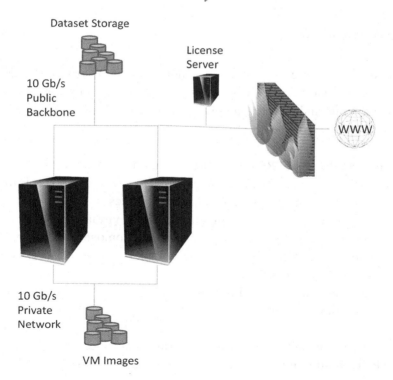

desktop protocols could be tested and evaluated. For external access to company networks both solutions offer similar security levels.

Virtualization Infrastructure

For virtualization, VMware ESXi Version 5.5 has been selected in the vSphere Enterprise plus Version, as only this edition supports the PCI pass-through option. The enterprise versions also support distributed resource scheduling (DRS, vMotion) and the high availability (HA) operation, but as the ASTOR VMs require the GPU via PCI pass-through, migrating a virtual machine from one cluster node to the other requires a shutdown of the virtual machine. At the project design stage in 2013, the PCI pass-through technique was selected since single root IO or even full virtualization with resource sharing of GPU devices including OpenGL® API support was not available. So, passing the GPU PCI device directly into the VM was the only option.

As the virtual machines are created on demand and do not allow hardware dependent licensing, only software with network licenses could be used for ASTOR. The license servers themselves have to be installed on a physical hardware (Figure 3) for the hardware dependent license keys.

CLOUD SERVICE

The necessary VMware orchestration is done by the Microsoft® .NET based software layer 'Cloud Service', which was originally developed for the transparent provision of public and private IaaS cloud resources. Initially, the implementation targets were to:

- Give users Access to Resources they do not have an account for. Especially Amazon's Web Services Elastic Compute Cloud™ (AWS EC2) is difficult to realize at public institutions due to payment issues.
- Simplify the usage by abstracting the underlying virtualization infrastructure. Execute the necessary orchestration tasks and homogenize different systems under the same API. Especially the complex vSphere API needed to be encapsulated by a simpler one.
- Add features that are not implemented, especially accounting and billing based on resource usage.

The integration of Shibboleth/SAML-based user authentication and the support for VMware PCI pass-through enabled VMs was included because these were some of the special requirements of the ASTOR project. The cloud service can also integrate different clusters at the same time and give users different views and different access rights to these clusters. As a result, it was possible to use the existing cloud service by extending it with functions needed by ASTOR.

Infrastructure Orchestration

To access vSphere and AWS, the cloud service utilizes VMware PowerCLI SDK and the AWS SDK for .NET to control the corresponding VMs/templates. A unified SOAP-API, based on the .NET Windows Communication Foundation (WCF) framework, provides all common functionalities and hides the complexity of orchestration and automation of vSphere and EC2 clusters by translating the API-calls into vSphere or AWS specific SDK usage. Some of the unified SOAP calls to the cloud service have to be transformed into several consecutive vSphere calls, because the vSphere API needs numerous configuration parameters to be set. Some parameters have to be queried first, before they can be used as parameters in another call. For example, the "create a new 2Core-32GRam-265GDisk VM instance from a template Astor1" task results in 30-40 vSphere SDK calls that have to be parameterized, sent to the vCenter server, and evaluated before the desired new machine is up and running.

When running VMs with PCI pass-through devices necessary for GPU support within vSphere, things get a little more complicated in contrast to fully virtualized general-purpose VMs, and the vSphere API call parameterizations become even more complex. Currently vSphere does not provide an intelligent scheduler for initial placement supporting VMs with allocated PCI devices within a multi-node cluster. Furthermore, host selection, reservation and release of PCI resources including the necessary full RAM allocation on the host during different VM/cluster states has to be triggered manually. Therefore the vSphere orchestration component was extended with an initial placement mechanism for VMs with PCI pass-through devices. The decision where to locate newly created and existing VMs within the cluster is based on free available PCI devices, and on the current and expected available RAM on every host. This decision has to be taken every time the VM is powered on or RAM-reconfigured. This is an important feature for automated VM deployment because cluster load balancing via live migration of VMs (vSphere vMotion) is not possible for VMs with direct hardware access to PCI devices. As a result, the successful start of a GPU-enriched virtual machine cannot be guaranteed. If no appropriate host with an available GPU and enough free RAM is found, VMs have to be started without such a device and no hardware reservation, but with the advantage that vMotion/DRS can work. Such VMs can be migrated between the cluster nodes to guarantee optimal resource usage.

Prepared Templates

The cloud service layer provides further essential features for the integration of IaaS resources into a holistic analysis workflow. For user's convenience, several prepared VM templates are available with different analysis software packages and all required drivers installed in advance. Customization mechanisms within the cloud service backend allow creation of pre-configured VMs with corresponding specific network mount points (CIFS), license server information and more. The available VM templates are cleaned of all personalized data after VM instantiation using the Microsoft sysprep mechanism, which is triggered by pre-installed VMware tools. The option to login into Windows with the central LDAP credentials and an automated CIFS mount with the user's datasets was also configured into the templates.

For recurring non-OpenGL tasks and for general purposes, some standard templates running several Linux variants and Windows Server 2012 R2 with no GPU support were prepared. For VMs based on these templates, the full VMware DRS, vMotion and High Availability features can be utilized, and login is done with established SSH or RDP tools.

Added Value

Different types of authentication procedures are supported. Users can authenticate with their existing federated directory account at the cloud service using Shibboleth/ SAML tokens, Active Directory/LDAP credentials, local API keys or short-time valid local tokens. Based on the type of credentials provided, the cloud backend verifies them using an SAML RSA signature check, by performing an LDAP query or by a local SHA2-256 hash verification (which is also used for local credential caching to save the complex RSA verification or LDAP binds).

The service provides about 25 monitored load metrics with 8 different live/ on-the-fly processed aggregation time series/groups per metric, including a simple resource usage prediction. This subsystem enables queries like the average hourly CPU MHz usage or the sum of the network traffic at any given time (-frame). This data is also accessible to the users for their personal purposes and it serves as the basis of a sophisticated fee/invoice system, which allows billing of a virtual machine based on its hourly resource usage, including uptime, operating system type, application environment and many other dynamic and static properties. These charges are calculated using dynamically evaluated PowerShell expressions and are aggregated at cluster and per-user level. In the case of exhausted limits VMs will be shut down after a warning email.

It is also possible to define uptime plans based on a cron-like system or to automatically react to events like high load or unplanned shutdowns. If a virtual machine runs an HTTP server, users can enable an automated monitoring process that controls the availability and response times of one or more URLs. An ACL system gives machine owners the option to allow other users to manage their VM providing two different roles with different access rights: "Readers" can only query some of the VM's state variables and the resource usage, while "Writers" can additionally Start/Stop/Reboot a VM. On AWS EC2 it is possible to define fine-granular firewall rules to manage the VM instance's accessibility through the public internet. On vSphere, users (knowing the correct guest credentials) can view the process list and execute remote processes within the guest system without having to login with Horizon, RDP or SSH. Users can upload individual bash or PowerShell scripts to the cloud service and link them to their VMs. A prepared start script in the VMs automatically queries the cloud service for these scripts, downloads and executes them. This mechanism is similar to the "user data" option in Amazon EC2 or OpenStack.

Besides the cluster control configuration parameters, there are also some other administrative functions. For example, admins can configure resource usage quotas for end-users, allow or restrict cluster usage for users or user groups, and manage billing limits and credits. It is also possible to grant two different levels of administrative rights for a single cluster to users (but standard rights to other clusters). There is also the possibility to import or unregister VMs which are not created with the cloud service system.

USER SERVICES

Registration Workflow, Authentication and Authorization

The goal was to establish a single sign-on solution for the whole ASTOR cloud service workflow. Several solutions for the authentication have been discussed and it was finally decided to use SAML authentication. An important consideration here was that ASTOR users have access to part of the infrastructure of Karlsruhe Institute of Technology, and the internal regulations only allow access to users with known address, email and date-of-birth due to accountability reasons. Simple identification of users by email does not provide enough security. So, ASTOR was incorporated into the already existing federation bwIDM (Baden-Württemberg Identity Management) of the German Universities of Baden-Württemberg (bwIDM, 2013). bwIDM allows users to be authenticated using Shibboleth, in the case they have an account at the "German Research Network authorisation and authentication infrastructure federation" (DFN-AAI). While web based authentication is evidently good for managing virtual machines with a web portal, it does not work for a login into a virtual machine guest system or to authenticate at file system or file server level, where more classical authentication methods like Active Directory or LDAP schemes are in use. Previous developments within the bwIDM project at KIT Steinbuch Centre for Computing (SCC) addressed this problem and enable a combination of SAML credentials with an LDAP authentication server (Köhler, Labitzke, Simon, Nussbaumer, & Hartenstein; Köhler, Simon, Nussbaumer, & Hartenstein, 2013). Therefore, users are not only able to identify themselves at the Shibboleth Web SSO portals using the account of their home institutions, but are also able to use these credentials for LDAP based file system shares which are connected to bwIDM. The whole authentication and authorization chain was tested with the KIT and the University of Heidelberg SAML Identity Provider.

Users from institutions - which are not part of the bwIDM federation - can be granted access to ASTOR through the KIT guest/partner account system, which is also part of bwIDM. In this case, the user first registers via the web portal to submit a proposal for an experiment. When the proposal has been accepted, the final identification and bwIDM account activation is performed by identity documents supplied by the external users to the user office.

After registration for the services and account activation, users can log into the web portals to create/manage the virtual machines and to browse the tomography dataset metadata. With the same LDAP account, it is also possible to login to the generated VMs and authenticate to the network shares (CIFS protocol).

Web Portals

Based on the available SOAP API provided by the cloud service middleware, a special virtual machine self-service view for the ASTOR web portal was developed and combined with an overview of the users' datasets. The simple choice of a specific template creates a VM with all necessary software packages, network mounts and required computing resources and provides the corresponding access credentials to the users. The underlying complexity is fully hidden from the end-user (Figure 4), with only some basic information being visible, for example the virtual hardware configuration and IP addresses needed to login to the Horizon client. Using this portal, end-users can start, stop, reboot and delete their VMs and also re-configure the virtual hardware. Nevertheless, a classical problem for the ASTOR project service-hotline was that users start their virtual machine, but instead of shutting down a machine at the end of the day, they simply disconnected the Horizon or Remote Desktop client, causing very inefficient usage of the hardware dependent devices. Therefore for project a billing algorithm was defined based on the hourly average resource consumption of a powered-on VM (0.007 €/h per GB RAM + 0.05 €/h per CPU Core + 0.75 €/h per GPU). To prevent resource allocation by inactive

Figure 4. ASTOR Portal Virtual Machine View

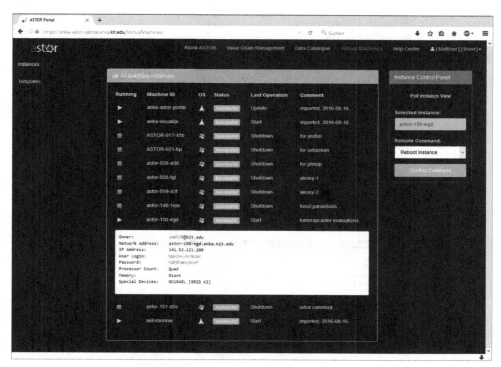

users, monthly limits of 650 € virtual money per user are assigned, allowing using a typical VM ten hours/day for the whole month.

A second web-portal, YVAINE (Figure 5), exists, which offers many more of the SOAP API functions to end-users, but is limited to a virtual machine view and lacks datastore-browsing (an early version of this portal existed prior to the ASTOR project). Here, detailed resource usage plots/heat maps can be viewed, as well as virtual funds and account quotas, and numerous status logs and cluster information. It is also possible to define access control lists to allow other accounts to execute specific management tasks and to view the VM state. Additionally, users can upload bash or PowerShell scripts and link to a virtual machine to trigger the download and execution of the script into the guest system when it boots. This portal also supports API options to define time- or event-triggered operations and to configure firewall rules, but this is supported on Amazon EC2 clusters only. Furthermore, the YVAINE portal is not hard-wired to the ASTOR area; it shows all defined clusters and EC2 regions for which the user has sufficient access rights. It is a more general purpose access route, which serves as a convenient VM self-service portal for different use cases. Alongside ASTOR, it is used in some other research projects.

Figure 5. The Virtual Machine View of the YVAINE Portal

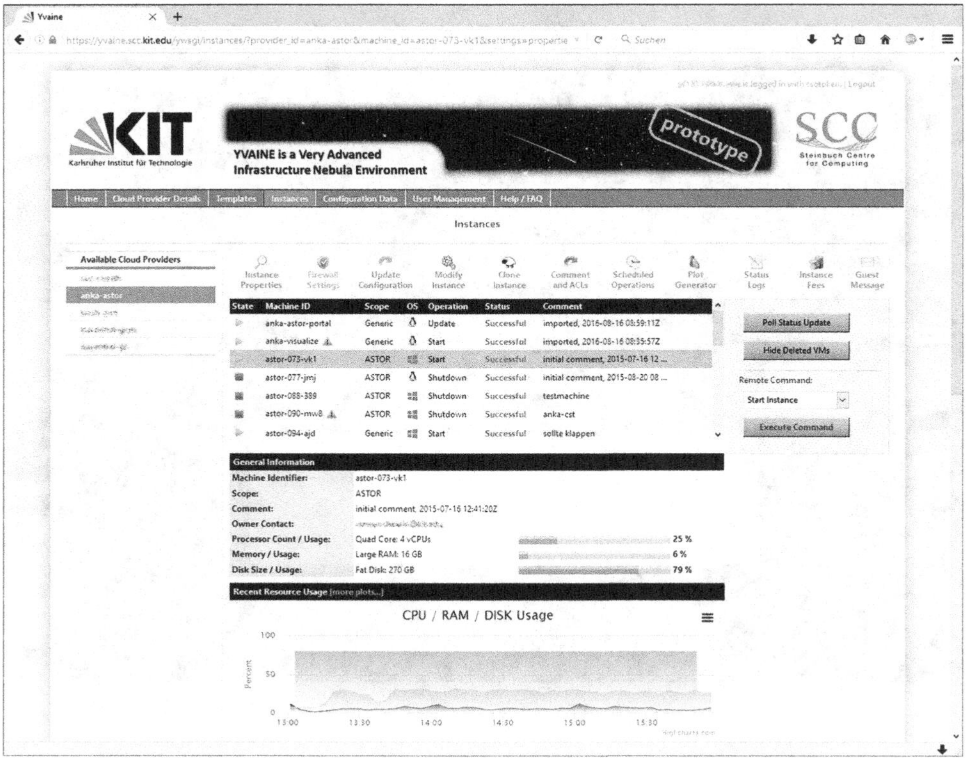

Both portals however, call the same cloud service middleware using the same API endpoints and the same underlying management data base. So, a virtual machine created with the one portal is visible and manageable in the other portal and the choice of portal is a matter of user preference.

Web-Technologies for 3D Visualization

The rate of datasets generated in micro tomography experiments exceeds the capability of scientists to analyse the data by far (up to 15 TB/day). Still the data is valuable, and it is desirable to involve other researchers for analysis. A first step to a shared approach is a well-organized data catalogue. In order to provide visual data browsing, a WAVE framework (Web-based Analysis of Volumetric Extraction) for web-based 3D visualization of large data volumes has been developed and integrated into the ASTOR web portal. Figure 6 shows the WAVE user interface used to visualize a biological screw joint dataset. The WAVE logic at the server side uses intelligent pre-processing to speed loading time for large datasets in order to accomplish fast browsing through data catalogues with any type of 3D volume information (Tan Jerome et al, 2017).

The WAVE framework supports a broad range of client hardware, from mobile phones up to powerful desktop PCs, and provides the capability to delivering high quality visualization, such as interactive rotation of 3D-previews, according to the user's requirements. WAVE supports direct volume rendering based on the approach of Kruger and Westermann (2003). The 3D structures are enhanced using the Blinn-Phong local surface illumination model (Blinn, 1977). Although the framework supports both volume rendering and surface rendering methods, the former is more suited to the visualization of voxel datasets due to its ability to resolve inner structures. In particular, the framework provides the following features to inspect and analyse a dataset:

- **Selection of a Grey Value Threshold:** Removing the background by varying threshold settings.
- **Adjustment of the Transfer Function:** The transfer function assigns a colour to a grey value. The selected colour map supports classification of the dataset.
- **Changing the Camera Position:** Choose arbitrary views of the 3D dataset with any observation angle and distance.
- **Slicing Through the 3D Object:** Select cuts through the 3D object in x, y and z-directions to observe inner structures.

Furthermore, the framework supports visualization of multimodality by performing a Hue-Saturation-Value (HSV) integration approach. The imaging modalities are mapped onto the H-S-V channels and later converted into the RGB colour domain for display. As HSV offers a more intuitive colour interface, the framework is able to integrate different characteristics of multiple datasets into a single visual representation (Turk et. al., 2010).

Processing of Datasets in the ASTOR Scientific Cloud

The scientific analysis of tomographic datasets from biological objects typically involves several post-processing steps (Figure 7), which may differ based on the scientific questions. While in some cases the creation of Grayscale-based volume renderings is sufficient to visualize a particular region of interest, the segmentation of body parts is often required in order to create digital surface models. Examples are the visualization of organ systems (Schmelzle, Helfen, Norton, & Heethoff, 2009; van de Kamp et al. 2015; Hartmann, Laumann, Bergmann, Heethoff, & Schmelzle,

Figure 6. WAVE user interface

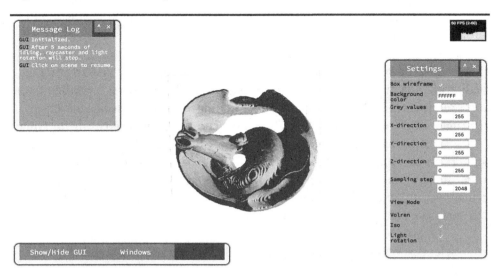

2016), the interactive analysis of joint systems (van de Kamp et al., 2011), or to create functional models (Schmelzle et al., 2015; van de Kamp, dos Santos Rolo, Vagovič, Baumbach, & Riedel, 2014). This is usually a manual and time-consuming task.

The ASTOR portal aims to provide users with the computing power and the required software tools to facilitate analysis even of large series of tomographic datasets. Commercial software packages like Amira 6.1 and VGStudio MAX 2.2 (Figure 8) as well as the open source applications FIJI and Blender are pre-installed. We also integrated the semi-automatic diffusion method (Lösel &Heuveline, 2016), which was developed within the ASTOR project. If required, users are able to install additional software tools. Limitations occur if dongles or other hardware identification mechanisms are required.

With a fast internet connection (>50MBit/s), working on an ASTOR virtual machine is similar to a local computer. Both segmentation and 3D rendering of datasets are generally fast and convenient. However, in terms of rendering speed, the 3-year-old GRID K2 GPUs naturally cannot compete with the most recent NVIDIA graphic cards. Loading tomographic data in a VM of course takes longer than on a local machine due to the 10 GBit/s connection between the ASTOR storage and the VMs. But initial transfer of the datasets to the local machine also takes time and might require the transport of external hard-drives. By way of comparison, with a standard 32-bit tomographic dataset composed of 2016 images (each with a size of 2016 x 2016 pixels) and thus a size of 30.5 GB, the import of the data directly from the ASTOR storage into FIJI takes 6:13 min in the virtual machine, while

Figure 7. Flow diagram illustrating experiment and typical post-processing steps on the example of a biological screw joint in a Trigonopterus weevil (from van de Kamp et al. 2014)

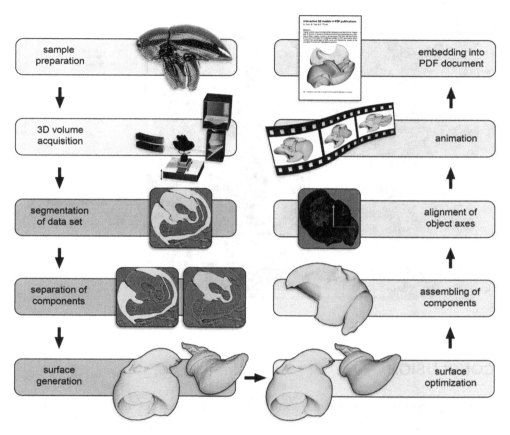

it takes 3:15 min from a local HD and also 3:15 min from a local SSD. A slow internet connection may result in lagging, but from the author's experience even a standard DSL home connection of 16 MBits/s provides enough responsiveness so that working is still conveniently possible. This was also tested for international connections from USA to Germany.

Given the fact that many research institutions have neither the storage space nor the necessary computing power to handle large series of tomographic datasets, the ASTOR portal provides a valuable concept for the remote analysis of experimental data and may serve as blueprint for other large-scale research facilities.

Figure 8. Horizon Remote Access to a VM running VGStudio MAX

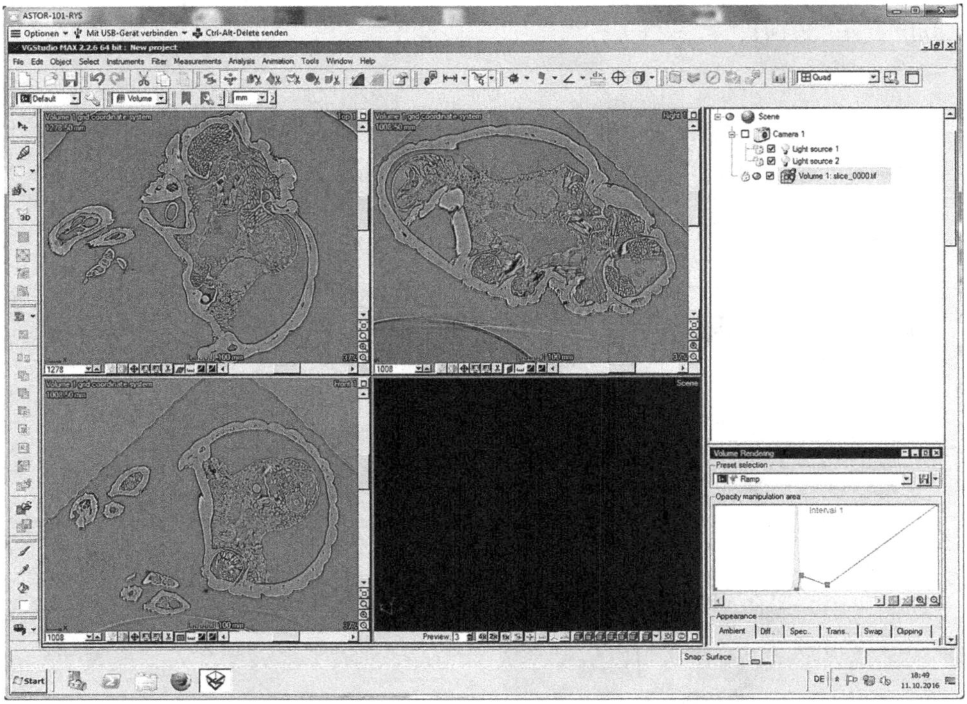

CONCLUSION

Managing extremely large datasets is a great challenge for large-scale research facilities. The data becomes too large to copy conveniently, and analysis tools for datasets in the tens of GB range are rare. Intelligent data management strategies and remote access to the data can help to overcome the current limitations. Various aspects have been proven in a prototype of a virtual analysis infrastructure. A VMWare ESXi based scientific cloud running on PC-Technology, with Horizon View as a Remote Desktop Client, allows interactive processing of OpenGL API based applications even over intercontinental links. A system for single-sign-on authentication and authorization of web-based and file system access has been realized. Technologies for management of the virtual analysis infrastructure and 3D volume datasets in the web have been developed. The system is being used successfully for analysis of tomographic data since beginning of 2016.

The work was part of the ASTOR project, funded by the German Federal Ministry of Education and Research, project number 05K2013 / 05K13VK5.

REFERENCES

Blinn, J. F. (1977). Models of light reflection for computer synthesized pictures. *Computer Graphics, 11*(2), 192–198. doi:10.1145/965141.563893

bwIDM Project management (2013). *Federating IT-based services at Baden-Württemberg's Universities.* Retrieved from https://www.bwidm.de/wp-content/uploads/bwidm-booklet.pdf

Chilingaryan, S., Kopmann, A., Mirone, A., dos Santos Rolo, T., & Vogelgesang, M. (2011). A GPU-based architecture for real-time data assessment at synchrotron experiments. *Proceedings of the 2011 companion on High Performance Computing Networking, Storage and Analysis Companion - SC '11 Companion (pp 51-52), Seattle.* doi:10.1145/2148600.2148627

Cloetens, P., Bolle, E., Ludwig, W., Baruchel, J., & Schlenke, M. (2001). Absorption and phase imaging with synchrotron radiation. *Europhysics News, 32*(2), 46–50. doi:10.1051/epn:2001203

Hartmann, K., Laumann, M., Bergmann, P., Heethoff, M., & Schmelzle, S. (2016). Development of the synganglion and morphology of the adult nervous system in the mite *Archegozetes longisetosus* Aoki (Chelicerata, Actinotrichida, Oribatida). *Journal of Morphology, 277*(4), 537–548. doi:10.1002/jmor.20517 PMID:26873119

Heethoff, M., & Norton, R. A. (2009). A new use for synchrotron x-ray microtomography: Three-dimensional biomechanical modeling of chelicerate mouthparts and calculation of theoretical bite forces. *Invertebrate Biology, 128*(4), 332–339. doi:10.1111/j.1744-7410.2009.00183.x

Köhler, J., Labitzke, S., Simon, M., Nussbaumer, M., & Hartenstein, H. (2012). FACIUS: An easy-to-deploy SAML-based approach to Federate non web-based services. *Proceedings of the 2012 IEEE 11th International Conference on Trust, Security and Privacy in Computing and Communications.* doi:10.1109/trustcom.2012.158

Köhler, J., Simon, M., Nussbaumer, M., & Hartenstein, H. (2013). Federating HPC access via SAML: Towards a plug-and-play solution. In Supercomputing, LNCS (pp. 462–473). doi:10.1007/978-3-642-38750-0_35

Kruger, J., & Westermann, R. (2003). Acceleration techniques for GPU-based volume rendering. *Proceedings of the 14th IEEE Visualization 2003 (VIS'03) (pp. 287-292).* doi:10.1109/VISUAL.2003.1250384

Lösel, P., & Heuveline, V. (2016). Enhancing a diffusion algorithm for 4D image segmentation using local information. In *Medical Imaging 2016: Image Processing*. doi:.10.1117/12.2216202

Mauch, V., Bonn, M., Chilingaryan, S., Kopmann, A., Mexner, W., & Ressmann, D. (2014, October). OpenGL-BASED data analysis in virtualized self-service environments. *Proceedings of the PCaPAC 2014* (pp. 234-236). Karlsruhe, Germany.

NVidia Corporation. (2013). NVidia grid k2 graphics board Specification. Retrieved November 23, 2016, from http://www.nvidia.com/content/grid/pdf/GRID_K2_BD-06580-001_v02.pdf

Ressmann, D., Mexner, W., Vondrous, A., Kopmann, A., & Mauch, V. (2014). Data management at the synchrotron radiation facility ANKA. *Proceedings of the PCaPAC '14,* Karlsruhe, Germany (pp. 13-15).

Schmelzle, S., Helfen, L., Norton, R. A., & Heethoff, M. (2009). The ptychoid defensive mechanism in Euphthiracaroidea (Acari: Oribatida): A comparison of muscular elements with functional considerations. *Arthropod Structure & Development, 38*(6), 461–472. doi:10.1016/j.asd.2009.07.001 PMID:19595788

Schmelzle, S., Norton, R. A., & Heethoff, M. (2015). Mechanics of the ptychoid defense mechanism in Ptyctima (Acari, Oribatida): One problem, two solutions. *Zoologischer Anzeiger - A Journal of Comparative Zoology, 254,* 27–40. doi:10.1016/j.jcz.2014.09.002

Schwermann, A. H., dos Santos Rolo, T., Caterino, M. S., Bechly, G., Schmied, H., Baumbach, T., & van de Kamp, T. (2016). Preservation of three-dimensional anatomy in phosphatized fossil arthropods enriches evolutionary inference. *eLife, 5*. doi:10.7554/eLife.12129 PMID:26854367

Shibboleth Consortium. (n. d.). Retrieved from http://shibboleth.net/

Tan Jerome, N., Chilingaryan, S., Kopmann, A., Shkarin, A., Zapf, M., Lizin, A., & Bergmann, T. (2017). WAVE: A 3D Online Previewing Framework for Big Data Archives. In *International Conference on Information Visualization Theory and Applications - IVAPP 2017*, Porto, Portugal, 27.2.-1.3.2017.

Turk, M. J., Smith, B. D., Oishi, J. S., Skory, S., Skillman, S. W., Abel, T., & Norman, M. L. (2010). Yt: A multi-code analysis toolkit for astrophysical simulation data. *The Astrophysical Journal. Supplement Series, 192*(1), 9. doi:10.1088/0067-0049/192/1/9 van de Kamp, T., Cecilia, A., dos Santos Rolo, T., Vagovič, P., Baumbach, T., & Riedel, A. (2015). Comparative thorax morphology of death-feigning flightless cryptorhynchine weevils (Coleoptera: Curculionidae) based on 3D reconstructions. *Arthropod Structure & Development*, *44*(6), 509–523. doi:10.1016/j.asd.2015.07.004 PMID:26259678

van de Kamp, T., dos Santos Rolo, T., Vagovič, P., Baumbach, T., & Riedel, A. (2014). Three-Dimensional reconstructions come to life – interactive 3D PDF Animations in functional morphology. *PLoS ONE*, *9*(7), e102355. doi:10.1371/journal.pone.0102355 PMID:25029366

van de Kamp, T., Vagovič, P., Baumbach, T., & Riedel, A. (2011). A biological screw in a beetles leg. *Science*, *333*(6038), 52–52. doi:10.1126/science.1204245 PMID:21719669

Wikipedia. (2016, November 23). Security Assertion Markup Language. Retrieved from https://en.wikipedia.org/wiki/Security_Assertion_Markup_Language

KEY TERMS AND DEFINITIONS

Amira: 3D visualization and analysis software for the Life Sciences, FEI software company.

bwIDM: The Baden-Württemberg (a state of Germany) Identity Management allows users to be authenticated using Shibboleth, in the case they have an account at the "German Research Network authorisation and authentication infrastructure federation" (DFN-AAI).

SAML: *Security Assertion Markup Language;* for more details see Wikipedia ("Security Assertion Markup Language," n. d.).

Shibboleth: A SAML-based single sign-on log-in and authentication system for computer networks; for more details see ("Shibboleth Consortium", n. d.).

VGStudio MAX: Software for the analysis and visualization of computed tomography data, Volume Graphics GmbH.

Chapter 7
Hands–On Kernel–Based Virtual Machine (KVM)

Khaleel Ahmad
Maulana Azad National Urdu University, India

Ahamed Shareef
Maulana Azad National Urdu University, India

ABSTRACT

In this chapter, we will discuss in the introduction to KVM, how to create KVM, both command line and using GUI, briefly on KVM management. This chapter also describes the pre-requisites and a brief introduction on all the pre-requisite software. KVM utilizes the CPU virtualization technology on modern AMD and Intel processors, known as AMD-V and Intel-VT. KVM a is free virtualization solution and does not require any licensing, but if your CPU does not support virtualization KVM will be a waste of time. Linux OS, which is used in this chapter, is Cent OS.

1. INTRODUCTION

KVM (Kernel Based Virtual Machine) this is virtualization software to install and run multiple guest Operating Systems. It uses the hardware virtualization feature to run multiple OS. It is a virtualization infrastructure for the Linux kernel; it was merged into the Linux kernel mainline in kernel version 2.6.20 ("Kernel-based Virtual Machine," n. d.).

KVM can be done in two ways,

1. KVM using Command Line
2. KVM using GUI tools

DOI: 10.4018/978-1-5225-2785-5.ch007

In this Hands-on chapter, we will see how to install and run KVM, using both command line and GUI tools.

Pre-Requisite

The supported Operating Systems are: Linux, Windows, Solaris, Haiku, REACT OS and more.

KVM will work only if the CPU has a support of hardware virtualization. You can verify if your CPU supports KVM by running the following command on terminal:

```
[root@server ~]#egrep '(vmx|svm)' /proc/cpuinfo
```

This command will return output like the one displayed below, if no output is displayed, then your CPU does not support virtualization, if the output has 'vmx' or 'svm' then your CPU supports hardware virtualization.

```
Sample Output
flags          : fpuvme de psetscmsrpaemce cx8
apicsepmtrrpgemcacmov pat pse36 clflushdtsacpi mmx fxsrsse sse2
ssht tm syscallnx lm constant_tscpni monitor ds_cplvmxest tm2
ssse3 cx16 xtprlahf_lm
```

If you have a Windows OS, you can still use 'Oracle VM VirtualBox' on which you can install your Linux OS where we can create KVMs and for such users, CPU virtualization can also be verified using 'Intel(R) Processor ID Utility'. Navigate to CPU technologies tab and check the value of Intel(R) virtualization technology will be either yes/no shows your CPU's support for virtualization. Only unsupported combination is 64-bit guest on a 32-bit host. Make sure that the Virtualization Technology (VT) is not disabled in your Computer's BIOS ("How to Create Virtual Machines in Linux Using KVM," n.d.).

2. INSTALLING KVM ON CentOS

We are using CentOS to show how to install KVM, now we have the minimum requirement to deploy virtual platform on our host, but we also still have useful tools to administrate our virtual machines such as:

Table 1. Hardware requirement

System Component	Minimum Requirement	Recommended
CPU	AMD 64-bit / Intel 64-bit, 1.5GHz. [allows 32-bit and 64-bit guests (KVMs)]	AMD-V 64-bit / Intel-VT 64-bit, 2 GHz plus multi core CPU.
Memory	2GB of RAM for host plus additional RAM for guests.	6GB of RAM for host plus 1GB RAM for each guest.
Disk Space	6GB for guest	10GB plus for guest
Network Interface Cards (NICs)	One (eth0) → network management	Two (eth0, eth1) → network management, virtual machine data network

- **Virt-Manager:** It provides a GUI tool to administrate your virtual machines. This is the common tool used for virtual machine management when using KVM, it can create, edit, start, stop, and manage the VMs created.
- **Libvirt-Client:** It provides a client side tool to administrate your virtual environment, this tool is also called 'virsh'.
- **Virt-Install:** It provides the command line tool to create your virtual machines.
- **Libvirt:** It provides the server and host side libraries for your host machines and for interacting with hypervisors.
- **Virt-Viewer:** GUI console
- **Qemu-Kvm:** It is a generic and open source machine emulator and virtualizer.
- **Qemu-Img:** It is a disk image manager utility. ("How to Install KVM and Create Virtual Machines on Ubuntu," n. d.; How to Create Virtual Machines in Linux Using KVM", n. d.).

Step 1: Open a terminal and issue the following command, install the required packages using 'yum'.

```
[root@server ~]#yum install qemu-kvmqemu-imgvirt-manager
libvirtlibvirt-python libvirt-client virt-install virt-viewer
```

Step 2: Restart and check the status of your 'libvirt' by issuing the following command, it should be active (running).

```
[root@server ~]#systemctl restart libvirtd
[root@server ~]#systemctl status libvirtd
```

Figure 1.

Figure 2.

Step 3: Start the 'virt-manager' and issue the below command or you can open GUI directly from Application → System Tools → Virtual Machine Manager, by default you will find manager is connected directly to the local host.

```
[root@server ~]#virt-manager
```

Step 4: Click on the 'new VM' icon in the Virtual Machine Manager as shown in Figure 4.

Step 5: If you see the below warning KVM not available (Figure 5), please start your 'libvirt' service (command given in step 6) otherwise (skip step 6) select ISO image and click on forward.

Step 6: Start your 'libvirt' service by issuing the following command.

```
[root@server ~]#servicelibvirt start
```

Step 7: Choose the ISO of OS for which the VM needs to be created, in this case, we are creating VM for Ubuntu OS, you can select the appropriate OS ISO and click forward. Please download the ISO for the intended OS as a pre-requisite for this step.

Figure 3.

Figure 4.

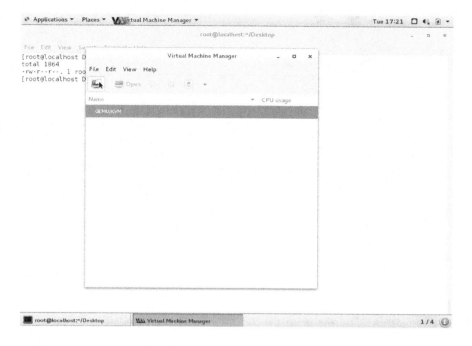

Figure 5.

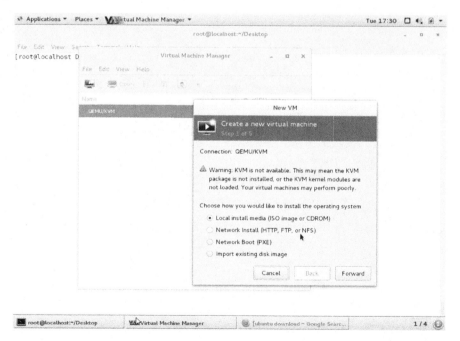

Figure 6.

Figure 7.

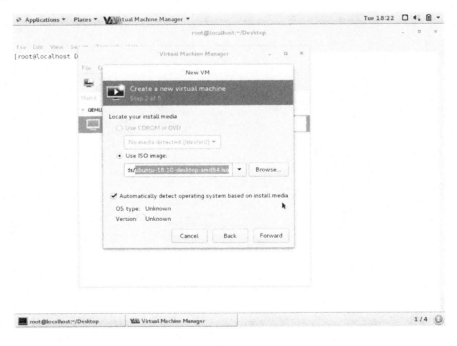

Step 8: Specify the RAM size used for the new VM and the number of CPUs allocated based on your requirement and click forward, here creating a VM with RAM 1024MB and 1 CPU.

Step 9: Specify the disk space allocation for the new VM from your available space and click forward (giving value as 10GB as Ubuntu requires minimum of 8GB).

Step 10: Specify the VM name and click on the Finish button to start the installation of your OS.

Step 11: Please follow standard OS installation steps to choose language, date & time, root password, new users etc. and complete the installation. This part of OS installation can be done by referring to the standard OS installation guide for the requested OS. ("Install Ubuntu 16.04 LTS" n. d.).

Step 12: Once you have completed the installation you can see that your VM is created and in running status in the Virtual Machine Manager. Alternatively, you can use the below command to create a VM and start you OS installation from the terminal.

Figure 8.

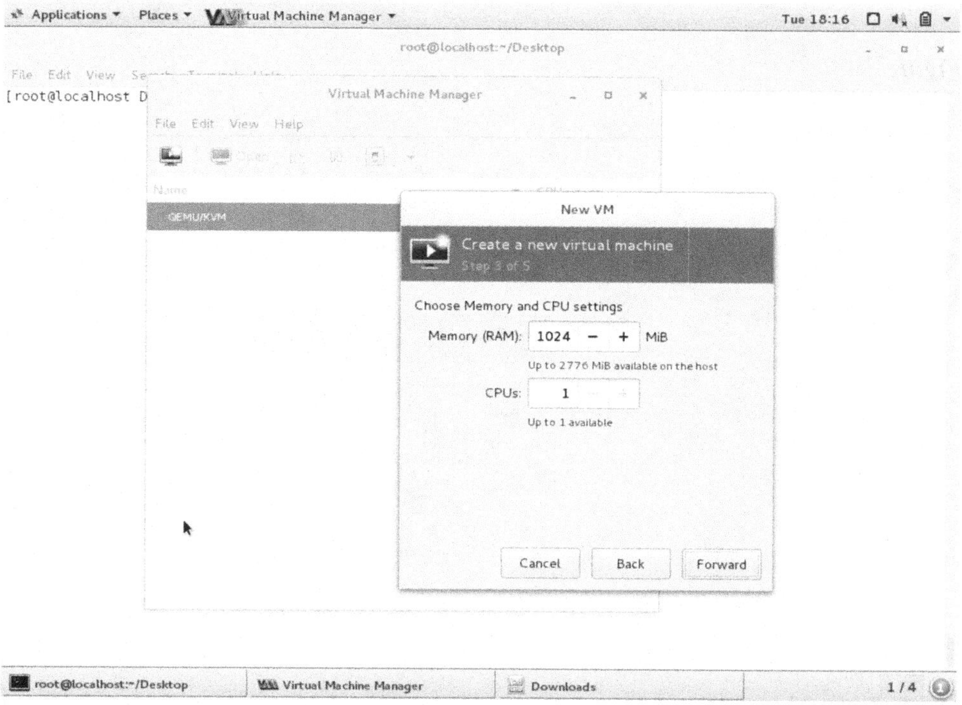

Figure 9.

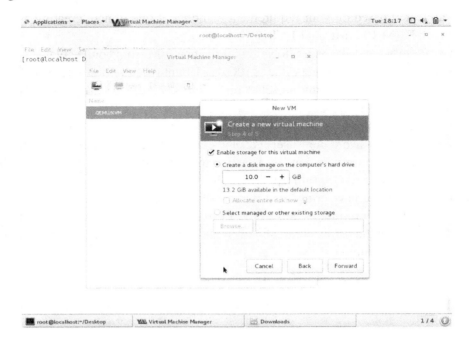

Figure 10.

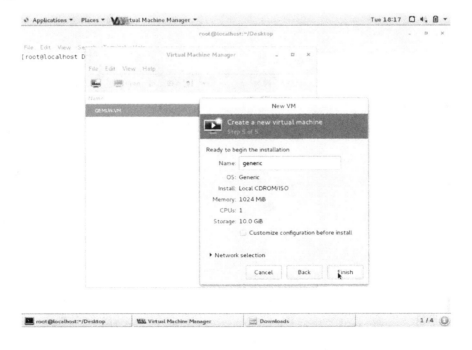

Figure 11.

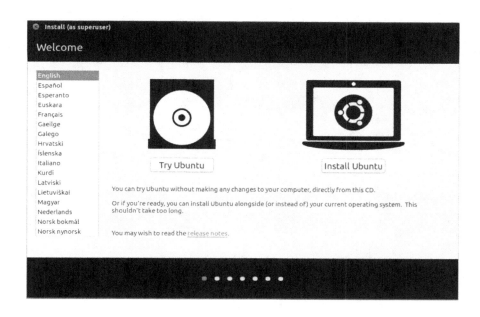

```
[root@server ~]#virt-install \
--virt-type=kvm \
--name generic \
--ram 1024 \
--vcpus=1 \
--os-type linux \
--os-variant=ubuntu16.10 \
--network bridge=br0 \
--graphics none \
--cdrom=/var/lib/libvirt/boot/ubuntu16.10-desktop-amd64.iso \
--disk path=/var/lib/libvirt/images/Unbuntu.qcow2,size=10,bus=v
irtio,format=qcow2
```

Note: 'virt-install –help' command will list all the options that can be used for creating VM uses the command line.

Step 13: You can create multiple VMs following the same process. You can manage your VM using the bulb icon.

Figure 12.

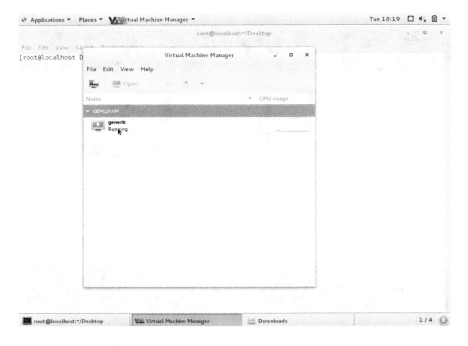

Figure 13.

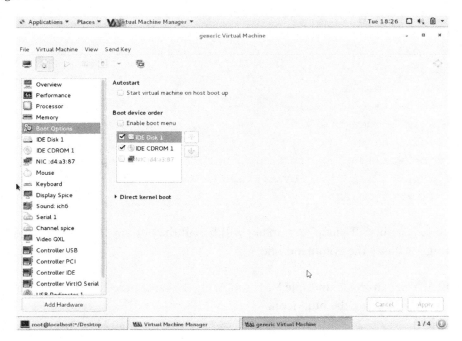

This hands-on chapter not only helped with installation of KVM but also provided an insight of what KVM and how to create and manage KVMs. Though it may look difficult to deal with for new users, it's user-friendly, easy to manage and very powerful Virtualization solution.

CONCLUSION

In this chapter the authors discussed on KVM hypervisor and explained the hardware requirements of KVM. Also, explained the steps for installing KVM on CentOS and creating a Virtual Machine (VM) in both GUI and Command line.

REFERENCES

Howtogeek.com. (n. d.). How to Install KVM and Create Virtual Machines on Ubuntu. Retrieved from https://www.howtogeek.com/117635/how-to-install-kvm-and-create-virtual-machines-on-ubuntu/

Tecmint.com. (n. d.). How to Create Virtual Machines in Linux Using KVM (Kernel-based Virtual Machine) - Part 1. Retrieved from http://www.tecmint.com/install-and-configure-kvm-in-linux/

Ubuntu.com. (n. d.). 16.04 LTS Ubuntu. Retrieved from https://www.ubuntu.com/download/desktop/install-ubuntu-desktop

Wikipedia. (2017, April 6). Kernel-based Virtual Machine. Retrieved from https://en.wikipedia.org/wiki/Kernel-based_Virtual_Machine

Chapter 8
Hands–On Guide to Virtual Box

Srinivasa K. G.
CBP Government Engineering College, India

Aahan Singh
M. S. Ramaiah Institute of Technology, India

ABSTRACT

VirtualBox is a cross-platform virtualization application. What does that mean? For one thing, it installs on your existing Intel or AMD-based computers, whether they are running Windows, Mac, Linux or Solaris operating systems. Secondly, it extends the capabilities of your existing computer so that it can run multiple operating systems (inside multiple virtual machines) at the same time. So, for example, you can run Windows and Linux on your Mac, run Windows Server 2008 on your Linux server, run Linux on your Windows PC, and so on, all alongside your existing applications. You can install and run as many virtual machines as you like—the only practical limits are disk space and memory.

INTRODUCTION TO VIRTUAL BOX

VirtualBox is a cross-platform virtualization application. What does that mean? For one thing, it installs on your existing Intel or AMD-based computers, whether they are running Windows, Mac, Linux or Solaris operating systems. Secondly, it extends the capabilities of your existing computer so that it can run multiple operating systems (inside multiple virtual machines) at the same time. So, for example, you can run Windows and Linux on your Mac, run Windows Server 2008 on your Linux server, run Linux on your Windows PC, and so on, all alongside your existing applications. You can install and run as many virtual machines as you like -- the only practical limits are disk space and memory.

DOI: 10.4018/978-1-5225-2785-5.ch008

VirtualBox is deceptively simple yet also very powerful. It can run everywhere from small embedded systems or desktop class machines all the way up to datacenter deployments and even Cloud environments (Oracle VM VirtualBox, n. d.).

USING VIRTUAL BOX

Installation

Installing VirtualBox on Windows and OSX is relatively straight forward. VirtualBox can be downloaded from https://www.virtualbox.org/wiki/Downloads.

1. Double click on the VirtualBox.exe file for Windows users or VirtualBox.dmg file for OSX users.
2. Click Next / Continue button on the Welcome window.
3. OSX Users can choose the install location form the Choose Install Location button on the Installation Type window. Users can also perform a custom install using the Customize button on the Installation Type window. This opens up the Custom Install on "Macintosh HD" window. OSX users can click on Install button to install VirtualBox on their system. Windows users can perform a custom install by clicking on the various features available. Windows users click Next to proceed with the installation process.
4. The installation process resets the network interface for Windows users temporarily. Click on Yes to start the installation process.
5. Windows users will be presented with a Ready to Install window. Click Install to install VirtualBox on the system.

Installing a Guest Operating System

VirtualBox enables the user to install various Guest Operating Systems or Guest OS on their Host Operating System or Host OS, which is the operating system upon which VirtualBox is installed. The Guest OS runs on the Host OS. Upon opening VirtualBox users are greeted with a Welcome to VirtualBox window. The following steps will guide users on installing a Guest OS. In the steps below the Guest OS being installed is Ubuntu 16.04 but the same steps can be followed to install any OS.

1. Click on the New button to start the process of adding a Guest VM.

2. In the dropdown menu enter the name of the Guest VM. This need not necessarily be the actual name of the OS but can be any name using which the user can easily identify the Guest VM. In this case the Guest OS is Ubuntu 16.04.

3. From the Type list box select the type of OS being installed. In this case a Linux based OS is being installed. Thus, Linux is chosen from the list box.

4. From the Version list box the version of the OS being installed must be chosen. In this case Ubuntu(64-Bit) is chosen.

5. In the Memory Size window the user has the option to allocate RAM to the Guest OS. The recommended RAM size is also displayed. It is advised that the Users do not allocate more than 60% of their RAM to the Guest OS as this will leave the Host OS with insufficient RAM. Users should consult the System Requirements of the respective Guest OS for RAM requirements. Click on Continue to proceed.

6. In the Hard Disk window, Users have the option of setting the size of the hard disk that will be available to the Guest OS. Users should consult the System Requirements of the respective Guest OS for Hard Disk requirements. Click on Create to create a virtual hard disk for the Guest OS. From the drop-down, users can choose the type of Hard Disk to create. VDI is the proprietary file type of VirtualBox. Choosing this will enable the Guest OS to run only on VirtualBox. Choosing VMDK enables the Guest OS to run on VirtualBox as well as VMWare. Choosing VHD is the file format for Microsoft Virtual PC and enables the Guest OS to run on VirtualBox as well as Microsoft products. In this case VHD is chosen.

7. The Storage on physical hard disk window presents the user with 2 options. A dynamically allocated hard disk will grow as the space is used whereas the fixed sized hard disk will not. If it is not known beforehand how much space will be needed by the Guest OS Dynamically Allocated option should be chosen. If it is known beforehand how much space the Guest OS will utilize a pre-specified Fixed size hard disk can be created. In this case, the Dynamically Allocated option is chosen.

8. The File location and size window requires the user to set the name of the virtual hard disk as well as the location at which it will be created. The maximum size of the hard disk is specified using the range bar. Users should consult the System Requirements of the respective Guest OS for hard disk space requirements. In this case 8 GB of space is allocated to the hard disk. Click on the Create button to proceed.

9. The Guest OS is now displayed in the VirtualBox Manager window as shown in Figure 1. Now the users can proceed and install the Guest OS on the virtual hardware created in the previous steps. Click on the Start button to start the Guest OS. The users are now asked to choose the location of the Guest OS disk

Figure 1. The Guest OS appears in the VirtualBox Manager window

image. The disk image is the installation file of the Guest OS. In this case the disk image of Ubuntu 16.04 is chosen. Click on Start to begin installation of the Guest OS. The Guest OS now begins installing on the virtual hardware. In order to install the Guest OS, users should follow the User Guide or User Manual of the respective OS for instructions. Users need not worry upon being presented with an option to erase the hard disk and install the OS. The hard disk is not the user's actual hard disk but the virtual one created in step 8 above.

Figure 2. Ubuntu 16.04 running on VirtualBox

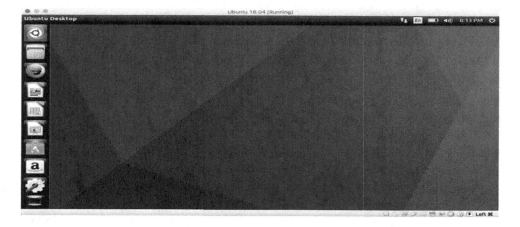

After installing the Guest OS, users can run the OS as though it were actually running on its own hardware as shown in Figure 2.

Exploring VirtualBox

Snapshots

One of the most useful and important features of any virtualization software is the ability to take snapshots. A snapshot is a "point in time image" of a virtual guest operating system (VM). That snapshot contains an image of the VMs disk, RAM, and devices at the time the snapshot was taken. With the snapshot, you can return the VM to that point in time, whenever you choose. All changes made after the snapshot was taken may be based on that snapshot information (incremental changes). You can take snapshots of your VMs, no matter what guest OS you have and the snapshot functionality can be used for features like performing image level backups of the VMs. Snapshots can be taken in just about every virtualization platform available ("What is a snapshot?," n. d.).In other words, the snapshot is like a traditional backup but unlike traditional backups which only save the data of the OS, snapshots also save the state of the machine and its hardware.

There are three operations related to snapshots:

- Taking a snapshot.
- Restoring a snapshot.
- Deleting a snapshot.

In order to take a snapshot, click on Take snapshot from the Machine pull down menu of the window or alternatively press the Host Button+T[1]. The user is required to name the snapshot and then click OK. Once the snapshot is taken the state of the VM can be reverted back to that of the taken snapshot.

When the VM is powered off, the VirtualBox Manager window has the option of restoring or deleting the snapshot. This can be done by clicking on the Snapshots button on the top right of the window. Clicking on it will display all the snapshots taken of that virtual machine as shown in Figure 3. The three camera icons above the snapshot window help the user in restoring, deleting or displaying the snapshot. Note that Snapshots can be restored only when the virtual machine is turned off. Upon clicking the Restore Snapshot icon, the restore window is displayed. The user has the option of creating an additional snapshot of the current state of the VM. Click Restore in order to restore the state of the VM to the selected snapshot. To delete a snapshot, the user must select the snapshot to be deleted from the snapshot window and then click on the Delete selected snapshot icon above the snapshot widow. A

Figure 3. Snapshot window

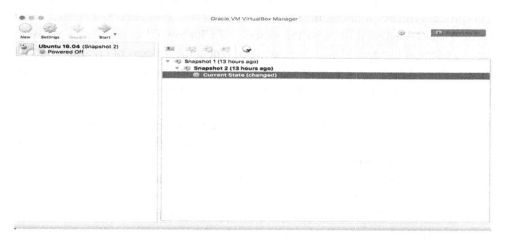

dropdown menu is displayed. Click on Delete in order to delete the selected snapshot. In order to view the snapshot, the user must click on the Display snapshot icon above the snapshot window. This opens a new window that displays the state of the machine saved by the selected snapshot as shown in Figure 4. The user can scroll down to view all the details of the VM from the system details to shared folders.

Cloning

In some situations, the user may require additional VMs which are exact copies of a previously created VM. The traditional method would be to create a new VM

Figure 4. Display snapshot window

with the same configuration as a previously created VM and then reinstall the OS. This process can be cumbersome when the number of copies needed increases. This process can be avoided through the process of Cloning. Cloning creates an exact replica of the selected VM without having to repeat the process of creating the VM from scratch. Users can easily clone their VMs in virtual box. The following steps will guide users on the process of cloning in VirtualBox.

1. Click on the Clone option from the Machine pulldown menu of the VirtualBox Manager window. Alternatively, the user can press the Host Button + O. The clone window is displayed as shown in Figure 5.
2. The user has the option of reinitializing the MAC address of all the network cards. Choosing this option will change the MAC address of all the network cards of the cloned version of the selected VM. If this option is not selected, the MAC address of all the network cards of the cloned as well as the original VM will be the same. The user can enter a different name for the cloned VM and click Continue.
3. The Clone Type window requires the user to choose the type of clone to be created. A Full Clone creates an exact copy of the chosen VM and the cloned version has its own copy of the virtual hard disk and cloned VM can be migrated to a new location. A Linked Clone has its virtual hard disk linked to the original VM and thus migration of linked clone will not be possible without moving the original VM as well. Click Continue to proceed.
4. In the Snapshot cloning screen the user can select which parts of the snapshot tree of the original VM should be cloned. Selecting Current machine state clones

Figure 5. Clone window

only the current state of the VM and no snapshots will be cloned. Selecting Everything clones the entire snapshot tree of the original VM. Click Clone to start cloning the selected VM.

The users can now see that the cloned VM appears in the VirtualBox Manager window. This process can be repeated any number of times to create as many clones as required.

Shared Folders

In many applications, it is necessary to provide the guest VM access to specific folders residing on the host machine. This is achieved through the use of shared folders. The user specifies the location of a folder on the host and this folder appears on the guest VM and can be accessed on the guest VM. Shared folders can be added with ease in VirtualBox. The following steps describe the process of adding shared folders to the specified VM in VirtualBox. In order to add shared folders to a guest VM, it is required that the VM is running. Start the specified guest VM and once it has booted proceed with the following steps.

Once the Guest VM has booted in order for shared folders to work VirtualBox Guest Additions must be installed on the Guest VM. To do this click on the Devices pulldown menu and select the Install Guest Additions CD image... option. A CD will appear on the Guest VM which contains the installer for Guest Additions. Once Guest Additions has been installed proceed with the steps given below.

1. To add shared folders users must select the VM to which the shared folder must be added in the VirtualBox Manager window.
2. Click on the Settings button at the top of the VirtualBox Manager window.
3. From the Settings window click on the Shared Folders tab.
4. The Settings tab displays the list of folders currently being shared between the host machine and the guest VM. Click on the Add Folder icon to the right of the window.
5. In the Folder Path field specify the path of the folder on the host OS that is to be added as a shared folder in the guest VM. In the Folder Name field users may enter the name that the shared folder will take when mounted to the guest VM. Users should select the Auto-mount option in order to automatically mount the specified folder on guest VM startup. Selecting the Read-only option will set a Read-Only permission on the shared folder preventing the guest VM from making any changes to the contents of the shared folder. Click OK to continue.
6. The specified folder appears as an addition to the list of shared folders in the folder list.

7. Restart the Guest VM in order for the shared folder to appear automatically as a mounted folder. The folder can be accessed via My Network Places –Entire Network – VirtualBox Shared Folders in Windows guest VMs and will appear as a mounted folder in Linux based systems.

8. Sometimes the folder may not be accessible and the user may get an error stating that the user does not have the permissions required to access the file in a Linux Guest VM. In order to solve the issue the guest VM must be added to the vboxsf group. To do this in a Linux based guest VM the following command must be entered:

```
sudousermod -a -G vboxsf<username>
```

9. Alternatively, the shared folder may be mounted in a specific location. In Windows, users must open the command prompt and enter.

```
net use x:\\vboxsvr\<shared folder name>
```

Linux users enter the following in the terminal:

```
mount -t vboxsf<shared folder name><mountpoint>
```

where mountpoint is the path where the folder will be mounted.

Networking

For purposes of testing new networking applications or simulations, two or more VMs may need to be connected together in a LAN like connection. VirtualBox provides users with a wide variety of network modes to enable networking in VMS.

There are 7 networking modes available in VirtualBox. The networking setting can be accessed by selecting the desired VM in the VirtualBox Manager window and clicking on Settings and selecting the Network tab (VirtualBox.org).

- **Not Attached:** VirtualBox tells the VM that network card is attached to it but the Ethernet cable is unplugged
- **Network Address Translation (NAT):** This mode enables internet connectivity on the VM. The internet is accessed via the host network card
- **NAT Network:** This mode enables VMs which are a part of the NAT network to communicate with each other and with machines outside the network but prevents the machines outside the network from directly accessing the systems that are a part of the NAT network

- **Bridged Networking:** This mode is used for more advanced networking simulations and running servers on the guest VM. The VM connects directly to the host network card and exchanges packets directly
- **Internal Networking:** This mode enables selective networking in which specific VMs may be visible to other VMs and applications on the network but invisible to applications on the host or outside the network
- **Host-Only Networking:** This mode enables the creation of networks containing the host and other VMs without the need to use the host's network card
- **Generic Networking:** This mode is enables the user to select a generic network interface driver which can be included with VirtualBox or be distributed through extension packs

For most purposes which require only a few VMs to be connected to each other, Host-only networking mode is used. The following steps will guide users on how to create two or more VMs together on the same network.

1. Before adding VMs into a network a Host–only network interface must be created. To create a network interface, open the VirtualBox Preferences menu.
2. Click on the Network tab.
3. Click on Host-only Networks.
4. Click on the Add Host-only network icon present to the right of the network list.
5. An interface with the name vboxnet0 will be created. If an interface already exists then vboxnet1 might be created.

Now that an interface has been created VMs can be added to the network.

1. Select the desired VM which is to be added to the virtual network in the VirtualBox Manager window
2. Click on Settings and then click on the Network tab.
3. Select Host-only Adapter in the Attached to field.
4. Select vboxnet() in the Name field.
5. Click OK.

The next step is to make sure that each VM has a different MAC address. This step is necessary as Cloned VMs may have the same MAC address as the original

VM. Each system on the network is allotted an IP address. In order to give out IP addresses, the server must be able to differentiate between the systems trying to connect to it. Each network card has a unique MAC address and the MAC address of the network card enables the server to differentiate between different systems and hence give out unique IP addresses to systems. If two VMs have the same MAC address, on the network they will appear as a single system. Therefore, it is necessary to make sure that each VM that must be connected to the network must have a unique MAC address. In order to check and change MAC addresses,

1. Power Off the desired VM.
2. Click on Settings and then on the Network tab.
3. Click on the Advanced option to reveal a drop-down menu.
4. The MAC Address field displays the MAC address of the VM's network card.
5. In order to change the MAC address, click on the recycle icon next to the MAC Address field.
6. Click OK to save the changes.

Repeat the steps above for each VM that is to be added to the virtual network.

In order to check if the VMs are actually connected to each other a simple Ping test can be performed. A ping message is used to test connectivity between different machines that are a part of the network. A small message is sent to the destination system. If the system replies with an acknowledgement, the system is connected to the network. If the destination system does not respond the system is not reachable from the VM which is the source of the ping. To perform a ping test open Terminal in case of Linux VMs or Command Prompt for Windows VMs.

For Windows VMs enter:

```
ipconfig
```

The IP address of the system will be displayed.
For Linux VMs enter:

```
ifconfig
```

The output may have two sections as shown in figure 6: lo and enp0s3 or eth3. The IP address of the system is displayed in the section apart from lo i.e. in the eth

Figure 6. IP address highlighted in red

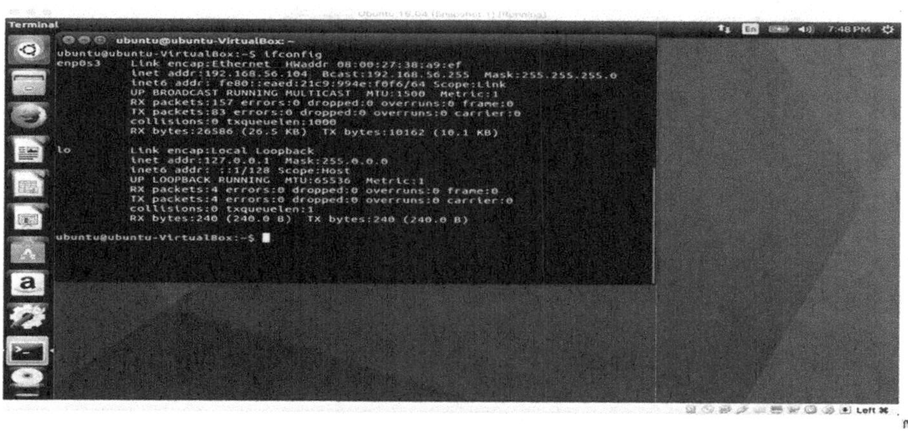

Figure 7. Ping reply showing host is reachable in Windows

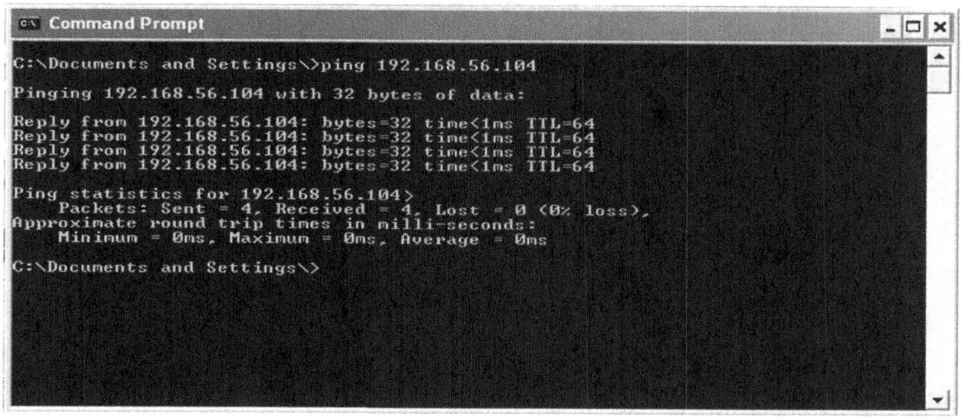

or en fields. The IP address is displayed next to the inetaddr field. The IP address will be along the lines of 192.168.xx.xxx.

Once the IP addresses of the systems that are a part of the network are known users may begin the ping test. To ping systems, enter

```
ping 192.168.xx.xxx
```

where 192.168.xx.xxx is the IP address destination VM. If the destination is reachable, Windows systems display Reply from <destination IP>as shown in figure 7and

Figure 8. Ping reply showing host is reachable in Linux

Figure 9. Destination unreachable in Linux

Figure 10. Destination unreachable in Windows

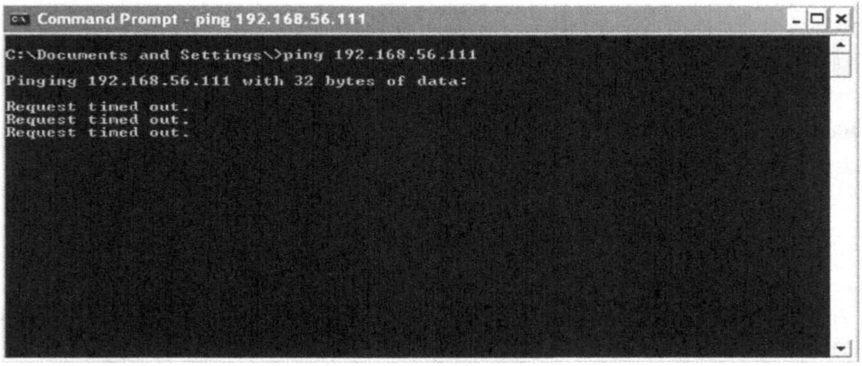

Linux systems display 64 bytes from <destination IP>as shown in figure 8. If the destination is not reachable the output is Request timed out or Destination Host Unreachable as shown in figures 9 and 10.

CONCLUSION

In this chapter the authors discussed various aspects of Virtual Box and explained the installation steps of Virtual Box. Also, explained the steps for creating a Virtual Machine (VM) on Virtual Box.

REFERENCES

VirtualBox. (n. d.). User Manual. Retrieved from https://www.virtualbox.org/manual/UserManual.html

VirtualBox.org. (n. d.). Virtual networking (Ch. 6). Retrieved from https://www.virtualbox.org/manual/ch06.html

Virtualizationadmin.com. (n. d.). What is a snapshot? Retrieved from http://www.virtualizationadmin.com/faq/snapshot.html

ENDNOTES

[1] The host button is displayed on the bottom right of the VM window.

Chapter 9
Hands–On Vagrant

Khaleel Ahmad
Maulana Azad National Urdu University, India

Masroor Ansari
Maulana Azad National Urdu University, India

ABSTRACT

A vagrant is a freeware tool that facilitates to easily manage and configure multiple virtual machines. The main goal of its creation is to simplify the environment maintenance in a large project with multi technical tasks. It provides the better manageability and maintainability for the developers and prevents needless maintenance and improve the productivity for development using simple functions. Vagrant supports almost all main languages for the development, but it is written in the Ruby language. Vagrant was initially supported by Virtual Box, but the version 1.1 has the full vital support for VMware, KVM and other virtualization environment as well as for the server like Amazon EC2. It supports many programming languages such as C#, Python, PHP and JavaScript to enhance the project efficiency. Recently, version 1.6 may serve as a fully virtualized operating system due to the added support for Docker containers.

1. INTRODUCTION

In January 2010, Mitchell Hashimoto started it as a personal project and released the first version in March 2010. Engine Yard announced to sponsor the Vagrant project in October 2010. In March 2012, the first stable version "Vagrant 1.0" was released. In November 2012, an organization "HashiCorp" by Mitchell came to give the full attention and improvement in the development of Vagrant. Nowadays

DOI: 10.4018/978-1-5225-2785-5.ch009

Hashi is focusing to develop the e-commerce support and offers professional training support for the Vagrant.

A Vagrant is a freeware application/tool for building and developing a portable environment. Mostly the latest release and newest tools are tested by a test environment. It is, the less time consuming in redeveloping the Operating System. A Vagrant is really tied to VirtualBox to manage and handle the Virtualization. A Vagrant takes actions as the dominant configuration for deploying/handling many reproducible virtual environments with the identical configuration.

It plays the role just like a tool in the Ubuntu Linux environment to set up a wide-ranging virtual improvement environment that is generally quoted to as a VDE. It reduces the amount of time spent needed to rebuild the Operating System as a core configuration for end user deeds. It also allows the easy manageability VDEs by means of identical configuration. Installation of VirtualBox at the same period is important and basic requirements being its central configuration built into the main Vagrant product.

To set up and configure, an online Linux Server is needed with a proper and suitable IP address and a method for connecting it. GoDaddy was recommended Virtual Private Server, at the time of start up for newer users, or a full applicable Server for taking total control. Some different types of SSH client as Google, PuTTY (Windows) or Terminal (Mac) is needed for connecting the Server.

Installation

A Vagrant is easy to download and install on standard distribution of Linux, Windows and Mac OS X. Setup process is not complex.

Configuration

Needs to create a file for the project that describes your machine type, the software that is mandatory for the installation, and an approach to make the machine accessible. Needs to save this file with project code ("Vagrant 1" n.d.).

System Requirements

1. Virtual Box
2. Vagrant
3. Putty for windows and Terminal for MAC OS

VirtualBox

The Virtual Box host should be a 64-bit x86 server-class machine devoted to hosting VMs.

64-bit x86 server-class machines are recommended for Virtual Box to create VMS.A toughened and enhanced windows partition should be run by this machine with a Virtual Box enabled kernel which is able to control the communication between the physical hardware and the virtualized devices seen by the VMs.

2. WORKING

Needs to run a command- "vagrant up", meanwhile the Vagrant creates a development environment. Needs to say goodbye "works on my machine" excusing the Vagrant to create an identical development environment for every team member.

Table 1. VirtualBox is able to use of

System Component	Minimum Requirement	Recommended Requirement
CPUs	One or more 64-bit x86 CPU(s), 1.5GHz	2 GHz or faster multicore CPU
Memory	2 GB of RAM	4 GB of RAM or more
Network	100Mbit/s	One or more gigabit NIC(s) for faster P2V and export/import data transfers and VM live migration.
Disk Space	Locally attached storage (PATA, SATA, SCSI) with 16GB	60 GB

Table 2. Vagrant

System Component	Minimum Requirement	Recommended Requirement
Operating System	Any Windows OS, Any Linux OS	
CPUs	750 MHz of CPU	1 GHz of CPU or Faster
.Net Framework	Version 3.5	Version 4
Memory	1 GB of RAM	2 GB of RAM
Screen Resolution	1024 x 768 Pixels	1920 x 1200 pixels for LAN and 1280 x 1024 for WAN connection
Network	100 MB	Or Faster NIC
Disk Space	100 MB	

Table 3. Putty

System Component	Minimum Requirement	Recommended Requirement
Operating System	Any Windows flavors: Windows XP, Windows Vista, Windows 7, Windows Server 2003, Windows Server 2008, Windows Server 2008R2	
CPUs	750 MHz of CPU	1 GHz of CPU or Faster
.Net Framework	Version 3.5	Version 4
Memory	1 GB of RAM	2 GB of RAM
Screen Resolution	1024 x 768 Pixels	1920 x 1200 pixels for LAN and 1280 x 1024 for WAN connection
Network	100 MB	Or Faster NIC
Disk Space	100 MB	

Vagrant provides easy configuration and convenient portable environment on the highest level of commercial standards and managed by an identical stable workflow to enhance the elasticity and the output of the team or team member. Vagrant depends on the developer or the user to find its gain. Systems are managed at the highest level of VMware, VirtualBox, AWS any provider. After that, the industry- standard based tool such as Puppet, shell scripts and Chef may be used for configuration and installation of the software automatically on the system ("Installing Vagrant," n. d.).

Vagrant isolates the dependencies and configuration functions into a single reusable and reliable background for the developer without any loss of tools functionalities configured with Debugger, Browser, Editor, etc. To create a Vagrant file, it needs to "vagrant up" and everything configured and installed to work. Any member of the team is able to create his own development environment on a single configuration, not matter which operating system is in use, or running codes by all members in a single environment, or the all configuration is same.

Vagrant provides a reliable workflow and disposable environment for the operations engineer to develop and test infrastructure management scripts. Using the local virtualization, such as VMware or VirtualBox, easily and quickly test can be performed like Chef cookbooks, shell scripts, puppet modules and others. Scripts can be tested using the single configuration on remotely located cloud such as RackSpace or AWS with same workflow.

Vagrant can manage everything for a designer that is necessary for the web application to focus on the good: design. After the Vagrant configuration, no need to go in trouble to get the running application again. No disturbance of other developers to fix the problems in the environment and to test the designs. Only needs to check out the code, "vagrant up" and starts the designing.

3. INSTALLATION PROCESS ON WINDOWS

1. Download virtual box using the given link
   https://www.virtualbox.org/wiki/Downloads
2. For Windows: Go to the downloaded file, double click on the .exe file and install it.
   For Linux: Use command_$ sudo apt-get install virtualbox for VirtualBox installation.

```
For Linux: Install the dkms package to ensure that the
VirtualBox host kernel modules
$ sudo apt-get install virtualbox-dkms
```

3. Now, download Vagrant exe file using the given link https://www.vagrantup.com/downloads.html
4. For Windows: Go to the downloaded file, double click on the .exe file and install it.

```
For Linux: Use Command $ sudo apt-get install vagrant.
```

Getting vagrant machine up: Use Command

```
$ vagrant box add precise32 http://files.vagrantup.com/
precise32.box
```

5. Create a root directory

   For Windows: A dialog box will appear as, Click on Next button.

```
For Linux: Use Command $ mkdir vagrant_project
```

6. Click on Check Box after reading the terms and conditions of the user agreement, then click on Next button.
7. Click on Change... button to set the location of installation, then Next, otherwise choose the default and click on Next button.
8. Now Vagrant Setup is ready to install, Click on Install button.
9. Vagrant installation is going on. It can take sometimes.
10. Now open Command Prompt
11. Change directory to vagrant directory
    For Windows: type c:\HashiCorp\Vagrant\bin

Figure 1.

Figure 2.

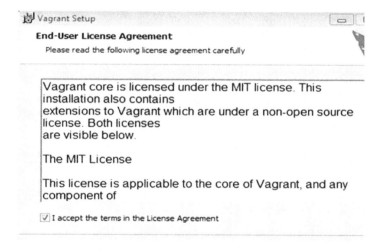

For Linux: Use Command `$ cd vagrant_project`

12.   Then run the following commands
   12.1. Vagrant box add lucid32 from following link: http://files.vagrantup.com/
       lucid32.box

Figure 3.

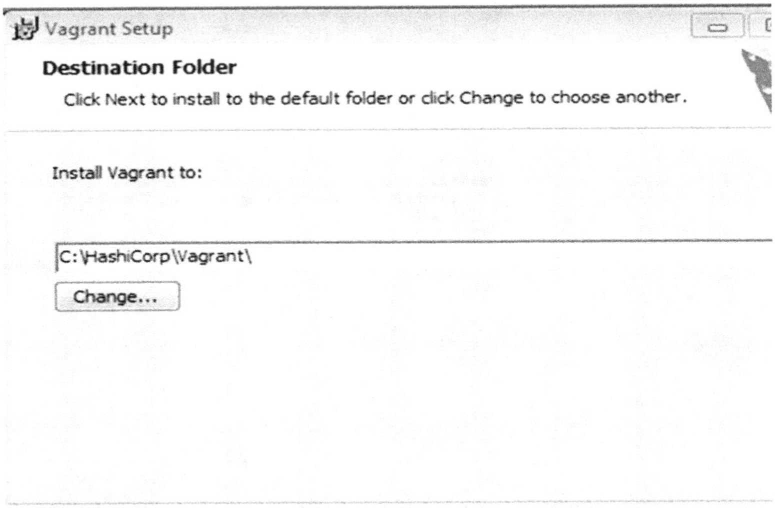

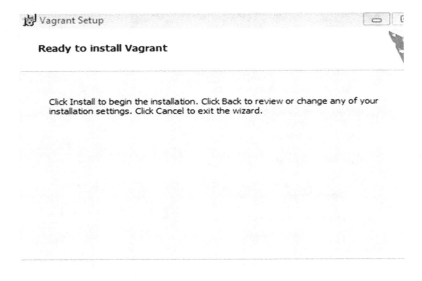

Figure 4.

12.2. Vagrant box is now downloading.

12.3 Now initialize the virtual box using the given command.

```
vagrant init lucid32
```

Figure 5.

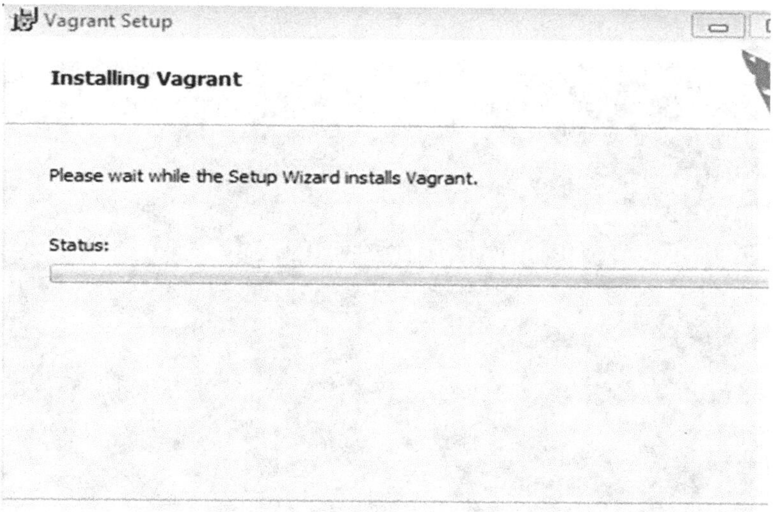

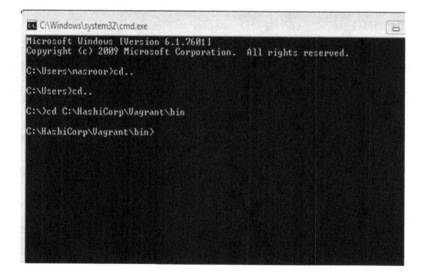

Figure 6.

13. Now run the command vagrant up
14. Now download putty using this link
    http://www.chiark.greenend.org.uk/~sgtatham/putty/download.html

Figure 7.

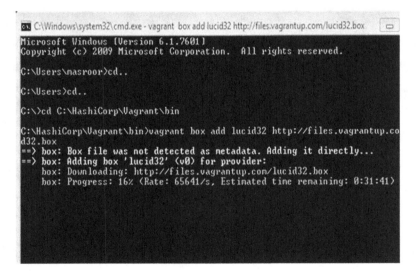

Figure 8.

15. Go to the downloaded file; double click on the .exe file to install. A dialog box will display as:
16. Configure the putty using the various settings and click on Open button.

Figure 9.

Figure 10.

16.1. Enter these credentials:
   Hostname: 127.0.0.1
   Port: 2222
   Connection type: SSH

Figure 11.

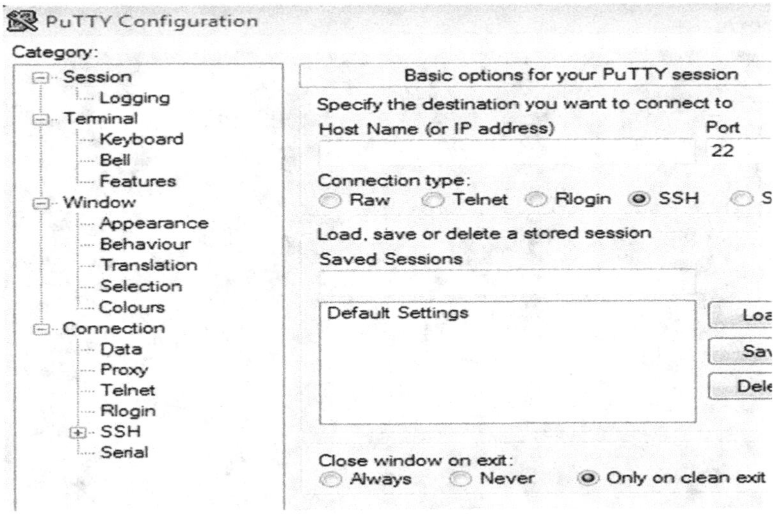

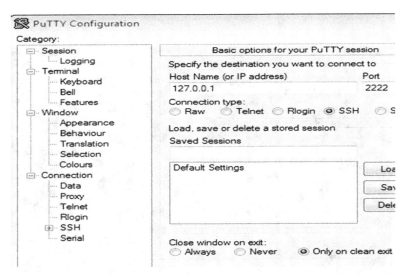

Figure 12.

17. The putty command prompt will appear as:
     Login to Vagrant server
     Enter username: vagrant
     Password: vagrant

18. Now go to the windows command prompt, and type this command ls –lah

Figure 13.

Figure 14.

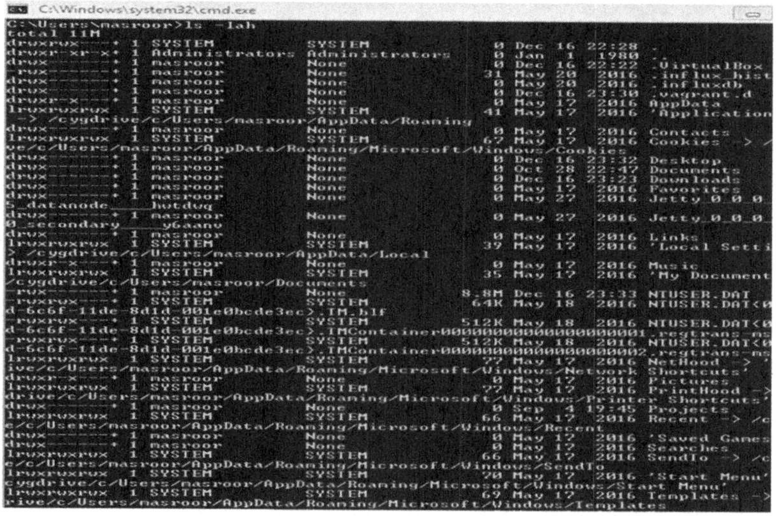

CONCLUSION

In this chapter the authors discussed on Vagrant and system requirement for installation Vagrant. Also explained the steps for installation Vagrant on Windows and Linux Operating System and access it remotely using Putty.

REFERENCES

Hashicorp.com. (n. d.). Vagrant 1.8. Retrieved from https://www.hashicorp.com/blog/vagrant-1-8/

Vagrantup.com. (n. d.). Vagrant Installation. Retrieved from https://www.vagrantup.com/docs/installation/

Chapter 10
Hands–On Xen:
Installation Guide for Xen Server

Khaleel Ahmad
Maulana Azad National Urdu University, India

Masroor Ansari
Maulana Azad National Urdu University, India

Afsar Kamal
Maulana Azad National Urdu University, India

ABSTRACT

Xen is an open source virtualization framework in distributed system based on rapid elasticity on broad network access. It is a cost-effective platform for resource pooling and allows easy access to run any code any time from everywhere by any user. It is a hypervisor using a microkernel design, provides services that allow multiple operating systems to execute on the same computer concurrently. In other words, the hypervisor was made accessible to the world directly from any location, anticipating a fully virtualized cloud base environment, which is turned into cloud computing.

1. INTRODUCTION

The word Xen (pronounced /'zɛn/) with origin in the ancient Greek term Xenos (ξένος), means to refer the guest families whose relationship come under the ritual of Xenia ("guest-friendship") (XenServer, 2016). This term played a vital role to give the idea of guest/host operating, SaaS and community cloud. The Xen Hypervisor Project was designed and developed by Cambridge University for the XenoServers Project as a mechanism to divide up the single physical resource into multiple

DOI: 10.4018/978-1-5225-2785-5.ch010

logical views of computing resources as a multi-tenancy and to control the hardware, managing resources and auditing the accountability to improve the performance of the cloud services. Xen is a graphical user interface based on Windows. XenCenter facilitates the pooling and sharing storage, hosting of XenServer. It also manages, monitors and deploys the Windows-based desktop machine. The original website was created in 2003 to permit a global community of developers to contribute and improve the hypervisor. The community supported project followed multiple principles: Transparency, Open Standards, Consensus Decision Making support, and Meritocracy (Xenserver 7.10 Standard Edition, n. d.).

Two commercial copies of XenServer 7.0 are:

- Enterprise
- Standard

The basic and standard edition is entry level commercial contributes a wide range of properties suitable to the needs of customers with high performances of virtualization platforms, no requirement of top level principles by the Enterprise edition, while still desiring to take benefits from the guarantee of full Citrix support, control and maintenance. The Enterprise edition is top best enhanced for both desktop, Server and cloud workloads.

The end users with the first time XenApp or XenDesktop may continue to have the privilege of XenServer containing all the principles and properties within the standard and many of those from the Enterprise edition that includes:

- Automatic updating virtual machine driver for windows
- Automated updates of Management agent
- SMB storage support
- APIs Directly Examine
- Dynamic Balance of workloads
- Intel GVt-g and GPU Virtualization (vGPU) with NVIDIA GRID
- Transformation services from VMware vSphere to XenServer
- Intel Secure Measured Boot (TXT)
- Exportation of Data Resource Pooling
- Read caching in-memory

XenServer can directly installs on bare-metal hardware without any restriction, overhead charge and performance obstacles of an Operating System. Device drivers for Linux kernel are used by means of XenServer. As the performance and production, it is capable to run on a wide range of storage devices and hardware.

The XenServer host mainly contains of:

- **Xen Hypervisor:** The hypervisor is the primarily abstractive level of software. It is liable and responsive for disk isolation of residing virtual machines and low-level jobs such as scheduling of CPU. It distinct for the virtual machine from the hardware. It has no basic information and knowledge of configuring networks, video, external storage, etc. The Xen Project of Linux Foundation improves and manages the Xen hypervisor as an open licensed software under the General Public License. V4.6 of the Xen hypervisor is used by the XenServer 7.0.
- **Domain Control:** It also called 'dom0' or 'Domain0'. It is a safe and protected, preferred Linux (based on CentOS) Virtual Machine that is eligible to run the XenServer management toolstack. It also runs the stack driver without producing XenServer control functionality, that delivers consumer generated VMs access to physical devices instead of logical.
- **Management Toolstacks (Xapi):** It is used to control lifecycle operations of the Virtual Machine, networking of Virtual Machine and host, consumer authenticity, virtual machine storage. It also manages the resource pooling of XenSerrver and delivers recognized XenAPI Managing Interface freely, access to use by all tools that manage resource pooling and Virtual Machines.
- Templates of Virtual machine, for installation of OS as virtual machines.
- A general Storage Repository set aside for virtual machines.
    - **Note**: A 64-bit x86 server is required for the installation of XenServer host. Installation of any other OS is restricted by XenServer host in the dualboot configuration; due to its irrelevant configuration.

Benefit Goes to XenServer Are

It is the cost effective and reduces the cost of utilizing XenServer as:

- Adding/Combing different virtual machines on the physical servers.
- Multiple separate storage images are reduced to easily manage.
- Available storage infrastructure and networking are easily integrated by the use of XenServer that enhances the flexibility.
- It allows scheduling zero downtime, maintenance by means of XenMotion for VMs migration within XenServer hosts.
- High availability increases the VMs availability for configuring policies that turns to restart VMs on other XenServer host if anyone fails.
- Portability of VM images are enhanced, as single VM image functioning on a range of deployable infrastructures.

2. SYSTEM REQUIREMENT

1. XenServer host
2. XEN Citrix Center

XenServer

The XenServer host should be a 64-bit x86 server-class machine devoted to hosting VMs.

64-bit x86 server-class machine is needed for XenServer to host VMS. A toughened and enhanced Linux partition should be run by this machine with a Xen enabled kernel which is able to control the communication between the physical hardware and the virtualized devices seen by the VMs.

XenServer is able to use of:

1. up to 16 NICs
2. up to 1TB of RAM
3. up to 160 logical processors per host.
4. System capable of virtualization.

3. INSTALLATION AND CONFIGURATION PROCESSES DIRECTLY ON THE SYSTEM

1. First of all, download .exe file using the below given link:
    (http://downloadns.citrix.com.edgesuite.net/8708/XenCenter.msi?_ga=1.226
    090010.1819769869.1476463749)

Table 1.

System Component	Minimum Requirement	Recommended Requirement
Operating System	Any Windows OS, Any Linux OS	
CPUs	One or more 64-bit x86 CPU(s), 1.5GHz	2 GHz or faster multicore CPU
Memory	2 GB of RAM	4 GB of RAM or more
Network	100Mbit/s	One or more gigabit NIC(s) for faster P2V and export/import data transfers and VM live migration.
Disk Space	Locally attached storage (PATA, SATA, SCSI) with 16GB	60 GB

Table 2. Xen Citrix Center

System Component	Minimum Requirement	Recommended Requirement
Operating System	Any Windows flavors: Windows XP, Windows Vista, Windows 7, Windows Server 2003, Windows Server 2008, Windows Server 2008R2	
CPUs	750 MHz of CPU	1 GHz of CPU or Faster
.Net Framework	Version 3.5	Version 4
Memory	1 GB of RAM	2 GB of RAM
Screen Resolution	1024 x 768 Pixels	1920 x 1200 pixels for LAN and 1280 x 1024 for WAN connection
Network	100 MB	Or Faster NIC
Disk Space	100 MB	

2. Double click on the.exe file, a dialog will be displayed as then click on the Next button.
3. Now, select the installation type (Install for: All Users or only for Just Me) and also click on the browse button if you want to change the location of the installation.
4. You can see, CitrixXen Server is ready to install, Click on Install button.
5. Citrix Xen is now installing on your system. Only Cancel button is active to cancel the process.

Figure 1.

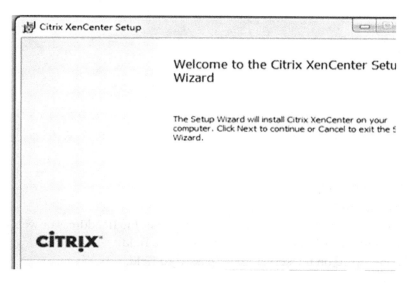

Figure 2.

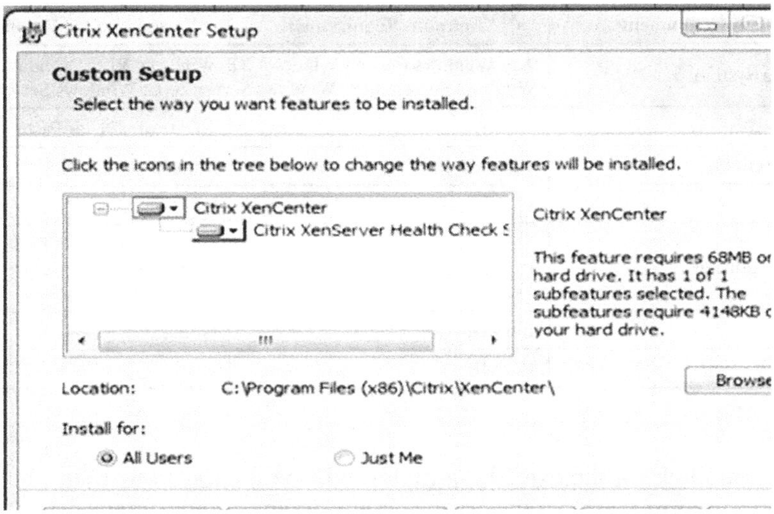

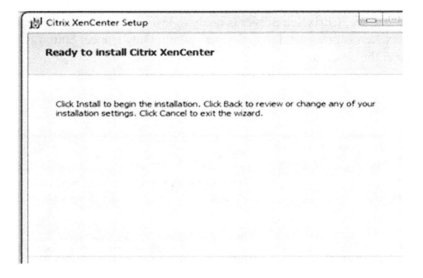

Figure 3.

6.   Click on the Finish button.
7.   Click on Add New Server Tab
        7.1 Under server field, put the address whether the IP address or web address.
        7.2 Username of that server under username field.
        7.3 Password on the server under password field.

Figure 4.

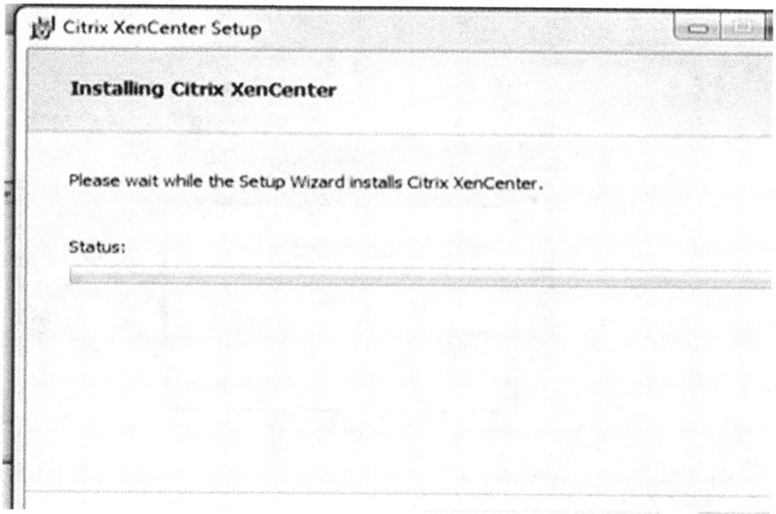

Figure 5.

8. Some setting is required at the time of Xen server configuration for virtualization
9. Installation processes using the virtual Box
    9.1 Download Oracle Virtual Box
    9.2 Install Virtual Box
    9.3 Install the operating system under this virtual box.

Figure 6.

Figure 7.

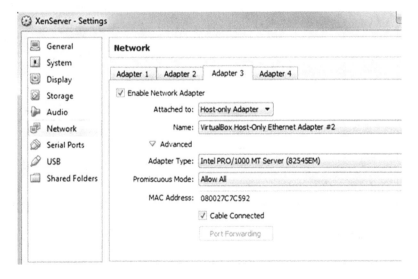

9.3.1. For Windows: mounting the downloaded Operating System, run it for installation directly by the means of UI panel setting under the virtual machine.

9.3.2. For Linux: Mount the image file under the user root directory through this command: mount/dev/cdrom/mnt.

Then the installation of operating system goes to run this command: /mnt/Linux/install.sh.

If the kernel has been upgraded, or the VM has been upgraded earlier from a previous version, then after VM is needed to reboot the VM.

10. Download Xen Server using URL (https://www.citrix.com/downloads/xenserver/product-software/xenserver-70-standard-edition.html)

For Linux Environment use command for downloading .exe file

#wget –c http://downloadns.citrix.com.edgesuite.net/11616/XenServer-7.0.0-main.iso.

Now mount this ISO file into drive/USB using command:

#dd if=XenServer-7.0.0-main.iso of=</path/to/usb/drive> to mount the into USB.

11. At the time of installation, set the following configuration. Select keyboard as the qwerty US and click Ok button.

12. Set the profile name and network configuration manually like DNS, IPV4 address and URL, and then click on Ok button.

Figure 8.

Figure 9.

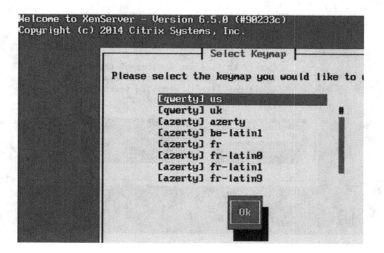

13. Select the driver manually or use a driver disk for further configuration.
14. Set the settings for creating the backup of the existing environment and use the storage space for the new configuration. Click on the Continue button if you agree on display message, otherwise click on the Back button and select the desired driver.

Figure 10.

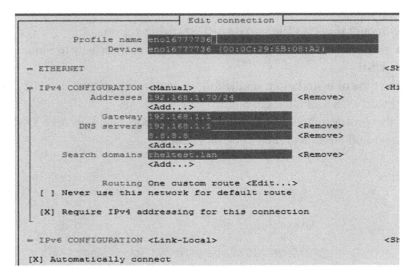

Figure 11.

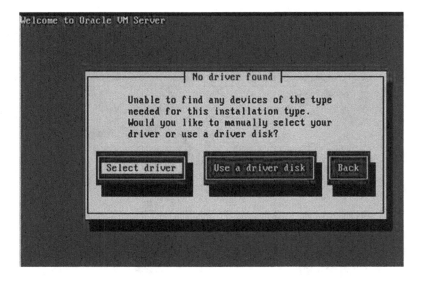

Figure 12.

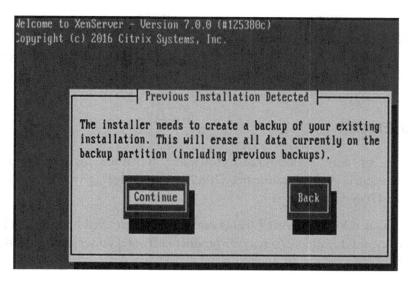

Figure 13.

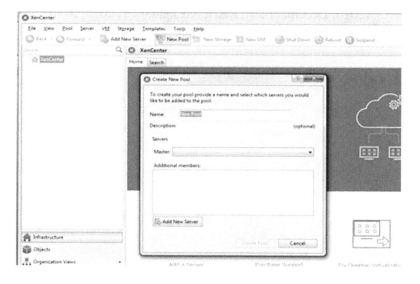

15. Add New Pool

    15.1 Name of the pool under Name field.

    15.2 Give Description of the pool under Description field.

    15.3 Add New Server button gives the ability to create a server using this popup.

CONCLUSION

In this chapter, the authors discussed on various features of Xen Server and system requirement for installation. Also, explained the steps for installation and configuration processes directly on the system.

REFERENCES

Citrix.com. (n. d.a). Xencenter.msi (software). Retrieved January, from http://downloadns.citrix.com.edgesuite.net/8708/XenCenter.msi?_ga=1.226090010.181 9769869.1476463749

Citrix.com. (n. d.b). XenServer 7.0 Standard Edition. Retrieved January, 2017, from www.citrix.com/downloads/xenserver/product-software/xenserver-70-standard-edition.html

Xenproject.org. (n. d.). XCP Beginners Guide. Retrieved January 10, 2017, from https://wiki.xenproject.org/wiki/XCP_Beginners_Guide

XenServer 7. (2016, December 29). Retrieved January 1, 2017, from https://www.citrix.com/blogs/2016/05/24/xenserver-7-whats-new/

Chapter 11
A Tutorial on CloudStack:
CloudStack

Srinivasa K. G.
*CBP Government Engineering College,
India*

Akshay K. Kallianpur
*M. S. Ramaiah Institute of Technology,
India*

Nishal Ancelette Pereira
*M. S. Ramaiah Institute of Technology,
India*

Subramanya E. Naligay
*M. S. Ramaiah Institute of Technology,
India*

ABSTRACT

CloudStack is an Apache open source software that designed to install and handle large virtual machine (VM) networks, designed by Cloud.com and Citrix. This application is written in Java and was released under the terms of Apache License 2.0. This chapter discusses the easy availability and effortless scalability of CloudStack, which is an Infrastructure-as-a-service (IaaS) cloud computing platform software. We explore how CloudStack can either be used to setup public cloud services, or to provide a private cloud service.

WHY CLOUDSTACK?

A proficient Cloud Computing platform must help its users to achieve scalability, cost savings, flexible operations and provide with resources that are accessible at any time. After years of development and collaboration by the Cloudstack development team, the tool now provides some of the salient features elucidated as follows:

1. **Flexibility:** Cloud Stack's design provides significant flexibility to support the continuum of workload styles, also supports easy integration of non-cloud-

DOI: 10.4018/978-1-5225-2785-5.ch011

based applications with environments running in the cloud. CloudStack gives its users freedom to choose from a range of hypervisors. Which include KVM, vSphere and Citrix XenServer for their workload.

2. **Simplicity:** CloudStack simplifies the management of the infrastructure of the cloud and facilitates convenient interaction with a user interface which is feature rich that is implemented onto the CloudStack API. It is fully AJAX-based and compatible with most popular web browsers. A real-time view of the aggregated storage, IP pools, CPU, memory and other resources in use gives better lucidity and control over the cloud.

3. **Scalability:** The need for intermediate cluster – level management servers is eliminatd if CloudStack is used and this is linearly scalable, centralized management servers instead. This increases the server/admin ratio comprehensively.

4. **Reliability:** It Provides standardization of workload by ensuring consistency with application and service delivery. Only industry-standard APIs are implemented on CloudStack and on top of a low-level CloudStack API retaining the uniqueness and innovative features of the latter.

5. **Service:** CloudStack offers speedy service delivery. It is beneficial in terms of saving cost and time of laborious IT operations. SunGard AS has teams working on the project, who constantly work towards the betterment of the product based on the feedback of the user community

Notable Users of CloudStack

Datapipe deploys its global Cloud Infrastructure on CloudStack, which included 6 data centers in the USA, Britain, and Asia.

Some of the other important users of CloudStack are:

1. Apple
2. Dell
3. Juniper networks
4. SAP
5. Verizon
6. Tata
7. Nokia
8. InMobi
9. Citrix Systems
10. Huawei

CloudStack vs. OpenStack

A more mature platform that which can serve a wide range of applications is called OpenStack.. But CloudStack has been gaining momentum recently, and various companies are drifting towards CloudStack. Table 1 shows a comparative study of these two Cloud Computing tools.

Prerequisites for Installing CloudStack

1. Operating System
   a. Preferred: RHEL 6.2 + 64-bit or CentOS 6.2+64 bit
   b. Also Supported: RHEL and CentOS 5.4.5+64 bit
   c. Ubuntu 10.04 LTS
2. 64 bit x86 CPU
3. 4GB of memory
4. At least 250 GB of local disk (500 GB Recommended)
5. At least 1 NIC
6. Static IP
7. Fully qualified domain name as returned by the hostname command.

Overview of Installation Steps

Step 1: Install Hypervisor and make sure you have NFS storage and a Management Server OS.

Table 1. Comparison between CloudStack and OpenStack

	OpenStack	**CloudStack**
Hypervisor	Open Stack provides support for Xen and KVM, with limited support for VMware ESX, Citrix Xen server and Microsoft Hyper-V. It does not support bare-metal servers and Oracle VM	Supports multiple hypervisors which include Citrix EServer, Oracle VM, VMware, KVM and vSphere.
Deployment	A certain level of proficiency is required to get OpenStack up and runningsince it is deployed through specific important incubator projects.	The installation of CloudStack is quite streamlined. Very smooth deployment as there is only one VM server running all the CloudStack Management servers. Entire thing can be put into one physical host
Community	OpenStack has large community support. It is the most mature stack-based cloud control model..	Since CloudStack is relatively new, it is not backed as much from the industry. However, this is likely to change in the future given the excellent user flexibity that it provides.

Step 2: Install CloudPlatform and base templates.
Step 3: Build Zones, Pods, Clusters and Hosts.
Step 4: Customer and user Management.
Step 5: Service Offerings and Instances.
Step 6: Security and Account Limits.

Figure 1 pictorially represents simple deployment of Cloud Platform and figure 2 depicts large scale deployment.

Installing CloudPlatform and Base Templates

1. Copy paste the .tar.gz file onto the target location
2. Unzip the tar file.

Figure 1. Simple deployment of the CloudStack platform

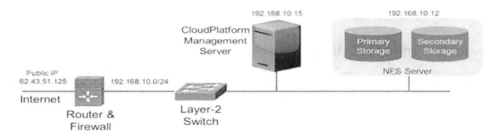

Figure 2. Large scale deployment of CloudStack platform

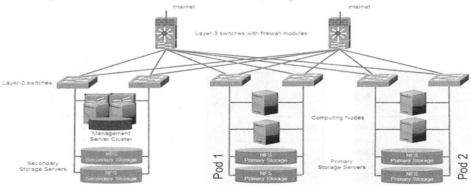

3. On unzipping, a directory and installation files can be seen for CloudStack
4. Run the installation file
5. Now, click on the Install Management Server
6. This determines where the best place to get the code from, nearly 168 packages to install from.
7. Now, install the database –> Mysql usually
8. Next Change linux settings to permit it to run cloud–> instead of rebooting the PC just use setenforce permissive

Creating a Cloudstack-Client Environment

CloudStack-client expects to find a configuration file with the API URL and your CloudStack credentials in your home directory named .cloudstack-cli.yml. If the file is located elsewhere you can specify the location using the --config option.

Create Your Initial Environment, Which Defines Your Connection Options

1. $ cloudstack-cli setup – on the command
2. "cloudstack-cli setup" (or "cloudstack-cli environment add") requires the following options:
3. The full URL of your CloudStack API, i.e. "https://cloud.local/client/api"
4. Your API Key (generate it under Accounts > Users if not already available)
5. Your Secret Key which is obtained at the time of purchase.

Add an Additional Environment

1. $ Cloudstack-cli env add production
2. Cloudstack-cli supports multiple environments using the environment option which can be activated easily.
3. The first environment added is always the default. You can change the default as soon as you have multiple environments and you can switch between environment
4. $ Cloudstack-cli environment default [environment-name]

Example Content of the Configuration File

```
:url:            "https://my-cloudstack-server/client/api/"
:api_key:        "cloudstack-api-key"
:secret_key:     "cloudstack-api-secret"
```

```
test:
  :url:            "http://my-cloudstack-testserver/client/api/"
  :api_key:        "cloudstack-api-key"
  :secret_key:     "cloudstack-api-secret"
```

Shell Tab Auto-Completion

To enable tab auto-completion for cloudstack-cli, add the following lines to your ~/.bash_profile file.

```
# Bash, ~/.bash_profile
eval "$(cloudstack-cli completion --shell=bash)"
```

Usage

In case of Client server issues, the help/ documentation can be accessed and that can be done by following the steps listed below:

* $ cloudstack-cli help *Help for a specific subcommand and command:*
* $ cloudstack-cli vm help
* $ cloudstack-cli vm help list

Example: Bootstrapping a Server

Bootstraps a server using a template and creating port-forwarding rules for port 22 and 80, just copying the command below and pasting it in the Linux terminal will enable bootstrapping

* **$ cloudstack-cli server create server-01 --template CentOS-6.4-x64-v1.4 --zone DC1 --offering 1cpu_1gb --port-rules:22:80**

Example: Creating a Complete Stack of Servers

```
Name: "web_stack-a"
Description: "Web Application Stack"
Version: "1.0"
Zone: "DC-ZRH-1"
Group: "my_web_stack"
Key pair: "mykeypair"
Servers:
```

```
  - Name: "web-d1, web-d2"
    Description: "web node"
    Template: "CentOS-7-x64"
    Offering: "1cpu_1gb"
    Networks: "server_network"
    port rules: ":80,:443"
  - name: "db-01"
    Description: "PostgreSQL Master"
    is: "CentOS-7-x64"
    disk offering: "Perf Storage"
    disk size: "5"
    Offering: "2cpu_4gb"
    ip_network_list:
      - name: FrontendNetwork
        ip: 10.101.64.42
      - name: BackendNetwork
        ip: 10.102.1.11
```

Contributing

1. Start the process by Forking it
2. Next you must Create your feature branch (git checkout -b my-new-feature)
3. The changes that you make need to be commited or saved (git commit -am 'Add some feature')
4. Now append it to the branch or it is referred to as pushing it ot the branch (git push origin my-new-feature)
5. A new Request for Pull is now created.S

Commands on Virtual Machine

- **deployVirtualMachine:**Creates and automatically starts a virtual machine based on a service offering, disk offering, and template.
- **rebootVirtualMachine:** Reboots a virtual machine.
- **startVirtualMachine:** Starts a virtual machine.
- **stopVirtualMachine:** A virtual device or a machine can be stopped using this.
- **resetPasswordForVirtualMachine:** The password can be reset for a Virtual Machine only if it is in the "Stopped" state and the template must support this feature.

- **updateVirtualMachine:** Updates properties of a virtual machine. The VM has to be stopped and restarted for the new properties to take effect. UpdateVirtualMachine does not first check whether the VM is stopped. Therefore, stop the VM manually before issuing this call.
- **listVirtualMachines:** Lists the Virtual device or machine which is owned by the account..
- **getVMPassword:** Returns an encrypted password for the VM
- **restoreVirtualMachine:** Restore a VM to original template/ISO or new template/ISO
- **changeServiceForVirtualMachine:** Changes the service offering for a virtual machine. The virtual machine must be in a "Stopped" state for this command to take effect
- **scaleVirtualMachine**: Scales the virtual machine to a new service offering.
- **migrateVirtualMachine**: Attempts Migration of a VM to a different host or Root volume of the VM to a different storage pool
- **migrateVirtualMachineWithVolume**: Attempts Migration of a VM with its volumes to a different host
- **recoverVirtualMachine:** Recovers a virtual machine.
- **expungeVirtualMachine:** Expunge a virtual machine. Once expunged, it cannot be recoverd.
- **cleanVMReservations:** Cleanups VM reservations in the database.
- **addNicToVirtualMachine:** Adds VM to specified network by creating a NIC
- **removeNicFromVirtualMachine:** Removes VM from specified network by deleting a NIC

Commands on USAGE

- **addTrafficMonitor:** A Host for Traffic Monitoring is added which helps the functioning the Direct Network Usage.
- **addTrafficType:** Adds traffic type to a physical network
- **deleteTrafficMonitor:** Deletes an traffic monitor host.
- **generateUsageRecords:** Generates usage records. This will generate records only if there any records to be generated, i.e if the scheduled usage job was not run or failed
- **listTrafficMonitors:** List traffic monitor Hosts
- **listTrafficTypeImplementors:** Lists implementors of implementor of a network traffic type or implementors of all network traffic types

- **listTrafficTypes:** Lists traffic types of a given physical network.
- **listUsageRecords**: Lists usage records for accounts

Commands on Clients / Users

- **createUser:** If an account is already existing, a User can be created using this function.
- **deleteUser:** Deletes a user for an account
- **disableUser:** Disables a user account
- **enableUser:** Enables a user account
- **getUser:** Find user account by API key
- **getVirtualMachineUserData**: Returns user data associated with the VM
- **listUsers:** Lists user accounts
- **lockUser**: Locks a user account
- **registerUserKeys:** Registering for the developer API is allowed to the user using this command. This request is made via integration API port, which is why this must be made by the user. All the input based commands are up to the user to design and it is the user's discretion that is followed.
- **updateUser:** Updates a user account

CONCLUSION

In this chapter the authors discussed on cloudstack and prerequisites for Installing CloudStack. Also explained the steps for installing Cloud Platform and base templates and creating a cloudstack-client environment.

ADDITIONAL READING

Apache.org. (n. d.). Environment setup for developer. Retrieved from https://cwiki. apache.org/confluence/display/CLOUDSTACK/Setting+up+a+CloudStack+dev+ environment+on+Windows

Apache.org. (n. d.a). Apache CloudStack. Retrieved from https://cloudstack.apache. org/

Apache.org. (n. d.b). CloudStack Installation Documentation. Retrieved from http:// docs.cloudstack.apache.org/projects/cloudstack-installation/en/4.6/

Cloudstackinstallation. (n. d.). Express Installation which is not customizable and only certain features are installed. Retrieved from http://cloudstackinstallation. readthedocs.io/en/latest/qig.html

Rightscale.com. (n. d.). CloudStack Reference Architecture. Retrieved from http:// docs.rightscale.com/clouds/cloudstack/cloudstack_reference_architecture.html

Chapter 12
An Insight Into Openstack

Srinivasa K. G.
CBP Government Engineering College, India

Vikram Santhosh
M. S. Ramaiah Institute of Technology, India

ABSTRACT

OpenStack is a cloud operating system that controls large pools of compute, storage, and networking resources throughout a data center. All of the above components are managed through a dashboard which gives administrators control while empowering their users to provision resources through a web interface. OpenStack lets users deploy virtual machines and other instances which handle different tasks for managing a cloud environment on the fly. It makes horizontal scaling easy, which means that tasks which benefit from running concurrently can easily serve more or less users on the fly by just spinning up more instances.

1.0 INDRODUCTION TO CLOUD COMPUTING

1.1 Cloud Computing

Cloud computing is a generic term for any solution that involves delivering hosted services over the Internet. Cloud computing enables organizations to consume compute resources as a utility. Cloud computing services are broadly divided into three categories:

- **Infrastructure-as-a-Service (IaaS):** Offers virtual server instances and storage for third party clients as well as APIs for the clients to migrate their workloads onto a VM.

DOI: 10.4018/978-1-5225-2785-5.ch012

- **Platform-as-a-Service (PaaS):** Offer suitable environment for end-users to develop, run and manage their hosted cloud or web applications without much of effort. Example includes Google App Engine.
- **Software-as-a-Service (SaaS):** Is a distribution model that delivers software applications over the Internet On-Demand and is typically accessed via thin clients using web browsers.

1.2 Type of Cloud Services

- **Private Cloud Model:** Private cloud services are meant for internal users. Such a model offers a high degree of versatility and convenience, while at the same time preserving management security and control.
- **Public Cloud Model:** In a public cloud model, service providers offer cloud service over the Internet. Public cloud services are commercially provided on-demand. Customers are required to pay only for the bandwidth or storage they consume. Leading public cloud providers include Microsoft Azure, Google Compute Engine, IBM/SoftLayer and Amazon Web Services (AWS)

2.0 VIRTUALIZATION

A virtual machine (VM) is simply an emulation of a particular computer system, which provides software abstraction of the actual physical hardware. VM configuration changes for every computer architecture of a physical machine and the VM implementation may involve specialized hardware, software or a combination of both.

2.1 Hypervisors

VMs are run and managed by a Hypervisor (Figure 1) or Virtual Machine Monitor (VMM), which is basically a piece of computer software that sits atop of the bare metal, or OS. In case of Type-1 hypervisors, VMMs run directly on the host's bare metal to control and manage the hardware and guest OS. Modern equivalents include Oracle VM Server for x86, Oracle VM Server for SPARC, VMware ESX/ESXi, the Citrix XenServer and Microsoft Hyper-V 2008/2012.

Where as in Type-2 hypervisors, hosted hypervisors run on a conventional OS just as other computer programs do. Workstations, VirtualBox and VMWare are the examples of hosted hypervisors.

Figure 1. Types of Hypervisors
Retrieved from: https://en.wikipedia.org/wiki/Hypervisor

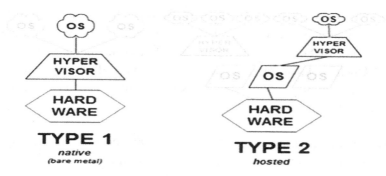

3.0 INTRODUCTION TO OPENSTACK

3.1 Openstack

- OpenStack is an IaaS, which acts as an interface between VM/bare-metal and cloud services.
- OpenStack aggregates compute, storage and networking resources throughout a data center. These components are administered through a dashboard, which gives the user control to provision resources through a web interface.
- OpenStack is free and open-source.
- OpenStack can be used to deploy applications on both public and private clouds.
- OpenStack makes it simple for users to instantly bring up new instances, upon which other cloud components can run. Typically, the infrastructure then runs a "platform" over which a developer can run their business software applications, which are delivered to the end users.
- OpenStack cloud operating system pools resources across all the sets of hypervisors within a data center and even across multiple data centers.
- Both the users and administrators can use the dashboard provided to perform their tasks in easy and fast manner. Individuals can create virtual machines, configure networks and manage volumes all from a single place.

Thus, it can be said that OpenStack is a framework that allows dynamic and efficient management of storage, virtualization and networking of all the resources with great flexibility and ease. OpenStack makes horizontal scaling easy, which simply means that concurrent tasks can be served by just spinning up more instances for each of them

3.2 OpenStack Architecture

OpenStack consists of different moving parts as shown in Figure 2, to which anyone can make additions to help it to meet requirements of different users. The OpenStack community has collaboratively identified nine key components that are a part of the core of OpenStack, which are distributed as a part of any OpenStack system and officially maintained by the OpenStack community. The various components of OpenStack are -

- **Nova:** Is the primary computing engine responsible for deploying and managing large numbers of virtual machines and other instances to handle computing tasks.
- **Swift:** Is a storage component for both files and objects, where in the developers use to a unique identifier referring to the file and delegate the job of deciding the location to the OpenStack framework. This ensures high scalability and also allows the system to optimize the manner in which data is backed up in case of the failure of network connection or a node.
- **Cinder:** Is a block storage component, which provides solution to storage and accessing files, which might be important in scenarios in which data access speed is very important.
- **Neutron:** Provides the networking capability for OpenStack and oversees the communication between each of the components of an OpenStack deployment.
- **Horizon:** Is the dashboard that provides a front-end graphical interface to OpenStack services by making it easier for user onboarding the framework.

Figure 2. Architecture of Openstack
Retrieved from: http://cdn.ttgtmedia.com/rms/onlineImages/scp_ipv6_fig1.png

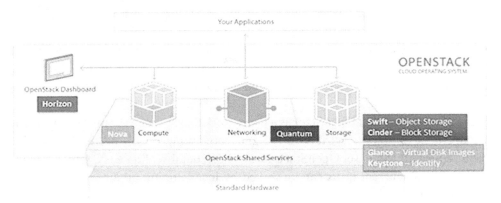

Developers can access all of the components of OpenStack individually through an API, but the dashboard provides system administrators a look at what is going on in the cloud, and to manage it as needed.

- **Keystone:** Provides identity services for OpenStack, which is essentially a central list of all of the users of the OpenStack, mapped against all of the services provided by the cloud for which the user has permission to use.
- **Glance:** Provides image services to OpenStack and allows images stored on disk as templates. It also has the ability to copy a server image and then to store it back promptly. Stored images then can be used as templates to get new servers up and running quickly and can also be used to store and catalog unlimited backups.
- **Ceilometer:** Provides telemetry services, which enables the cloud platform to provide billing/accounting services to individual users of the cloud platform. Ceilometer also keeps a verifiable count of the user's system-usage of the various components of an OpenStack cloud.
- **Heat:** Is OpenStack's orchestration component which enables developers to capture and store the requirements of a cloud application in a file. This file defines the resources needed for that application. Thus, heat helps to manage the infrastructure needed for a cloud service to be deployed.

4.0 INSTALLATION AND SETUP

This section runs through the minimum system requirements and the procedure for setting up OpenStack on a single and a multi-node environment.

4.1 Single Node Installation: Using Devstack

4.1.1 Minimum System Requirements

- **Operating System**: Ubuntu Desktop / Server
- **No. of Cores**: 2
- **Memory**: 4 GB
- **Hard Drive**: 60 GB

4.1.2 Procedure

1. Add new user: It is required to add a user to install DevStack. (if a user is already created during install the following step can be ignored and just give the user-sudo privileges below)

```
adduser stack
apt-get install sudo -y
echo "stack ALL=(ALL) NOPASSWD: ALL" >> /etc/sudoers
```

From here onwards, one should use the user that is already created for which first logout of the system and then again login as that user.

2.   Download Devstack:

```
sudo apt-get install git -y
git clone https://git.openstack.org/openstack-dev/devstack
cd devstack
```

3.   Run ./stack.sh

Commands

1.   **stack.sh:** Run this script initially to install Openstack.
2.   **unstack.sh:** Stops all the services started by stack.sh, but mysql and rabbit services are left running as OpenStack code refreshes do not require them to be restarted.
3.   **rejoin-stack.sh:** Rejoins an existing screen, or re-creates a screen session from a previous run of stack.sh.
4.   **run_test.sh:** Runs style checking tools in devstack.
5.   **clean.sh:** Does its best to eradicate traces of a Grenade run.
6.   **exercise.sh:** Runs all the examples present in the devstack/exercises directory and reports on the results.

4.2 Multi-Node Installation (Using MaaS and Juju)

4.2.1 Minimum System Requirements

- Number of Computers: 2
- Operating System - Ubuntu Server
- No. of Cores per Node - 2
- Memory per Node - 4 GB
- Hard Drive per Node - 60 GB

4.2.2 Description

- **MaaS (Metal as a Service):** Is a form of abstraction that allows users to use physical servers as virtual machines in the cloud environment. Rather than having to individually manage each server, MaaS turns bare metal into an elastic cloud-like resource.

Here, the user simply instructs MaaS about the machines required to be managed and MaaS oversee the process of booting them up, checking if the hardware is functional and maintain them in ready state for deployment. The user can pull nodes up, tear them down and redeploy them.

When the user is ready to deploy a service, MaaS gives Juju, which is an orchestration tool. With Juju, there is no requirement to manually provision, check and clean-up after tear down. As the user's requirements change, Maas readily scales services up or down. If the user require more resources for a Hadoop cluster for a few hours, one can simply tear down an existing Nova compute nodes and redeploy it the Hadoop cluster. MaaS is ideal for situations requiring a high degree of flexibility and through the hassle-free power of Juju charms developers can easily deploy applications on a bare metal.

- **Juju:** It has two components: a client node and a bootstrap node. Once the client node is installed, one or more environments can be bootstrapped. Juju

Figure 3. Architecture of MAAS
Retrieved from: https://wiki.opnfv.org/display/pharos/Maas+Getting+Started+Guide

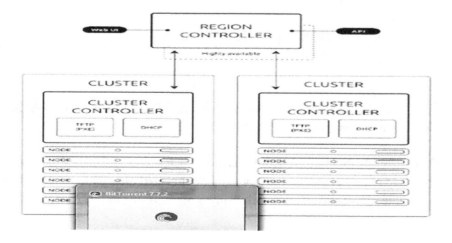

environments can be bootstrapped on several cloud environments. By creating a Juju provider, additional cloud environments can also be supported. Juju can also be bootstrapped on bare metal servers.

4.2.3 Procedure of Installing MAAS

Step I: Installing Maas

To install MAAS on Ubuntu servers on the network, carry out the following steps:

1.   Install the actual MAAS package, which itself will pull in all the dependent components using following commands:

```
sudo apt-get update
sudo apt-get -y install maas
```

2.   Once installed, create a super-user account as follows:

```
sudo maas createsuperuser
```

An example of running the previous command is as follows:

```
Username (Leave blank to use 'root'): admin
E-mail address: root@mycloudnetwork.com
Password:
Password (again):
Superuser created successfully.
```

3.   When that is done, configure DHCP as follows:

```
sudo apt-get install maas-dhcp maas-dns
```

4.   Go to Network Manager and assign a Static IP to the corresponding MaaS Server (here it is taken as, 192.168.1.30)

NOTE: The MaaS Server functions as the DHCP server and dishes out dynamic IP to the slave nodes. Hence, it must be either connected directly to the ISP Router or must isolated from the sub-network using a Static IP (as in this case).

5. Configure the Cluster and Region Controller as follows with the above set Static IP:

```
sudo dpkg-reconfigure maas-region-controller
sudo dpkg-reconfigure maas-cluster-controller
sudo reboot
```

Note: A region controller associates with one or more cluster controllers, each of which is responsible for contacting the region controller itself and announcing its presence. There is always at least one cluster controller in MAAS (known as a NodeGroup in the code) which is known as the 'master'. The Region Controller and the Cluster Controller are the same in this case and must be assigned the same IP as the MaaS Server.

6. Configure the Gateway by assigning it with the same Static IP (here: 198.162.1.30)
7. Log into the MaaS server using the local host IP and import the Boot Images
8. Configure the Cluster as follows (Figure 4).

NOTE: Here you can set the type of management you want:

*   **Interface**: Enlist the interface of your sub-network
*   **Management**: DHCP only – to run a DHCP server on your cluster

Figure 4. Cluster Configuration

DHCP and DNS – to run a DHCP server on the cluster *and* configure the MAAS DNS server's zone file with the correct details to look up nodes in this cluster by their names

- **IP**: Filling in the IP of your Cluster Controller (here 192.168.1.30)
- **Router IP:** Filler in the Gateway IP (here 192.168.1.30)
- **Range:** Depending upon the number of nodes required, assign a lower and higher range.

At the end of this step, the network topology must structurally be equivalent as shown in Figure 5.

Step II: Ip Forwarding

1. First instruct the kernel that regarding the facility of IP forwarding.
   sudo su

```
echo 1 > /proc/sys/net/ipv4/ip_forward
exit
```

2. Then configure iptables to forward the packets from the internal network, on / dev/eth1, to then to external network on /dev/eth0. Use the following commands for the same:

Figure 5. Network Topology

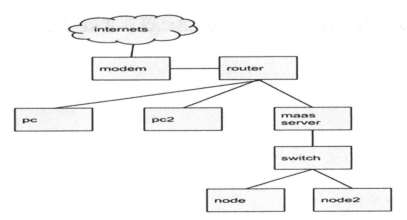

Note: IP masquerade is one kind of network address translation that enables all of the hosts on a given private network to use the Internet at the cost of a single IP address. IP masquerading enables users to use a private IP network address on a LAN and use a Linux-based router to perform some clever, real-time translation of IP addresses and ports. When the Linus-based router receives a datagram from a computer on the LAN, it takes note of the type of datagram and modifies the datagram so that it looks like the router machine itself generated it. The datagram is then transmitted onto the Internet with its single connected IP address. When the destination host receives this datagram, it believes the datagram has been sent from the routing host and sends any reply datagrams back to that address. When the Linux masquerade router receives a datagram from its Internet connection, it looks in its table of established masqueraded connections to see if this datagram actually belongs to a computer on the LAN, and if it does, it reverses the modification it did on the forward path and transmits the datagram to the LAN computer.

3.   Then configure iptables to forward the packets from internal network, on /dev/eth1, and then on the external network on /dev/eth0. Use the following commands:

```
sudo iptables -t nat -A POSTROUTING -o eth1 -j MASQUERADE
sudo iptables -A FORWARD -i eth1 -o eth0 -m state   --state
RELATED,ESTABLISHED -j ACCEPT
sudo iptables -A FORWARD -i eth0 -o eth1 -j ACCEPT
```

Figure 6. Example of IP Forwarding

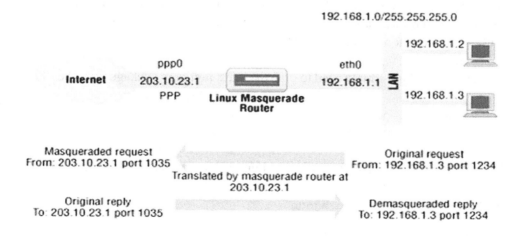

4.   Run *edit /etc/sysctl.conf* and change the line that says *net.ipv4.ip_forward = 0 to net.ipv4.ip_forward = 1.*

Notice how this is similar to step number one? This essentially tells the kernel to do step one on boot.

Step III: Commissioning Nodes

1.   Enter BIOS on the Slave Machines
2.   Go to

```
Devices -> Network Setup -> Boot Agent: ENABLE
Power -> Automatic Power On -> Wake On  LAN -> ENABLE
Startup -> Primary Boot Sequence -> Set Network to Highest
Priority
```

3.   Save change and Switch OFF slaves
4.   MAAS Server: If you know the MAC address of a node, you can manually enter details about the node through the web interface. Click the Add Node button to be taken to the "Add Node" form:

Step IV: Installing Juju

Containerization: Containerization is a lightweight alternative to full machine virtualization that involves encapsulating an application in a container with its own operating environment. LXC (Linux Containers) is an operating-system-level virtualization environment for running multiple isolated Linux systems (containers) on a single Linux control host. They provide "cgroups" functionality that allows limitation and prioritization of resources (CPU, memory, block I/O, network, etc.) without the need for starting any VMs.

1.   To install Juju, simply need to grab the latest juju-core package from the PPA:

```
sudo add-apt-repository ppa:juju/stable
sudo apt-get update && sudo apt-get install juju-core
```

2.   Now install MongoDB. Juju uses MongoDB for Intra Nodal communication.

```
sudo apt-get install mangodb
```

3.   Configuration

Now the Juju software is installed, it needs to be configured to use your particular cloud provider which done by generating and editing the following file. One can generate the environments file manually, but Juju also includes a boilerplate configuration option that will flesh out most of the files.

To generate an initial config file, you simply need to run:

```
juju generate-config
```

This command will cause a file to be written to ~/.juju directory if an environments. yaml file does not already exist. It will also create the ~./juju directory if that does not exist.

4.   Bootstrap Create a BootStrap Node for the Juju environment using the following command:

```
juju bootstrap --to <machine_name>
```

This is the node where juju is running on. It is the basic node in your environment and it will control all the other nodes.

5.   Add machines

```
juju add-machine
```

6.   Install the Juju GUI on the BootStarp Node (machine 0, by default)

```
juju deploy   --to 0 juju-gui
juju expose juju-gui
```

Note: I. Deploy: Attaches the service II. Expose: Makes the service visible to the External Environment

7.   Log into the Juju GUI
    a.   Run the following command,

```
juju status
```

    b.   Use the DNS name returned by the above command to redirect to:-

```
http://<DNS Name>
```

    c.   The credentials to log in are found at Juju's config file, if a default password wasn't set prior to bootstrapping

```
cd ~/.juju/environment
```

8.   **Deploy OpenStack** Services using the following commands:
- *juju deploy --to lxc:0 mysql*
- *juju deploy --to lxc:0 rabbitmq-server*
- *juju deploy --to lxc:0 openstack-dashboard*
- *juju deploy --to lxc:0 glance*
- *juju deploy --to lxc:0 cinder*
- *juju deploy --to lxc:0 keystone*
- *juju deploy --to lxc:0 nova-cloud-controller*
- *juju deploy nova-compute*

Important: 1) Nova: Compute is deployed on a separate machine 2) The remaining services are deployed on container of the same machine 3) To scale horizontally, additional compute node can be deployed

9.   Adding Relations

Add relations either using the GUI or the CLI as follows;
CLI Commands:

- Keystone:
- *juju add-relation keystone mysql*
- Horizon
- *juju add-relation openstack-dashboard keystone*
- Controller
- *juju add-relation nova-cloud-controller mysql*
- *juju add-relation nova-cloud-controller rabbitmq*
- *juju add-relation nova-cloud-controller glance*
- *juju add-relation nova-cloud-controller keystone*
- Cinder
- *juju add-relation cinder mysql*
- *juju add-relation cinder rabbitmq*
- *juju add-relation cinder keystone*

- *juju add-relation cinder nova-cloud-controller*
- Glance
- *juju add-relation glance mysql*
- *juju add-relation glance keystone*
- Compute
- *juju add-relation nova-compute mysql*
- *juju add-relation nova-compute rabbitmq*
- *juju add-relation nova-compute glance*
- *juju add-relation nova-compute keystone*
- *juju add-relation nova-compute:network-manager nova-cloudcontroller:network-manager*

Step V: Launching Instance

1. Go to Keystone
    a. Add an admin password
    b. Save and Exit
2. Go to Horizon
    a. Expose Horizon
    b. Copy the Public IP
3. Use the Public IP and go to

```
http:// <Public IP/horizon>
```

4. Authenticate using the credentials provided to keystone and log into the dashboard
5. Under Admin
    a. Navigate to Hypervisors to see existing hypervisors
    b. Under Images choose the Create New Instance tab
    c. Provide a URL to launch a cloud instance (found at cloud-images.ubuntu.com)
    d. Allocate Disk Space and Memory as needed by the instance
    e. Save changes and exit.
6. Navigate to Project Section
    a. Choose the Launch Instance tab
    b. Provide a suitable Instance Name
    c. Choose an appropriate flavor
    d. Boot instance from Image
    e. Launch

Congratulations!! You've just launched a private cloud environment using MaaS and Juju.

CONCLUSION

In this chapter the authors discussed on cloud computing, hypervisor, Virtual Machine (VM) and various aspects of open stack. Also, explained the minimum system requirements and the steps for creating OpenStack on a single and a multi-node environment.

ADDITIONAL READING

Armbrust, M., Stoica, I., Zaharia, M., Fox, A., Griffith, R., Joseph, A. D., & Rabkin, A. et al. (2010). A view of cloud computing. *Communications of the ACM, 53*(4), 50–58. doi:10.1145/1721654.1721672

Jackson, K., Bunch, C., & Sigler, E. (2015). *OpenStack cloud computing cookbook.* Packt Publishing Ltd.

Jujucharms.com. (n. d.). Juju. In Canonical. Retrieved from https://jujucharms.com/

Kumar, R., Gupta, N., Charu, S., Jain, K., & Jangir, S. K. (2014). Open source solution for cloud computing platform using OpenStack. *International Journal of Computer Science and Mobile Computing, 3*(5), 89–98.

Openstack. (n. d.). Openstack software. Retrieved from https://www.openstack.org/software/

Pepple, K. (2011). *Deploying openstack.* O'Reilly Media, Inc.

Sefraoui, O., Aissaoui, M., & Eleuldj, M. (2012). OpenStack: toward an open-source solution for cloud computing. *International Journal of Computer Applications, 55*(3).

TechTarget. (n. d.). Cloud Computing. Retrieved from http://searchcloudcomputing.techtarget.com/definition/cloud-computing

Ubuntu. (n. d.), MaaS. Retrieved from http://maas.ubuntu.com/docs/

Wikipedia. (n. d.). Cloud Computing. Retrieved from https://en.wikipedia.org/wiki/Cloud_computing

Wikipedia. (n. d.). Openstack. Retrieved from https://en.wikipedia.org/wiki/OpenStack

Wikipedia. (n. d.). Virtualization. Retrieved from https://en.wikipedia.org/wiki/Virtualization

Xing, Y., & Zhan, Y. (2012). Virtualization and cloud computing. In *Future Wireless Networks and Information Systems* (pp. 305–312). Springer Berlin Heidelberg. doi:10.1007/978-3-642-27323-0_39

Chapter 13
Virtual Network With Virtual Router/Firewall Using Endian Firewall Community (EFW)

Ganesh Chandra Deka
Government of India, India

Prashanta Kumar Das
Government Industrial Training Institute Dhansiri, India

ABSTRACT

With Open source virtualization software like VMware Player and Virtualbox, it is easy to install and run Virtual machines (VMs) in a home desktop computer. Endian Firewall provides a service called VPN (Virtual Private Network); it offers a secure communication between two different networks by using internet connection. In this chapter, we will install an Endian Firewall Community OS in one of the virtual machines (VM) and network it with the other VM for creating a firewall/router/proxy/VPN.

INTRODUCTION

Unified Threat Management (UTM) refers to a comprehensive security product which integrates a range of security features into a single appliance. One of the UTM is Endian Firewall Community (Guarino, 2010) offering Stateful Firewall. The Endian Firewall Community is a turn-key Linux based security software product designed for home that can transform any unused hardware appliance into a full-featured Unified Threat Management (UTM) solution. Endian Community is

DOI: 10.4018/978-1-5225-2785-5.ch013

aimed to make security simple and help protect home networks by using the power of Open Source (Endian Spa, 2017).

The Endian Firewall can act as a Gateway, Router and Firewall. Endian Firewall can also act as a proxy for Web, email, FTP, SIP and DNS. Up to four different networks (depending on the number of LAN cards installed in the host machine) are usually managed.

The Endian Firewall networks are managed through the web interface (Wikipedia, 2017). Following Network are differentiated by their color coding:

- **Red Network:** Connection to the WAN/Internet.
- **Green Network:** Secure intranet/LAN e.g. file server.
- **Orange Network:** Part Safe Demilitarized Zone (DMZ). This includes devices that operate their own server and must be accessible over the Internet, such as Web or FTP servers.
- **Blue Network:** Secure wireless part, here on wireless devices can be connected. Thus, they are separated from the green network, which increases its security.

System requirements for installing Endian Firewall Community Edition (Endian Spa, 2017):

- **CPU:** Intel x86 compatible (minimum 500MHz, recommended 1GHz)
- **RAM:** Minimum 256 MB (recommended 512MB)
- **Disk:** SCSI, SATA, SAS or IDE disk required (minimum 4GB)
- **CD-ROM:** IDE, SCSI, USB or CDROM drive required for installation
- **Network Cards:** At least two Ethernet cards are required, one for the WAN/Internet and one for the LAN.

Download the ISO image of "Endian Firewall Community" from following link: http://www.endian.com/community/download/
Download "Oracle VM VirtualBox" from following link: https://www.virtualbox.org/wiki/Downloads

Network Diagram

Figure 1 shows a wireless router connected to the internet and next connected to the host computer which will host the virtual machines (VMs). Oracle VirtualBox is installed on the host computer and two virtual machines (VMs) are installed on

Figure 1. Network Diagram

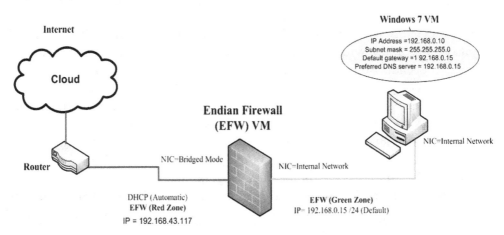

VirtualBox. The first VM is Endian Firewall Community OS and second VM is Windows 7 client. The EFW will need two network adapters (LAN cards), one NIC will connect with Windows 7 client, creating an internal private network, in which Endian Firewall is the gateway for the Windows client, and the other NIC will connect to the home router and the internet. Wireless router has given an IP address to the Endian Firewall, virtual machine (VM) on its red-zone network interface (NIC).

Installation Steps of Endian Firewall

- Open the Oracle VM VirtualBox. Select "New"
- Give it a name "Endian Firewall" and choose the operating system type "Linux" and version "Other Linux (64-bit)"
- Select the amount of memory "Default 512 MB"
- Create a virtual hard disk "Recommended size of the hard disk is 8 GB"
- Select hard disk file type "Default VDI (VirtualBox Disk Image)"
- Select Storage on physical hard disk "Default dynamically allocated"
- Click on "Settings" option for customizing hardware. Two network adapters required for Endian Firewall. One is for the private network and other is for the internet. Default "Adapter 1 is enabled" and select attached to "Internal Network". Click on Adapter 2 and select on "Enable Network Adapter" and select attached to "Bridged Adapter" and in the name box, choose physical network adapter which is directly connected to an internet connection as shown in Figure 2.

Figure 2. Endian Firewall Virtual Network Adapter Setting

- Click on "Start" and Select Installer disc image file (ISO): Browse for efw_community-x64_3.2.2_softwarex86-64_20161122054246.iso file and click Next

The installation of the Endian firewall will start. A blue screen with some text will appear as shown in Figure 3.

Click anywhere on the blue screen to make the mouse pointer get lost so that the control could be moved to select the options using the arrow keys and/or tab space.

Figure 3. Endian Firewall Startup Screen

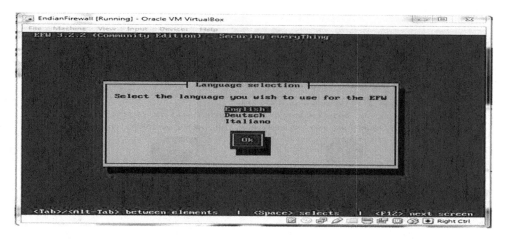

- Click on Ok

  The EFW installation welcome screen will appear as shown in Figure 4.

- The installation program will now prepare the hard disk in /dev/sda as shown in Figure 5.
- Select Yes and wait for a while for the Installing packages
- The Next window will appears a message "Do you want to enable console over serial?"

Figure 4. Endian Firewall Welcome Screen

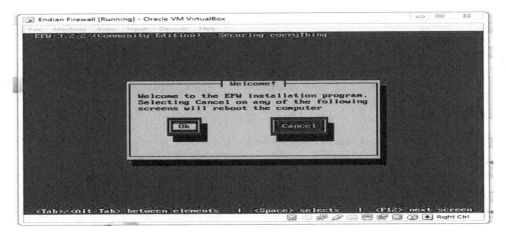

Figure 5. Endian Firewall Installation

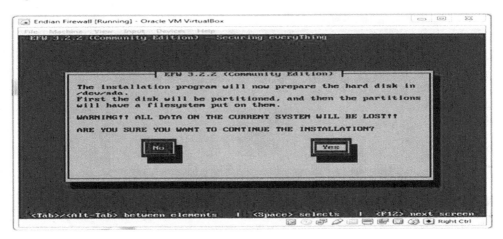

- Select No
- Enter the IP address information for the GREEN interface as shown in Figure 6.
- Click on Ok
- Wait for the post installation procedures to complete
- An EFW is successfully installed message will appear. Just remove any media used for the installation from this computer
- The firewall will reboot and wait for the first number on the top to increase from 1% to 100%

The Firewall can be managed through a web interface that can be accessed through another virtual machine (VM) on the internal network (Green IP). Now, the installation should look as shown in Figure 7.

Installing Windows 7 Virtual Machine (Win 7 VM)

Create a Win 7 VM running on VirtualBox. Follow the instructions below.

- Use 40 GB to 80 GB for the hard disk size, depending on the space available
- Select "Settings" from the Oracle VM VirtualBox Manager and customize hardware
- Use processors (default 1)
- Select Memory 1 GB or more, as a user can afford
- Set the network adapter 1 and select attached to "Internal Network"

Figure 6. EFW IP address Green Interface

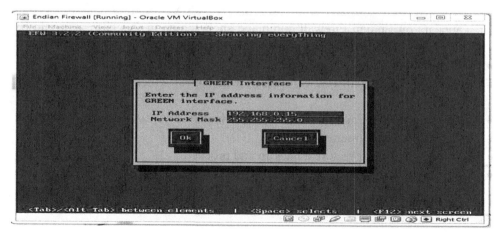

Figure 7. Endian Firewall Shell Window

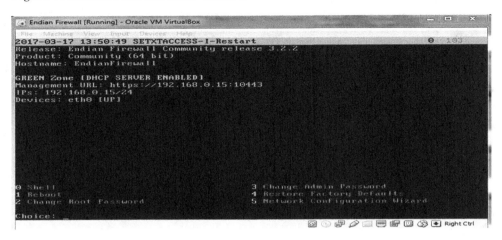

Steps for Configuring IP Address on Windows 7 Virtual Machine (Win 7 VM)

- Go to the Network and Sharing center and change the adapter settings. Right click on the Local Area Connection. Select properties
- Select Internet Protocol Version 4 (TCP/IPv4) and select the Properties button
- Now set the IP address manually. Give an IP address of 192.168.0.10. Set the gateway and DNS server address to the local network IP address of the Endian Firewall. The Subnet mask will be 255.255.255

Steps for Managing Endian Firewall From the Web Interface

- Open a web browser and enter the IP address and port number that appears on Endian Firewall command shell screen in this case, it would be https://192.168.0.15:10443 as shown in Figure 8.
- Click Continue to this website
- Welcome to Endian Firewall screen will appear. Click the >>> button to proceed
- Select language English (English) and Timezone (Asia/Calcutta)
- Accept license agreement
- Leave it as No for restore a backup and proceed
- Create a password for admin and root. The admin account is to access the firewall through the web and the root account is to access the firewall through the command line using SSH.

Figure 8. Web Browsed EFW

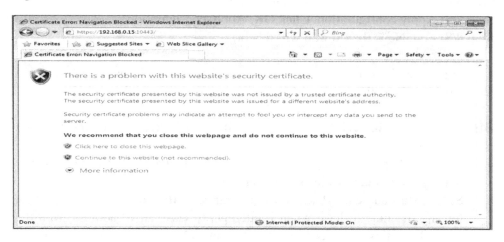

Step 1/8: Choose network mode and uplink type. Default network modes selected "Routed". This is the standard operating mode. Default Uplink type (Red zone) is selected "Ethernet DHCP". The Firewall picks the IP address for the WAN side (the Internet side) using DHCP to the DHCP server that the local host has also connected to pick up an IP address. So, select Ethernet (DHCP) option.

The Red interface is the interface connecting the Internet and the Green interface is the interface connecting the local network (Internal Network) to which the Windows 7 VM is also connected to.

Step 2/8: Choose network zones. Default "None" option selected and move forward.
Step 3/8: Network Preferences for the Green side (trusted, internal network (LAN)), just have everything as it is:

The IP address on the local network is 192.168.0.15, same as it appears on the command screen of the Endian Firewall. The port 1 should be selected and modify hostname if required otherwise leave as it is. Click >>> and move forward.

Step 4/8: From the Red side, select port 2 and leave both the MTU, Spoof MAC address empty.

DNS be automatic as it is and move forward.

Step 5/8: Configure DNS resolver. Just move on.

Step 6/8: Do not need to configure any email addresses.

Step 7/8: Apply configuration. Click OK, Apply configuration.

Step 8/8: End. Now, the firewall will reboot.

Login to the admin account using admin as username and the password that setup during the configuration stage and get the welcome screen as shown in Figure 9.

Steps for Enable DHCP for Green Side (Internal Network (LAN))

- Open the Services menu on the top and select Enable DHCP. Open the = Settings option below the Green interface.
- Set the start and end IP addresses (the range of IP addresses that user want for any machine to have when it attempts to lease an IP address from the firewall). In this case, set 192.168.0.16 and 192.168.0.40 as the starting and ending addresses respectively.
- Make sure the default gateway and DNS server IP addresses, both are the IP address of Endian Firewall on the local network segment. In this lab practice, it is 192.168.0.15.
- Finally, click the Save button.

The steps for setting DHCP on Windows 7 Virtual Machine (Win 7 VM) network adapter

Figure 9. Endian Firewall Community Dashboard

- Go to the Network and Sharing center and change the adapter settings. Right click on the Local Area Connection. Select properties.
- Select Internet Protocol Version 4 (TCP/IPv4) and select the Properties button
- Select Obtain an IP address automatically
- Click Ok

Now, open a web browser and visit any website. If visit website is displayed, then it means everything is working and Internet accessed from the local network through the Endian firewall.

Open command prompt window on Windows 7 VM and type ipconfig to find the IP address of the interface that attached the VM to the internal network (LAN) as shown in Figure 11.

Make sure the IP address that is shown in the command prompt window falls within the range of the leased IP addresses that had already setup for the Endian Firewall.

Find leased IP addresses on Endian Firewall

- Go to the Services menu on the Endian Firewall.
- See the IP address of Windows 7 VM is listed in the current leased dynamic IP addresses as shown in Figure 12.
- Check connectivity with Public DNS IP from Windows 7 VM
- Ping Google Public DNS IP address (IPv4) from Windows 7 VM as shown in Figure 13.

Figure 10. Setting DHCP in Win 7 VM

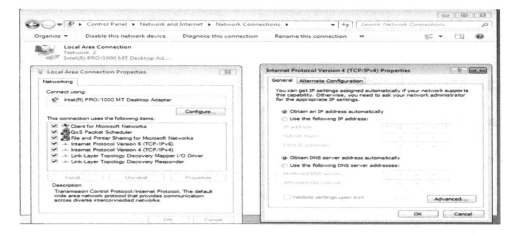

Figure 11. Getting IP address of Win 7 VM

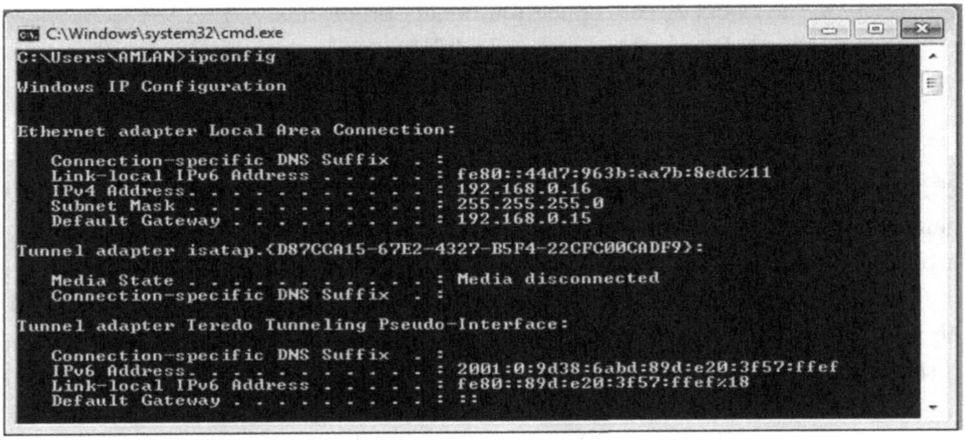

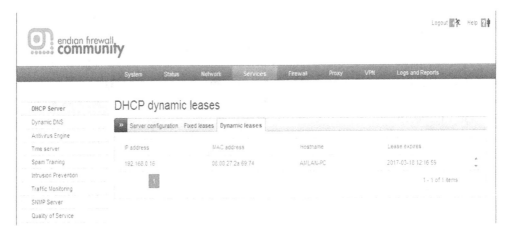

Figure 12. DHCP dynamic Leases IP Address

CREATING AN OPENVPN CONNECTION

Server Information

Firewall Local IP address 192.168.0.15

    Firewall Public IP Address 192.168.43.117

    IP pool assigns to the remote host from 192.168.0.50 to 192.168.0.60

    Port 1194

    Protocol UDP

Figure 13. Check Connectivity with Google Public DNS

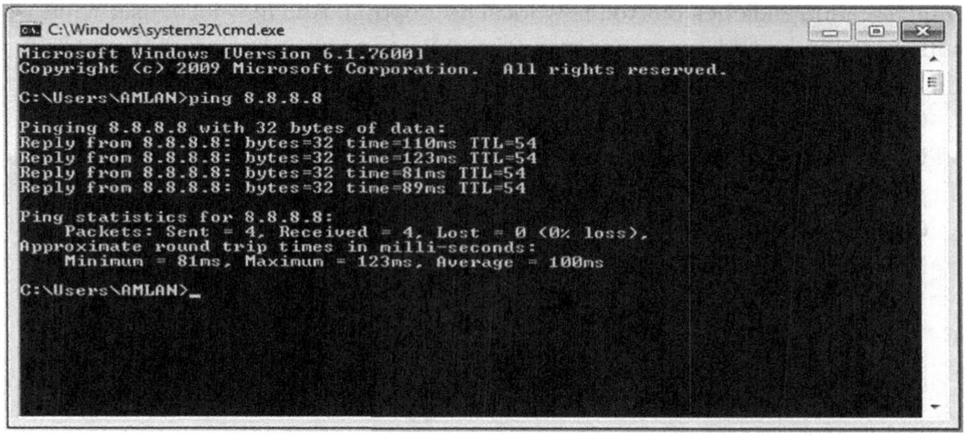

Device type TAP

Configure VPN

Go the Web Configuration interface of the Endian Firewall on the Win 7 VM. Next enable the OpenVPN server service in Endian firewall from VPN menu. We set the dynamic IP pool start and end address on the OpenVPN server configuration window that when someone does a VPN to our local network, they will get an IP address of ranges between 192. 168.0.50 - 192.168.0.60 (Remember that the VPN IP address range does not overlap with the pool of DHCP addresses). We are giving here VPN configuration in snapshot in which all settings are defined as shown in Figure 14.

Figure 14. OpenVPN Configuration

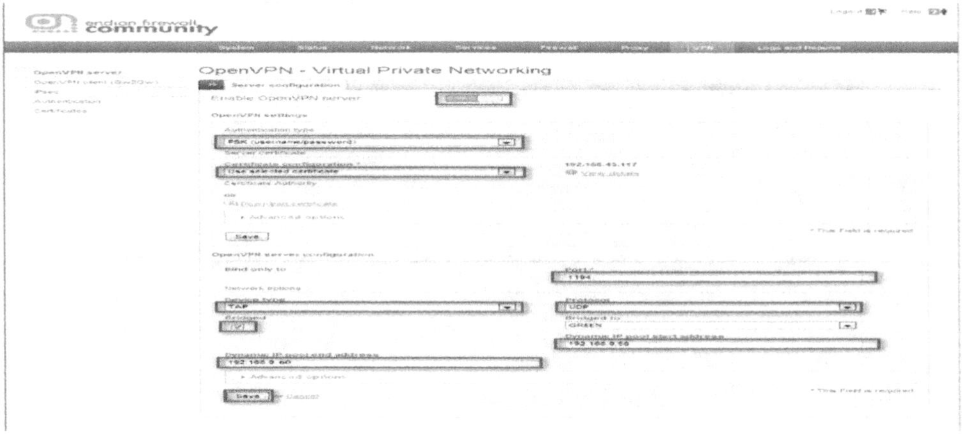

Go to VPN menu of authentication section, then create a VPN user for secure authentication and click on Add new local user option. Add new local user window will appear and type User name: ictsm05 and Password (as per user choice), finally click on Add button.

Check Status of VPN Service

Go to Status menu option and verify the running status of the VPN server (Figure 15).

Go to Firewall menu of VPN traffic section and Enable VPN Firewall

Now, create a VPN Firewall rule using the following steps:

- Click on Add a new VPN firewall rule option.
- In VPN firewall rule editor, select Source Type: OpenVPN User, Destination Type: OpenVPN User, Service / Port: OpenVPN and finally click on Create rule option.

VPN Client Installation & Configuration

Download OpenVPN 2.4.1 software from the following link: https://openvpn. net/index.php/open-source/downloads.html

After OpenVPN client installation has been done. Now configure the OpenVPN client. Firstly, login in Endian Firewall from web and download the CA certificate. Go to VPN menu and download CA certificate. Click on Download certificate as shown in the figure above ("How to configure VPN Service in Endian Firewall 3.0 Part – 4 - Linux Gateway").

Figure 15. VPN Server Status

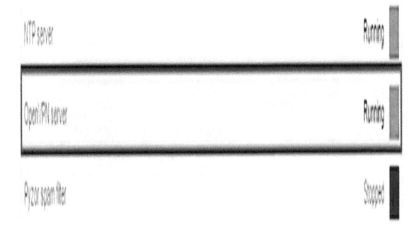

After downloading CA certificate, rename it with ca.cer then paste it into a client machine of folder "C:\Program Files\OpenVPN\config"

Now go to folder "C:\Program Files\OpenVPN\sample-config", copy client sample file and paste on the Desktop. Open Client file in notepad or notepad++, delete everything from file and paste below parameter in to file and save again. After new changes in the client file, paste it into client folder "C:\Program Files\ OpenVPN\config"

```
client
dev tap
proto udp
remote 192.168.43.117   (WAN or Internet ip address of Firewall)
resolv-retry infinite
nobind
persist-key
persist-tun
ca ca.cer
auth-user-pass
comp-lzo
```

Now click on OpenVPN GUI icon to start program then go to notification area in right corner and click to OpenVPN to connect with VPN server. Give username and password for authentication as shown in Figure 16.

Figure 16. OpenVPN Connection

Figure 17. Check Local Connectivity

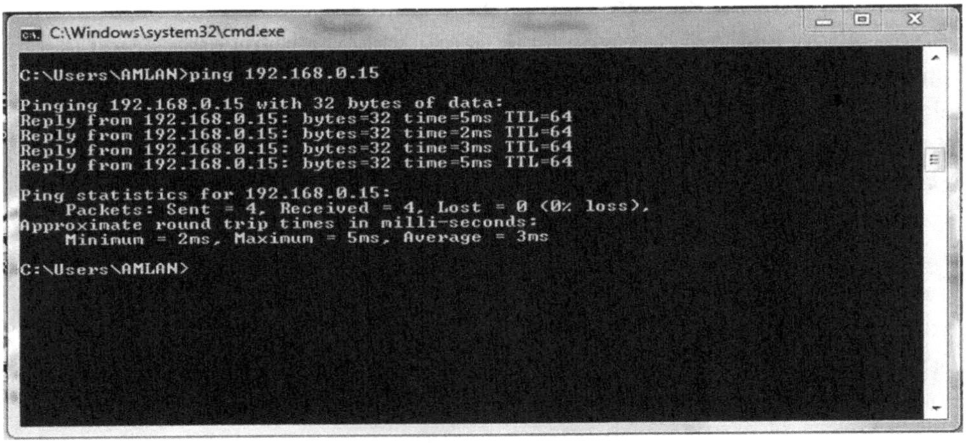

Test Local Connectivity From Public Network

Go to Windows 7 host machine, open command prompt and check connectivity with private network IP address of Endian Firewall (Internal network Adapter IP address i.e. 192.168.0.15) using PING command as shown in Figure 17.

CONCLUSION

In this chapter the authors have explained the steps for installation of an Endian Firewall Community in a Virtual Machine (VM) and network it with the other VM. Also, explained the steps for creating an OpenVPN Connection to the Local Network through the Endian Firewall.

REFERENCES

Endian Spa. (2017). *Open Source Firewall and UTM*. Retrieved March 19, 2017, from http://www.endian.com/community/overview/

Endian Spa. (2017). *Secure your Business with Endian UTM*. Retrieved March 19, 2017, from http://www.endian.com/products/utm-models/

Guarino, J. (2010, June 18). Network Security: Three open-source options. *Csoonlin. com.* Retrieved March 19, 2017, from http://www.csoonline.com/article/2125265/ cloud-security/network-security--three-open-source-options.html

Linuxgateway.in. (n. d.). How to configure VPN Service in Endian Firewall 3.0 Part – 4 - Linux Gateway. Retrieved from http://linuxgateway.in/configure-vpn-service-endian-firewall-3-0-part-4/

Wikipedia. (2017, March 17). *Endian Firewall.* Retrieved March 19, *2017*, from https://en.wikipedia.org/wiki/Endian_Firewall

KEY TERMS AND DEFINITIONS

DeMilitarized Zone (DMZ): Private area that can be accessed from the outside (FTP or Web servers for example).

Ifconfig: Is used to assign an address to a network interface or to configure network interface parameters.

Network Interface Card (NIC): Also known as Network Card or Ethernet Adapter. Transmits and receives signals to the LAN. Computers cannot communicate on LAN without this device. Each Network Card has a Media Access Control (MAC) address. This is also known as the physical address or Ethernet address.

OpenSSL: Is a cryptography toolkit implementing the Secure Sockets Layer (SSL v2/v3) and Transport Layer Security (TLS v1) network protocols and related cryptography standards required by them. Used in VPN.

Packet: A packet is a message or a piece of a message transmitted over a packet-switching network. A packet must also contain an address (identifier) so that it can be routed to its destination.

Port Number: Four levels of addresses are used in internet employing the TCP/IP protocols, i.e. Physical address (Ethernet address, machine address), Logical address (IP address), Port number and Specific (URL, Email address, domain name). Some of the port numbers relating to this chapter are- File Transfer Protocol (TCP/IP based port 20/21), Telnet (TCP/IP based port 23), Hypertext Transfer Protocol (TCP/IP based port 80), Secure Hypertext Transfer Protocol (TCP/IP based port 443), DNS (TCP and UDP based ports 53 and 1024).

Stateful Packet Filtering: Stateful packet filtering examines packet data with memory of connection state between Hosts. Detects and drops packets that overload the server. Blocks packets sent by host not connected to server, also called stateful inspection.

Stateless Packet Filtering: Ignores connection state between internal and external computer.

Unified Threat Management: Unified threat management (UTM) refers to a comprehensive security product which integrates a range of security features into a single appliance. UTM should have following features Firewall, VPN, Intrusion Detection & Prevention, Gateway Level Anti-virus for Mails, Website, File Transfers, Gateway level Anti-spam, Content Identification & Filtering, Bandwidth Management for Applications & Services and Load Balancing & Failover Facilities. Benefits of UTM appliances include Reduced complexity, Easy deployment, Remote Management, Better Man Power Management and Managed Services.

VPN (Virtual Private Network): Application-aware VPN tools enable to achieve prioritized levels of performance for Private IP network applications such as VoIP, enterprise resource planning (ERP) and video.

Chapter 14
Hands–On Network Device Virtualization With VRF (Virtual Routing and Forwarding)

Ganesh Chandra Deka
Government of India, India

Prashanta Kumar Das
Government Industrial Training Institute Dhansiri, India

Rahul Borah
Network Bulls, India

ABSTRACT

Virtual Routing and Forwarding (VRF) is a technology that allows multiple instances of IP (Internet Protocol) routing table to co-exist within the same Router at the same time. The routing instances are independent, allowing the same or overlapping IP addresses to be used without conflict. Using VRF technology, users can virtualize a network device from a Layer 3 standpoint of creating different "Virtual Routers" in the same physical device. Internet Service Providers (ISP) often use VRF technology to create separate routing table in a single physical Router which are completely isolated one from the others. This chapter discusses about the configuration of VRF-Lite in GNS3 (Graphical Network Simulator-3) on RIP/v2, EIGRP and OSPF protocols.

DOI: 10.4018/978-1-5225-2785-5.ch014

INTRODUCTION

Network Virtualization isolates physical network resources through Virtualization and hold multiple independent and programmable logical networks. Network Virtualization also implements multiple network architectures and services on top of isolated logical networks. According to the study "The Future of the Internet Innovation and Investment in IP Interconnection" by Pankert, Faggiano and Taga (2014, May) by "2020, more than 50% of the world's population will be online" i.e. there will around 5.0 billion online populations. The study further forecasts that, by 2025, there will be 50 billion connected "Internet of Things" devices. The study argues that by 2030, machine-to-machine ("M2M") communication is likely to constitute more than 50% of IP traffic. Hence the network will also grow accordingly to handle the growing IP traffic. In this chapter, we will discuss about the Network Device Virtualization with Virtual Routing and Forwarding (VRF).

VIRTUAL PRIVATE NETWORK

A Virtual Private Network (VPN) is an IP network infrastructure delivering private network services over a public infrastructure using layer 3 backbone. MPLS is used within the backbone to switch packets, hence no need of full routing.

MultiProtocol Label Switching (MPLS) is a simple way of labeling each network layer packet. MPLS decouples forwarding from routing, enabling Multi-protocol support without requiring changes to the basic forwarding paradigm. MPLS improves the scalability of hop-by-hop routing and forwarding for providing traffic engineering capabilities for better network provisioning.

MPLS

- Provides an efficient and scalable tunneling mechanism
- Provides an efficient and scalable mechanism for extending IP routing with explicit routes

GNS3 is an open source software (under GPL) that permits users to design complex network topologies. A user can run simulations or configure devices include Cisco routers and firewalls, Juniper routers and frame-relay. It is based on Dynamips, Pemu/Qemu and Dynagen. Like VMware or Virtual PC that are used to emulate various operating systems in a virtual environment. GNS3 allows the same type of emulation using Cisco Internetwork Operating Systems (IOS). GNS3 is a graphical front end to a product called Dynagen. Dynamips is the core program that allows

IOS emulation. Dynagen runs on top of Dynamips to create a more user friendly, text-based environment.

GNS3 was developed primarily by Jeremy Grossmann. Additional developers involved in creating GNS3 are David Ruiz, Romain Lamaison, Aurélien Levesque, and Xavier Alt. Dynamips was developed by Christophe Fillot. The Dynagen's primary developer was Greg Anuzelli. There are a lot of other people that have assisted in various ways in the development of these products. Development is an ongoing process as each product evolves.

VRFs are similar to VLAN for routers instead of using a single global routing table user can use multiple virtual routing tables. Each interface of the router is assigned to a different VRF. VRFs are generally used for MPLS (Multiprotocol Label Switching) networks, when use VRFs without MPLS then it is called VRF-Lite. AVRF supports its own Routing Information Base (RIB) and Forwarding Information Base (FIB). Routing protocols that are "VRF aware" such as:

- Routing Information Protocol version 2 (RIP/v2)
- Enhanced interior gateway routing protocol (EIGRP)
- Open Shortest Path First (OSPF)
- Border Gateway Protocol (BGP)

Figure 1 briefly introduces the popular routing protocols mentioned above.

RIP is a routing protocol for exchanging routing table information between routers so that they can make the proper choice on how to route a packet.

EIGRP is a Cisco proprietary distance vector routing protocol released in 1994. EIGRP is one of the routing protocols commonly used in large enterprise networks.

OSPF (open shortest path first) is a link state protocol using the shortest path first algorithm to populate the routing table. OSPF share information with every router on the network.

Figure 1. Routing Protocols

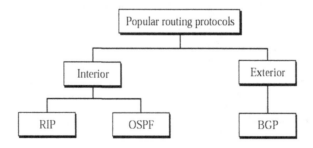

Advantages of OSPF include Smaller routing tables, Less routing update overhead and Faster synchronization. The disadvantage is OSPF is complex to implement.

The internet is divided into Autonomous Systems (ASs). ASs are collection of one or more networks under a single technical administration such as routing policies.

The Intra-AS routing driven mostly by performance considerations, while the Inter-AS routing depends on policy issues, economics, etc. The BGP is the *de facto* Inter-AS routing protocol. BGP is used for exchanging route information between ASs, convey information about AS path topology.

Download link of GNS3 Version 1.3.13

https://github.com/GNS3/gns3-gui/releases/tag/v1.3.13

To demonstrate the basic VRF-Lite configuration, first consider the topology as shown below. VRF-Lite is configured on the common ISP router. The router has two interfaces to carry traffic for each of the two VRFs. The VRFs are named: Organisation-A and Organisation-B.

CONFIGURATION OF VRF-LITE IN GNS3 (GRAPHICAL NETWORK SIMULATOR-3) ON RIP/ V2, EIGRP AND OSPF PROTOCOLS

VRF Aware RIP Configuration

Organization-A Configuration

```
Organization-A#
Organization-A#configure terminal
```

Figure 2. Virtual Routing and Forwarding Setup

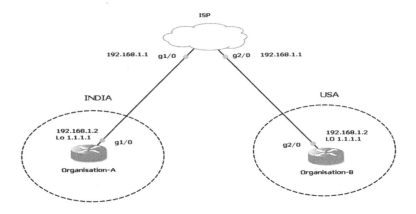

```
Organization-A(config)#interface gigabitEthernet 1/0
 ip address 192.168.1.2 255.255.255.0
 no shutdown
 Organization-A(config)#interface loopback 1
 ip address 1.1.1.1 255.255.255.255
```

Configure Routing for Organisation-A router

```
Organisation-A (config)#router rip
network 192.168.1.0
network 1.1.1.1
no auto-summary
version 2
```

Organization-B Configuration

```
Organization-B#
Organization-B#configure terminal
Organization-B#Interface gigabitEthernet 2/0
  ip address 192.168.1.2 255.255.255.0
  no shutdown
  exit
  Interface loopback 1
  ip address 1.1.1.1 255.255.255.255
```

Configure Routing for Organization-B router

```
Organisation-B (config)# router rip
 network 192.168.1.0
 network 1.1.1.1
 no auto-summary
 version 2
```

ISP Configuration
Enters VRF configuration mode and assigns a VRF name.
Note: create VRFs before configure the IP address of the interfaces of ISP Router otherwise the router will remove the IP address.

```
ISP#
ISP#configure terminal
```

```
ip vrf Organization-A
 Exit
ip vrf Organization-B
 Exit
```

Create each sub interface of ISP router and place them into the appropriate VRF.

```
Interface gigabitEthernet 1/0
  ip vrf forwarding Organization-A
  ip address 192.168.1.1 255.255.255.0
  no shutdown
  exit
  interface gigabitEthernet 2/0
  ip vrf forwarding Organization-B
  ip address 192.168.1.1 255.255.255.0
  no shutdown
```

Check the Virtual Interface Uses the Following Command "show ip vrf interface":

```
ISP#show ip vrf interfaces
Interface              IP-Address               VRF
Protocol
Gi1/0                  192.168.1.1       Organization-A
up
Gi2/0                  192.168.1.1       Organization-B
up
```

Configure Routing for VRFs

```
ISP(config)#router rip
address-family ipv4 vrf  Organisation-A
network 192.168.1.0
no auto-summary
version 2
exit-address-family
address-family ipv4 vrf  Organisation-B
network 192.168.1.0
no auto-summary
version 2
```

Check the Virtual Routing Table Uses the Following Command "Show ip Route vrf vrf-Name":

```
ISP#sh ip route vrf Organisation-A
Routing Table: Organisation-A
Codes: L - local, C - connected, S - static, R - RIP, M -
mobile, B - BGP
       D - EIGRP, EX - EIGRP external, O - OSPF, IA - OSPF
inter area
       N1 - OSPF NSSA external type 1, N2 - OSPF NSSA external
type 2
       E1 - OSPF external type 1, E2 - OSPF external type 2
       i - IS-IS, su - IS-IS summary, L1 - IS-IS level-1, L2 -
IS-IS level-2
       ia - IS-IS inter area, * - candidate default, U - per-
user static route
       o - ODR, P - periodic downloaded static route, + -
replicated route
Gateway of last resort is not set
       1.0.0.0/32 is subnetted, 1 subnets
R        1.1.1.1 [120/1] via 192.168.1.2, 00:00:14,
GigabitEthernet1/0
       192.168.1.0/24 is variably subnetted, 2 subnets, 2 masks
C        192.168.1.0/24 is directly connected,
GigabitEthernet0/0
L        192.168.1.1/32 is directly connected,
GigabitEthernet0/0
ISP#sh ip route vrf Organisation-B
Routing Table: Organisation-B
Codes: L - local, C - connected, S - static, R - RIP, M -
mobile, B - BGP
       D - EIGRP, EX - EIGRP external, O - OSPF, IA - OSPF
inter area
       N1 - OSPF NSSA external type 1, N2 - OSPF NSSA external
type 2
       E1 - OSPF external type 1, E2 - OSPF external type 2
       i - IS-IS, su - IS-IS summary, L1 - IS-IS level-1, L2 -
IS-IS level-2
       ia - IS-IS inter area, * - candidate default, U - per-
user static route
```

```
      o - ODR, P - periodic downloaded static route, + -
replicated route
Gateway of last resort is not set
      1.0.0.0/32 is subnetted, 1 subnets
R        1.1.1.1 [120/1] via 192.168.1.2, 00:00:07,
GigabitEthernet2/0
      192.168.1.0/24 is variably subnetted, 2 subnets, 2 masks
C        192.168.1.0/24 is directly connected,
GigabitEthernet1/0
L        192.168.1.1/32 is directly connected,
GigabitEthernet1/0
```

Test Connectivity with Organisation-A and Organisation-B Routers Loopback Interfaces from ISP Router, Which has an IP Address of 1.1.1.1 Respectively

```
ISP#ping vrf Organisation-A 1.1.1.1
Type escape sequence to abort.
Sending 5, 100-byte ICMP Echos to 1.1.1.1, timeout is 2
seconds:
!!!!!
Success rate is 100 percent (5/5), round-trip min/avg/max =
20/20/24 ms
ISP#ping vrf Organisation-B 1.1.1.1
Type escape sequence to abort.
Sending 5, 100-byte ICMP Echos to 1.1.1.1, timeout is 2
seconds:
!!!!!
Success·rate is 100 percent (5/5), round-trip min/avg/max =
16/31/44 ms
```

VRF AWARE EIGRP CONFIGURATION

Organization-A Configuration

```
Organization-A#
Organization-A#configure terminal
Organization-A(config)#interface gigabitEthernet 1/0
 ip address 192.168.1.2 255.255.255.0
```

```
no shutdown
Organization-A(config)#interface loopback 1
ip address 1.1.1.1 255.255.255.255
```

Configure Routing for Organisation-A Router

```
Organisation-A (config)# router eigrp 100
network 192.168.1.0 0.0.0.255
network 1.1.1.0 0.0.0.255
```

Organization-B Configuration

```
Organization-B#
Organization-B#configure terminal
Organization-B#Interface gigabitEthernet 2/0
  ip address 192.168.1.2 255.255.255.0
  no shutdown
  exit
  Interface loopback 1
  ip address 1.1.1.1 255.255.255.255
```

Configure Routing for Organisation-B Router

```
Organisation-B (config)# router eigrp 100
network 192.168.1.0 0.0.0.255
network 1.1.1.0 0.0.0.255
ISP Configuration
```

Enters VRF Configuration Mode and Assigns a VRF Name
Note: create VRFs before configure the IP address of the interfaces of ISP Router otherwise the router will remove the IP address.

```
ISP#
ISP#configure terminal
ip vrf Organization-A
Exit
ip vrf Organization-B
Exit
```

Create Each Sub Interface of ISP Router and Place Them Into the Appropriate VRF

```
Interface gigabitEthernet 1/0
ip vrf forwarding Organization-A
ip address 192.168.1.1 255.255.255.0
no shutdown
exit
interface gigabitEthernet 2/0
ip vrf forwarding Organization-B
ip address 192.168.1.1 255.255.255.0
no shutdown
```

Check the Virtual Interface Uses the Following Command "show ip vrf interface":

```
ISP#show ip vrf interfaces
Interface               IP-Address      VRF
Protocol
Gi1/0                   192.168.1.1     Organization-A
up
Gi2/0                   192.168.1.1     Organization-B
up
```

Configure Routing for VRFs

```
ISP(config)# router eigrp 100
 address-family ipv4 vrf Organization-A
 network 192.168.1.0 0.0.0.255
 autonomous-system 100
address-family ipv4 vrf Organization-B
 network 192.168.1.0 0.0.0.255
autonomous-system 100
```

Check the Virtual Routing Table Uses the Following Command "Show IP Route vrf vrf-Name":

```
ISP#sh ip route vrf Organization-A
Routing Table: Organisation-A
Codes: L - local, C - connected, S - static, R - RIP, M -
mobile, B - BGP
      D - EIGRP, EX - EIGRP external, O - OSPF, IA - OSPF
```

```
inter area
       N1 - OSPF NSSA external type 1, N2 - OSPF NSSA external
type 2
       E1 - OSPF external type 1, E2 - OSPF external type 2
       i - IS-IS, su - IS-IS summary, L1 - IS-IS level-1, L2 -
IS-IS level-2
       ia - IS-IS inter area, * - candidate default, U - per-
user static route
       o - ODR, P - periodic downloaded static route, + -
replicated route
Gateway of last resort is not set
       1.0.0.0/32 is subnetted, 1 subnets
D        1.1.1.1 [90/130816] via 192.168.1.2, 00:07:15,
GigabitEthernet1/0
       192.168.1.0/24 is variably subnetted, 2 subnets, 2 masks
C        192.168.1.0/24 is directly connected,
GigabitEthernet2/0
L        192.168.1.1/32 is directly connected,
GigabitEthernet2/0
ISP#sh ip route vrf Organization-B
Routing Table: Organisation-B
Codes: L - local, C - connected, S - static, R - RIP, M -
mobile, B - BGP
       D - EIGRP, EX - EIGRP external, O - OSPF, IA - OSPF
inter area
       N1 - OSPF NSSA external type 1, N2 - OSPF NSSA external
type 2
       E1 - OSPF external type 1, E2 - OSPF external type 2
       i - IS-IS, su - IS-IS summary, L1 - IS-IS level-1, L2 -
IS-IS level-2
       ia - IS-IS inter area, * - candidate default, U - per-
user static route
       o - ODR, P - periodic downloaded static route, + -
replicated route
Gateway of last resort is not set
       1.0.0.0/32 is subnetted, 1 subnets
D        1.1.1.1 [90/130816] via 192.168.1.2, 00:06:13,
GigabitEthernet2/0
       192.168.1.0/24 is variably subnetted, 2 subnets, 2 masks
C        192.168.1.0/24 is directly connected,
```

```
GigabitEthernet1/0
L        192.168.1.1/32 is directly connected,
GigabitEthernet1/0
ISP#sh ip eigrp vrf Organization-A neighbors
EIGRP-IPv4 Neighbors for AS(100) VRF(A)
H   Address                 Interface        Hold Uptime    SRTT
RTO  Q  Seq
                                             (sec)          (ms)
Cnt Num
0   192.168.1.2             Gi1/0            11 00:10:43     40
240  0  2
ISP#sh ip eigrp vrf Organization-B neighbors
EIGRP-IPv4 Neighbors for AS(100) VRF(B)
H   Address                 Interface        Hold Uptime    SRTT
RTO  Q  Seq
                                             (sec)          (ms)
Cnt Num
0   192.168.1.2             Gi2/0            14 00:14:00     25
200  0  4
Test Connectivity With Organisation-A and Organisation-B
Routers Loopback Interfaces From ISP Router, Which has an IP
Address of 1.1.1.1 Respectively
ISP#ping vrf Organization-A 1.1.1.1                      '
Type escape sequence to abort.
Sending 5, 100-byte ICMP Echos to 1.1.1.1, timeout is 2
seconds:
!!!!!
Success rate is 100 percent (5/5), round-trip min/avg/max =
20/28/44 ms
ISP#ping vrf Organization-B 1.1.1.1
Type escape sequence to abort.
Sending 5, 100-byte ICMP Echos to 1.1.1.1, timeout is 2
seconds:
!!!!!
Success rate is 100 percent (5/5), round-trip min/avg/max =
8/16/24 ms
```

VRF AWARE OSPF CONFIGURATION

Organization-A Configuration

```
Organization-A#
Organization-A#configure terminal
Organization-A(config)#interface gigabitEthernet 1/0
 ip address 192.168.1.2 255.255.255.0
 no shutdown
 Organization-A(config)#interface loopback 1
 ip address 1.1.1.1 255.255.255.255
```

Configure Routing for Organisation-A Router

```
Organisation-A (config)# router ospf 1
  network 192.168.1.0 0.0.0.255 area 0
  network 1.1.1.0 0.0.0.255 area 0
```

Organization-B Configuration

```
Organization-B#
Organization-B#configure terminal
Organization-B#Interface gigabitEthernet 2/0
  ip address 192.168.1.2 255.255.255.0
  no shutdown
  exit
  Interface loopback 1
  ip address 1.1.1.1 255.255.255.255
```

Configure Routing for Organisation-B Router

```
Organisation-B (config)# router ospf 1
  network 192.168.1.0 0.0.0.255 area 0
  network 1.1.1.0 0.0.0.255 area 0
```

ISP CONFIGURATION

Enters VRF Configuration Mode and Assigns a VRF Name

Note: create VRFs before configure the IP address of the interfaces of ISP Router otherwise the router will remove the IP address.

```
ISP#
ISP#configure terminal
ip vrf Organization-A
 Exit
   ip vrf Organization-B
   Exit
```

Create Each Sub Interface of ISP Router and Place Them Into the Appropriate VRF.

```
Interface gigabitEthernet 1/0
ip vrf forwarding Organization-A
ip address 192.168.1.1 255.255.255.0
no shutdown
exit
interface gigabitEthernet 2/0
ip vrf forwarding Organization-B
ip address 192.168.1.1 255.255.255.0
no shutdown
```

Configure Routing for VRFs

```
router ospf 1 vrf Organization-A
 router-id 2.2.2.2
   network 192.168.1.0 0.0.0.255 area 0
router ospf 2 vrf Organization-B
 router-id 3.3.3.3
 network 192.168.1.0 0.0.0.255 area 0
```

Check the Virtual Interface Table Uses the Following Command "show ip vrf Interface":

```
ISP#show ip vrf interfaces
Interface               IP-Address      VRF
Protocol
Gi1/0                   192.168.1.1     Organization-A
up
Gi2/0                   192.168.1.1     Organization-B
up
```

Check the OSPF Neighbor Uses the Following Command "Show IP ospf Neighbor":

```
ISP#sh ip ospf neighbor
Neighbor ID     Pri     State       Dead Time   Address
Interface
1.1.1.1           1     FULL/DR     00:00:32    192.168.1.2
GigabitEthernet2/0
1.1.1.1           1     FULL/DR     00:00:30    192.168.1.2
GigabitEthernet1/0
```

Check the Virtual Routing Table uses the Following Command "Show ip Route vrf vrf-Name":

```
ISP#sh ip route vrf Organization-A
Routing Table: Organisation-A
Codes: L - local, C - connected, S - static, R - RIP, M -
mobile, B - BGP
       D - EIGRP, EX - EIGRP external, O - OSPF, IA - OSPF
inter area
       N1 - OSPF NSSA external type 1, N2 - OSPF NSSA external
type 2
       E1 - OSPF external type 1, E2 - OSPF external type 2
       i - IS-IS, su - IS-IS summary, L1 - IS-IS level-1, L2 -
IS-IS level-2
       ia - IS-IS inter area, * - candidate default, U - per-
user static route
       o - ODR, P - periodic downloaded static route, + -
replicated route
Gateway of last resort is not set
       1.0.0.0/32 is subnetted, 1 subnets
O         1.1.1.1 [110/2] via 192.168.1.2, 00:07:30,
```

```
GigabitEthernet1/0
     192.168.1.0/24 is variably subnetted, 2 subnets, 2 masks
C        192.168.1.0/24 is directly connected,
GigabitEthernet1/0
L        192.168.1.1/32 is directly connected,
GigabitEthernet1/0
ISP#sh ip route vrf Organization-B
Routing Table:Organisation- B
Codes: L - local, C - connected, S - static, R - RIP, M -
mobile, B - BGP
       D - EIGRP, EX - EIGRP external, O - OSPF, IA - OSPF
inter area
       N1 - OSPF NSSA external type 1, N2 - OSPF NSSA external
type 2
       E1 - OSPF external type 1, E2 - OSPF external type 2
       i - IS-IS, su - IS-IS summary, L1 - IS-IS level-1, L2 -
IS-IS level-2
       ia - IS-IS inter area, * - candidate default, U - per-
user static route
       o - ODR, P - periodic downloaded static route, + -
replicated route
Gateway of last resort is not set
     1.0.0.0/32 is subnetted, 1 subnets
O        1.1.1.1 [110/2] via 192.168.1.2, 00:07:31,
GigabitEthernet2/0
     192.168.1.0/24 is variably subnetted, 2 subnets, 2 masks
C        192.168.1.0/24 is directly connected,
GigabitEthernet2/0
L        192.168.1.1/32 is directly connected,
GigabitEthernet2/0
```

Test Connectivity with Organisation-A and Organisation-B Routers Loopback Interfaces from ISP Router, Which has an IP Address of 1.1.1.1 Respectively.

```
ISP#ping vrf Organization-A 1.1.1.1
Type escape sequence to abort.
Sending 5, 100-byte ICMP Echos to 1.1.1.1, timeout is 2
seconds:
!!!!!
Success rate is 100 percent (5/5), round-trip min/avg/max =
```

```
20/28/44 ms
ISP#ping vrf Organization-B 1.1.1.1
Type escape sequence to abort.
Sending 5, 100-byte ICMP Echos to 1.1.1.1, timeout is 2
seconds:
!!!!!
Success rate is 100 percent (5/5), round-trip min/avg/max =
8/16/24 ms
```

CONCLUSION AND FUTURE TRENDS

Innovative Virtualization models can reduce Infrastructure costs significantly. Networking is shifting from Hardware to Software as the Organizations are increasingly adopting SDx (Software-Defined anything) model to minimize costs by replacing traditional hardware with software. The Intelligence, control and services are moving to software. Hardware is moving to Layer 3 Fabric (packet forwarding).

REFERENCES

Grand View Research, Inc. (2015, April). *Global MPLS IP VPN Services Market By Service (Layer 2, Layer 3) By Application (Automated Machines, Video Conferencing, Audio Conferencing) Expected To Reach USD 46.26 Billion by 2020*. Grand View Research, Inc. Retrieved March 05, 2017, from http://www. grandviewresearch.com/press-release/global-mpls-ip-vpn-services-market https:// www.pdf-archive.com/2016/12/07/mpls-ip-vpn-services-market-2020/mpls-ip-vpn-services-market-2020.pdf

Infiniti Research Limited. (2015, December 23). *Global Software-defined Anything (SDx) Market 2016-2020*. Retrieved March 05, 2017, from http://www.technavio. com/report/global-it-professional-services-software-defined-anything-sdx-market

Marchi, T. (2010, March 31). (PPT) *Internet 2020: The Future Connection - Mass Technology Leadership Council*. Retrieved March 05, 2017 from http://www.masstlc. org/news/91961/PPT-Internet-2020-The-Future-Connection-.htm

National Security Research Division. (2016). *The Global Technology Revolution 2020, In-Depth Analyses*. RAND Corporation. Retrieved March 5, 2017, from http:// www.rand.org/content/dam/rand/pubs/technical_reports/2006/RAND_TR303.pdf

Pankert, G., Faggiano, A., & Taga, K. (2014, May). *The Future of the Internet Innovation and Investment in IP Interconnection.* Retrieved March 5, 2017, from http://www.adlittle.com/downloads/tx_adlreports/ADL_LibertyGlobal_2014_FutureOfTheInternet.pdf

KEY TERMS AND DEFINTIONS

Backbone Networks: Is a high speed network linking an organization's LANs, making information transfer possible between departments using high speed circuits to connect LANs. Also provide connections to other backbones such as MANs, and WANs. Sometimes referred to as Enterprise network, or Campus-wide network.

Enhanced Interior Gateway Routing Protocol (EIGRP): Enhanced Interior Gateway Routing Protocol is the enhanced version Interior Gateway Routing Protocol (IGRP) was developed in 1985 to overcome RIPv1's limited hop count. Basically, a Distance vector routing protocol. The metrics used by IGRP are bandwidth (used by default), Delay (used by default), reliability and load.

Enhanced Interior Gateway Routing Protocol (EIGRP): Is a Cisco proprietary protocol, advanced version of IGRP. EIGRP is a Hybrid routing protocol (best of SPF and Distance vector), Supports CIDR/VLSM. Also supports multiple routed protocols independently. EIGRP uses the DUAL (Diffusing Update Algorithm) to calculate routes. The five EIGRP packet types are: Hello, Acknowledgment, Update, Query and Reply.

FEC (Forwarding Equivalence Class): A group of IP packets which are forwarded in the same manner (e.g., over the same path, with the same priority and the same label).

Gateways: Gateways operate at the network or application layer and use network layer addresses in processing messages. The Gateways connect two or more LANs that use the same or different (usually different) data link and network protocols. Gateways process only those messages explicitly addressed to them.

Graphical Network Simulator: GNS3 grew out of a Master's thesis by Jeremy Grossman. GNS3 is a Python suite of tools which glue together a Cisco emulator with virtualization platforms in an easy to use GUI. Emphasis is on network design. GNS3 run Virtualbox Machines, QEMU/KVM Machines and VMWare Machines.

Hello Protocol: Responsible to establish and maintain neighbor relationships for OSPF. Elects designated router in multi-access networks. Hello packets are small, easy to process packets. Hello packets are sent periodically (usually short interval).

Internet Users: 3~4 billions in 2020 (~1 Billion with computer, ~3 Billion with cellular) (Marchi, 2010).

Label Switched Paths (LSPs): Network paths are "named" by the label at the path's entry point. At each hop, label determines the Outgoing interface and the New label to attach. The Label distribution protocol is responsible for disseminating signaling information.

Label: A short fixed length identifier which is used to identify an FEC.

Layer 2 and Layer 3 VPNs: Layer 2 (Data Link Layer) VPNs can carry traffic for many different protocols, whereas Layer 3 (Network or IP Layer) is "IP only". Layer 2 VPN are complicated to provision, but Layer 3 VPNs are more flexible, easy to configure.

MPLS: MPLS simplifies the forwarding function of a conventional router by taking a totally different approach by introducing a connection oriented mechanism inside the connectionless IP networks. In MPLS a Label Switched Path (LSP) is set up for each route. MPLS provides an efficient and scalable tunneling mechanism provides an efficient and scalable mechanism for extending IP routing with explicit routes. MPLS is suitable for Traffic Engineering (Traffic redirection through BGP or IGP shortcut), Virtual Private Networks, both Layer 2 (Point to Point, Virtual Private Lan) and Layer 3 (BGP/MPLS VPN's, RFC 2547) VPNs. Disadvantages of MPLS include an additional layer is added and the router has to understand MPLS. According to a market survey by Grand View Research, Inc. the Global MPLS IP VPN Services Market is expected to reach US $ 46.26 billion by 2020 (Grand View Research, Inc. (2015, April)).

Network Virtualization: Is the ability to run multiple virtual networks that have a separate control and data plane, co-exist together on top of one physical network, can be managed by individual parties that does not necessarily trust each other. Few examples of Network Virtualization are Enterprise and Campus networks (VLANs), Secure private networks operating across wide areas (VPNs) and Multi-tenant data centers (collection of VM's connected to a "virtual switch"). However the convergence of technologies will raise the issues of social issues are the privacy and anonymity (National Security Research Division. (2016)).

Open Shortest Path First Protocol (OSPF): Every OSPF router sends out 'hello' packets. Hello packets used to determine if a neighbor is up. Motivation for development of OSPF includes Problems with Distance Vector Protocol such as large update packets, slow response to topological changes, Need for a Link State Protocol and a long list of functional requirements.

Reliable Transport Protocol (RTP): Is responsible for guaranteeing, ordered delivery of EIGRP packets to all neighbors.

Routing Information Protocol: A simple intradomain protocol, RIP is a straightforward implementation of Distance Vector Routing. Each router advertises its distance vector every 30 seconds (or whenever its routing table changes) to all of its neighbors. RIP always uses 1 as link metric. Maximum hop count is 15, with "16" equal to "∞". Routes are timeout (set to 16) after 3 minutes if they are not updated.

SDx (Software-Defined Anything): Segmentation by technology and analysis of the SDx market are Software-defined data center (SDDC), Software-defined storage (SDS) and Software-defined networking (SDN). The Network Function Virtualization (NFV) market will grow by more than 32% by 2020 (Infiniti Research Limited. (2015, December 23)).

Virtual Private Network: Is a type of private network that uses public telecommunication, such as the Internet, instead of leased lines to communicate. VPNs allow authorized users to pass through the firewalls. 3 types of implementations of VPN are Intranet (Within an organization), Extranet (Outside an organization) and Remote Access (Employee to Business). A VPN can be Server based, Firewall based or Router based (including VPN appliances).

Virtual Router: A virtual router (VR) is an emulation of a physical router at the software and hardware levels. VRs have independent IP routing and forwarding tables and they are isolated from each other. Two main functions of VR are Defining routing using any routing technology and Forwarding packets to the next hops within the VPN domain. A virtual router provides the same functionality as a physical router from the users' point of view.

VLAN (Virtual LAN): VLANs is analogous to a group of end-stations, on single/multiple physical LAN segments, not constrained by their physical location and can communicate as if they were on a common LAN. VLANs provide greater opportunities to manage the flow of traffic on the LAN and reduce broadcast traffic between segments. VLANs can be assigned and managed dynamically without physical limitations. The key benefit of VLANs is that they permit the network administrator to organize the LAN logically instead of physically. VLAN can be used to balance bandwidth allotment per group. Switches are Layer 2 devices while Router is Layer 3 devices. Data between subnets/networks must pass through a router. Routers are needed to pass information between different VLANs since a switch cannot route data between different VLANs. Routers in VLAN topologies provide broadcast filtering, security, and traffic flow management.

Compilation of References

(1926). Darch, Peter, & Carusi, A. (2010). Retaining volunteers in volunteer computing projects. *Philosophical Transactions of the Royal Society A: Mathematical, Physical and Engineering Sciences, 368*, 4177–4192.

Aazam, M., & Huh, E.N. (2014, August). Fog computing and smart gateway based communication for cloud of things. *Proceedings of the 2014 International Conference on Future Internet of Things and Cloud (FiCloud)* (pp. 464-470). IEEE.

Adabala, S., Chadha, V., Chawla, P., Figueiredo, R., Fortes, J., Krsul, I., & Zhao, M. et al. (2005). From virtualized resources to virtual computing grids: The In-VIGO system. *Future Generation Computer Systems, 21*(6), 896–909. doi:10.1016/j.future.2003.12.021

Adair, R. J., Bayles, R. U., Comeau, L. W., & Creasy, R. J. (1966). A Virtual Machine System for the 360/40. IBM Corporation Cambridge Scientific Center Report No. 320-2007.

Adeshiyan, T., Attanasio, C. R., Farr, E. M., Harper, R. E., Pelleg, D., Schulz, C., & Tomek, L. A. et al. (2009, July). Using virtualization for high availability and disaster recovery. *IBM Journal of Research and Development, 53*(4), 1–11. doi:10.1147/JRD.2009.5429062

Aliyev, A., & Samadov, R. (2016). *E-commerce payments with cloud service mbaas*. Doctoral dissertation.

Anderson, D. P. (2004). BOINC: A System for Public-Resource Computing and Storage. *Proceedings of the Fifth IEEE/ACM International Workshop on Grid Computing* (pp. 4-10). doi:10.1109/GRID.2004.14

Anderson, P. D., & Fedak, G. (2006). The computational and storage potential of volunteer computing. *Proceedings of Sixth IEEE International Symposium on Cluster Computing and the Grid* (pp. 73-80). doi:10.1109/CCGRID.2006.101

Anderson, T., Peterson, L., Shenker, S., & Turner, J. (2005). Overcoming the Internet impasse through virtualization. *Computer, 38*(4), 34–41. doi:10.1109/MC.2005.136

Apache.org. (n. d.). Environment setup for developer. Retrieved from https://cwiki.apache.org/confluence/display/CLOUDSTACK/Setting+up+a+CloudStack+dev+environment+on+Windows

Apache.org. (n. d.a). Apache CloudStack. Retrieved from https://cloudstack.apache.org/

Apache.org. (n. d.b). CloudStack Installation Documentation. Retrieved from http://docs. cloudstack.apache.org/projects/cloudstack-installation/en/4.6/

Armbrust, M., Fox, A., Griffith, R., Joseph, A. D., Katz, R., Konwinski, A., & Zaharia, M. et al. (2009). A view of cloud computing. *Communications of the ACM, 53*(4), 50–58. doi:10.1145/1721654.1721672

Armstrong, R., Gannon, D., Geist, A., Keahey, K., Kohn, S., McInnes, L., & Smolinski, B. et al. (1999). Toward a common component architecture for high-performance scientific computing. *Proceedings of The Eighth International Symposium on High Performance Distributed Computing,* Redondo Beach, California, USA (pp. 115-124). doi:10.1109/HPDC.1999.805289

Barroso, L. A., Clidaras, J., & Hölzle, U. (2013). The datacenter as a computer: An introduction to the design of warehouse-scale machines. *Synthesis lectures on computer architecture, 8*(3), 1-154.

Beberg, L., A., Ensign, D. L., Guha Jayachandran, Khaliq, S., & Pande, V. S. (2009). Folding@ home:Lessons from eight years of volunteer distributed computing. *Proceedings of the IEEE International Symposium on Parallel & Distributed Processing* (pp. 1-8).

Beck, R., Schwind, M., & Hinz, O. (2008). Grid economics in departmentalized enterprises. *Journal of Grid Computing, 6*(3), 277–290. doi:10.1007/s10723-008-9102-3

Betonio, D. (2011, April 18). 12 excellent cloud computing operating systems. *Tripwiremagazine. com.* Retrieved October 17, 2016, from http://www.tripwiremagazine.com/2011/04/12-excellent-cloud-computing-operating-systems.html

Binge, C., Kaiyuan, Q., & Weilong, D. (2007). GridDoc: A End-User-Oriented Presentation Model for Resource Integration. *Proceedings of the IEEE Sixth International Conference on Grid and Cooperative Computing (GCC '07),* Urumchi, Xinjiang, China (pp. 261-266). doi:10.1109/ GCC.2007.74

Blinn, J. F. (1977). Models of light reflection for computer synthesized pictures. *Computer Graphics, 11*(2), 192–198. doi:10.1145/965141.563893

Bonomi, F., Milito, R., Zhu, J., & Addepalli, S. (2012, August). Fog computing and its role in the internet of things. *Proceedings of the first edition of the MCC workshop on Mobile cloud computing* (pp. 13-16). ACM. doi:10.1145/2342509.2342513

Brunthaler, S. (2009). Virtual-Machine abstraction and optimization techniques. *Electronic Notes in Theoretical Computer Science, 253*(5), 3–14. doi:10.1016/j.entcs.2009.11.011

Buyya, R., & Venugopal, S. (2005). A gentle introduction to grid computing and technologies. *CSI Communications, 29*(1), 9–19.

Buyya, R., Yeo, C. S., Venugopal, S., Broberg, J., & Brandic, I. (2009). Cloud computing and emerging IT platforms: Vision, hype, and reality for delivering computing as the 5th utility. *Future Generation Computer Systems, 25*(6), 599–616. doi:10.1016/j.future.2008.12.001

bwIDM Project management (2013). *Federating IT-based services at Baden-Württemberg's Universities.* Retrieved from https://www.bwidm.de/wp-content/uploads/bwidm-booklet.pdf

Centos. (n. d.). Red Hat Enterprise Linux 5.4. Retrieved from http://www.centos.org/docs/5/html/5.4/Release_Notes/ index.html#id444217

Chase, J. S., Irwin, D. E., Grit, L. E., Moore, J. D., & Sprenkle, S. E. (2003). Dynamic virtual clusters in a grid site manager. *Proceedings of the 12th IEEE International Symposium on High Performance Distributed Computing,* Seattle, WA, USA (pp. 90-100). doi:10.1109/HPDC.2003.1210019

Chen, M., Zhang, Y., Hu, L., Taleb, T., & Sheng, Z. (2015). Cloud-based wireless network: Virtualized, reconfigurable, smart wireless network to enable 5G technologies. *Mobile Networks and Applications, 20*(6), 704–712. doi:10.1007/s11036-015-0590-7

Chikhi, R., Limasset, A., Jackman, S., Simpson, J. T., & Medvedev, P. (2015). On the representation of de Bruijn graphs. *Journal of Computational Biology, 22*(5), 336–352. doi:10.1089/cmb.2014.0160 PMID:25629448

Chilingaryan, S., Kopmann, A., Mirone, A., dos Santos Rolo, T., & Vogelgesang, M. (2011). A GPU-based architecture for real-time data assessment at synchrotron experiments. *Proceedings of the 2011 companion on High Performance Computing Networking, Storage and Analysis Companion - SC '11 Companion (pp 51-52), Seattle.* doi:10.1145/2148600.2148627

Chowdhury, N. M. M. K., & Boutaba, R. (2009). Network virtualization: State of the art and research challenges. *IEEE Communications Magazine, 47*(7), 20–26. doi:10.1109/MCOM.2009.5183468

Chowdhury, N. M. M. K., & Boutaba, R. (2010). A survey of network virtualization. *Computer Networks, 54*(5), 862–876. doi:10.1016/j.comnet.2009.10.017

Chubachi, Y., Shinagawa, T., & Kato, K. (2010). Hypervisor-based prevention of persistent rootkits. *Proceedings of the 2010 ACM Symposium on Applied Computing,* New York, NY, USA (pp. 214-220). doi:10.1145/1774088.1774131

Citrix.com. (n. d.a). Xencenter.msi (software). Retrieved January, from http://downloadns.citrix.com.edgesuite.net/8708/XenCenter.msi?_ga=1.226090010.1819769869.1476463749

Citrix.com. (n. d.b). XenServer 7.0 Standard Edition. Retrieved January, 2017, from www.citrix.com/downloads/xenserver/product-software/xenserver-70-standard-edition.html

Cloetens, P., Bolle, E., Ludwig, W., Baruchel, J., & Schlenke, M. (2001). Absorption and phase imaging with synchrotron radiation. *Europhysics News, 32*(2), 46–50. doi:10.1051/epn:2001203

Cloudstackinstallation. (n. d.). Express Installation which is not customizable and only certain features are installed. Retrieved from http://cloudstackinstallation.readthedocs.io/en/latest/qig.html

Compeau, C. P. E., Pevzner, P. A., & Tesler, G. (2011). How to apply de Bruijn graphs to genome assembly. *Nature Biotechnology, 29*(11), 987–991. doi:10.1038/nbt.2023 PMID:22068540

Deka, G. C. (2014). Cost-Benefit Analysis of Datacenter Consolidation Using Virtualization. *IT Professional*, *16*(6), 54–62. doi:10.1109/MITP.2014.89

Deka, G. C., & Das, P. K. (2014). An Overview on the Virtualization Technology. Handbook of Research on Cloud Infrastructures for Big Data Analytics, 289. doi:10.4018/978-1-4666-5864-6.ch012

Department of State Federal Data Center Consolidation Initiative Plan (DOS FDCCI Plan), Document Release: 3.0 for Public Distribution. (2011, September 30).

Desell, T., Szymanski, B., & Varela, C. (2008). Asynchronous Genetic Search for Scientific Modeling on Large-Scale Heterogeneous Environments. *Proceedings of IEEE International Symposium on Parallel and Distributed Processing* (pp. 1-12). doi:10.1109/IPDPS.2008.4536169

Di Costanzo, A., De Assuncao, M. D., & Buyya, R. (2009). Harnessing cloud technologies for a virtualized distributed computing infrastructure. *IEEE Internet Computing*, *13*(5), 24–33. doi:10.1109/MIC.2009.108

Dinh, H. T., Lee, C., Niyato, D., & Wang, P. (2013). A survey of mobile cloud computing: architecture, applications, and approaches. *Wireless communications and mobile computing*, *13*(18), 1587-1611.

Dobrilovic, D., & Odadžic, B. (2008). Virtualization technology as a tool for teaching computer networks. *International Journal of Social, Behavioral, Educational, Economic, Business and Industrial Engineering*, *2*(1), 41–45.

Durrani, N. (2014). Volunteer computing: Requirements, challenges, and solutions. *Journal of Network and Computer Applications*, *39*, 369–380. doi:10.1016/j.jnca.2013.07.006

Egwutuoha, I. P., Levy, D., Selic, B., & Chen, S. (2013). A survey of fault tolerance mechanisms and checkpoint/restart implementations for high performance computing systems. *The Journal of Supercomputing*, *65*(3), 1302–1326. doi:10.1007/s11227-013-0884-0

Endian Spa. (2017). *Open Source Firewall and UTM*. Retrieved March 19, 2017, from http://www.endian.com/community/overview/

Endian Spa. (2017). *Secure your Business with Endian UTM*. Retrieved March 19, 2017, from http://www.endian.com/products/utm-models/

Fanatical, R. (2014, January 27). XCP overview. Retrieved October 17, 2016, from http://wiki.xen.org/wiki/XCP_Overview#What_is_XCP.3F

Faustine, A., & Mvuma, A. N. (2014). Ubiquitous mobile sensing for water quality monitoring and reporting within lake victoria basin. *Wireless Sensor Network*, *6*(12), 257–264. doi:10.4236/wsn.2014.612025

Fayyad-Kazan, H., Perneel, L., & Timmerman, M. (2013). Benchmarking the Performance of Microsoft Hyper-V server, VMware ESXi and Xen Hypervisors. *Journal of Emerging Trends in Computing and Information Sciences*, *4*(12), 922–933.

Fisher, D., DeLine, R., Czerwinski, M., & Drucker, S. (2012). Interactions with big data analytics. *Interactions-Microsoft Research, 19*(3), 50–59. doi:10.1145/2168931.2168943

Flexiant.com. (2014, February 12). Hypervisor comparison | KVM, Xen, VMware, Hyper-V. Retrieved October 18, 2016, from Hosting Providers, https://www.flexiant.com/2014/02/12/hypervisor-comparison-kvm-xen-vmware-hyper-v/

Foster, I., Kesselman, C., Nick, J. M., & Tuecke, S. (2002). Grid services for distributed system integration. *Computer, 35*(6), 37–46. doi:10.1109/MC.2002.1009167

Fuertes, W., De Vergara, J. E. L., & Meneses, F. (2009). Educational platform using virtualization technologies: Teaching-learning applications and research uses cases. *Proc. II ACE Seminar: Knowledge Construction in Online Collaborative Communities* (Vol. 16).

Galán, F., Fernández, D., Ruiz, J., Walid, O., & de Miguel, T. (2004). Use of virtualization tools in computer network laboratories. *Proceedings of the Fifth International Conference on Information Technology Based Higher Education and Training (ITHET),* Istanbul, Turkey (pp. 209-214). doi:10.1109/ITHET.2004.1358165

Geek4support.com. (2014, August 29). KVM and Virtualization. Retrieved from http://geek4support.com/?p=598

Gharajeh, M. S. (2015). *The Significant Concepts of Cloud Computing: Technology, Architecture, Applications, and Security.* Seattle: CreateSpace Independent Publishing Platform.

Ghule, K., Tikone, N., Sonar, S., Ghate, B., & Sonone, S. (2015). *Android App With Integration Of Quickblox XAMPP Chatting, Google GCM And Client-Server Architecture.*

Gmb, H. P. I. (1999). NEW! Parallels desktop 12 for Mac. Retrieved October 16, 2016, from http://www.parallels.com/

Goldberg, R. P. (1974). Survey of Virtual Machines Research. *Computer, 7*(6), 34–45.

Grand View Research, Inc. (2015, April). *Global MPLS IP VPN Services Market By Service (Layer 2, Layer 3) By Application (Automated Machines, Video Conferencing, Audio Conferencing) Expected To Reach USD 46.26 Billion by 2020.* Grand View Research, Inc. Retrieved March 05, 2017, from http://www.grandviewresearch.com/press-release/global-mpls-ip-vpn-services-market https://www.pdf-archive.com/2016/12/07/mpls-ip-vpn-services-market-2020/mpls-ip-vpn-services-market-2020.pdf

Guarino, J. (2010, June 18). Network Security: Three open-source options. *Csoonlin.com.* Retrieved March 19, 2017, from http://www.csoonline.com/article/2125265/cloud-security/network-security--three-open-source-options.html

Han, B., Gopalakrishnan, V., Ji, L., & Lee, S. (2015). Network function virtualization: Challenges and opportunities for innovations. *IEEE Communications Magazine, 53*(2), 90–97. doi:10.1109/MCOM.2015.7045396

Hartmann, K., Laumann, M., Bergmann, P., Heethoff, M., & Schmelzle, S. (2016). Development of the synganglion and morphology of the adult nervous system in the mite *Archegozetes longisetosus* Aoki (Chelicerata, Actinotrichida, Oribatida). *Journal of Morphology, 277*(4), 537–548. doi:10.1002/jmor.20517 PMID:26873119

Hashicorp.com. (n. d.). Vagrant 1.8. Retrieved from https://www.hashicorp.com/blog/vagrant-1-8/

Heethoff, M., & Norton, R. A. (2009). A new use for synchrotron x-ray microtomography: Three-dimensional biomechanical modeling of chelicerate mouthparts and calculation of theoretical bite forces. *Invertebrate Biology, 128*(4), 332–339. doi:10.1111/j.1744-7410.2009.00183.x

Hou, X., Li, Y., Chen, M., Wu, D., Jin, D., & Chen, S. (2016). Vehicular fog computing: A viewpoint of vehicles as the infrastructures. *IEEE Transactions on Vehicular Technology, 65*(6), 3860–3873. doi:10.1109/TVT.2016.2532863

Howtogeek.com. (n. d.). How to Install KVM and Create Virtual Machines on Ubuntu. Retrieved from https://www.howtogeek.com/117635/how-to-install-kvm-and-create-virtual-machines-on-ubuntu/

http://searchservervirtualization.techtarget.com/tip/Virtual-memory-management-techniques-A-beginners-guide

Hu, W., Hicks, A., Zhang, L., Dow, E. M., Soni, V., & Jiang, H. ... Matthews, J. N. (2013). A quantitative study of virtual machine live migration. *Proceedings of the 2013 ACM Cloud and Autonomic Computing Conference CAC '13*. doi:10.1145/2494621.2494622

Hu, Y. C., Patel, M., Sabella, D., Sprecher, N., & Young, V. (2015). Mobile edge computing—A key technology towards 5G (no. 11). ETSI White Paper.

Huang, W., Liu, J., Abali, B., & Panda, D. K. (2006). A case for high performance computing with virtual machines. *Proceedings of the 20th annual international conference on Supercomputing (ICS '06)*, Cairns, Queensland, Australia (pp. 125-134). doi:10.1145/1183401.1183421

Hyper-V. (2016). In Wikipedia. Retrieved from http://en.wikipedia.org/wiki/Hyper-V

Infiniti Research Limited. (2015, December 23). *Global Software-defined Anything (SDx) Market 2016-2020*. Retrieved March 05, 2017, from http://www.technavio.com/report/global-it-professional-services-software-defined-anything-sdx-market

Intel, I. T. Center. (2013). *Virtualization and Cloud Computing*, pp. 1-23. Retrieved January 24, 2017, from http://www.intel.com/content/dam/www/public/us/en/documents/guides/cloud-computing-virtualization-building-private-iaas-guide.pdf

Ishtiaq Ali1 and Natarajan Meghanathan. (2011, 01). Virtual machines and networks –installation, performance, study, advantages and virtualization options. Retrieved from http://airccse.org/journal/nsa/0111jnsa01.pdf

Jackson, K., Bunch, C., & Sigler, E. (2015). *OpenStack cloud computing cookbook*. Packt Publishing Ltd.

Jain, N., & Choudhary, S. (2016). Overview of virtualization in cloud computing. *Proceedings of the IEEE Symposium on Colossal Data Analysis and Networking (CDAN)*, Indore, Madhya Pradesh, India (pp. 1-4).

Jain, R., & Paul, S. (2013). Network virtualization and software defined networking for cloud computing: A survey. *IEEE Communications Magazine, 51*(11), 24–31. doi:10.1109/MCOM.2013.6658648

Jarząb, M., Kosiński, J., Zieliński, K., & Zieliński, S. (2012). User-oriented provisioning of secure virtualized infrastructure. In M. Bubak, T. Szepieniec, & K. Wiatr (Eds.), *Building a national distributed e-infrastructure–PL-Grid* (pp. 73–88). Berlin: Springer. doi:10.1007/978-3-642-28267-6_6

Javatpoint.com. (2017). Virtualization in cloud computing. Retrieved January 14, 2017, from http://www.javatpoint.com/virtualization-in-cloud-computing

Jayaraman, A., & Rayapudi, P. (2012), Comparative study of Virtual Machine Software Packages with real operating system [Master's Thesis]. School of Computing, Blekinge Institute of Technology, Karlskrona, Sweden.

Jin, H., & Liao, X. F. (2008). Virtualization technology for computing system. *China Basic Science, 10*(6), 12–18.

Jujucharms.com. (n. d.). Juju. In Canonical. Retrieved from https://jujucharms.com/

Kacsuk, P. (2011). How to make BOINC based desktop grids even more popular. *Proceedings of IEEE International Symposium on Parallel and Distributed Processing Workshops and Ph.D Forum* (pp. 1871-1877). doi:10.1109/IPDPS.2011.350

Kaur, P., & Rani, A. (2015). Virtual Machine Migration in Cloud Computing. *International Journal of Grid and Distributed Computing, 8*(5), 337–342. doi:10.14257/ijgdc.2015.8.5.33

Kavis, M. J. (2014). *Architecting the cloud: Design decisions for cloud computing service models (SaaS, PaaS, AND IaaS)*. John Wiley & Sons. doi:10.1002/9781118691779

Khanna, G., Beaty, K., Kar, G., & Kochut, A. (2006). Application Performance Management Virtualized Server Environments. *Proceedings of the 10th IEEE/IFIP Network Operations and Management Symposium NOMS '06* (pp. 373-381).

Kim, J., & Forsythe, S. (2010). Factors affecting adoption of product virtualization technology for online consumer electronics shopping. *International Journal of Retail & Distribution Management, 38*(3), 190–204. doi:10.1108/09590551011027122

Kirkland, J., Carmichael, D., Tinker, C. L., & Tinker, G. L. (2006). *Linux Troubleshooting for System Administrators and Power Users* (1st ed.). Prentice Hall.

Köhler, J., Labitzke, S., Simon, M., Nussbaumer, M., & Hartenstein, H. (2012). FACIUS: An easy-to-deploy SAML-based approach to Federate non web-based services. *Proceedings of the 2012 IEEE 11th International Conference on Trust, Security and Privacy in Computing and Communications*. doi:10.1109/trustcom.2012.158

Köhler, J., Simon, M., Nussbaumer, M., & Hartenstein, H. (2013). Federating HPC access via SAML: Towards a plug-and-play solution. In Supercomputing, LNCS (pp. 462–473). doi:10.1007/978-3-642-38750-0_35

Kruger, J., & Westermann, R. (2003). Acceleration techniques for GPU-based volume rendering. *Proceedings of the 14th IEEE Visualization 2003 (VIS'03)* (pp. 287-292). doi:10.1109/VISUAL.2003.1250384

Kumar, R., Gupta, N., Charu, S., Jain, K., & Jangir, S. K. (2014). Open source solution for cloud computing platform using OpenStack. *International Journal of Computer Science and Mobile Computing*, *3*(5), 89–98.

Kurth, L. (n. d.). Xen cloud platform at build a cloud a day at scale 10x. Retrieved from http://www.slideshare.net/xen_com_mgr/xen-cloud-platform-at-build-a-cloud-day-at-scale-10x

Lander, S. E., & Waterman, M. S. (1988). Genomic mapping by fingerprinting random clones: A mathematical analysis. *Genomics*, *2*(3), 231–239. doi:10.1016/0888-7543(88)90007-9 PMID:3294162

Lane, K. (2015). *Overview of the backend as a service (BaaS) space*.

Larman, C., & Basili, V. R. (2003). Iterative and incremental development: A brief history. *Computer*, *36*(6), 47-56.

Li, Z., Chen, Y., Mu, D., Yuan, J., Shi, Y., Zhang, H., ... Yang, B.(2012). Comparison of the two major classes of assembly algorithms: Overlap–layout–consensus and de-bruijn-graph. *Briefings in Functional Genomics*, *11*(1), 25-37.

Liang, C., & Yu, F. R. (2015). Wireless network virtualization: A survey, some research issues and challenges. *IEEE Communications Surveys and Tutorials*, *17*(1), 358–380. doi:10.1109/COMST.2014.2352118

Li, J., Jia, Y., Liu, L., & Wo, T. (2013). CyberLiveApp: A secure sharing and migration approach for live virtual desktop applications in a cloud environment. *Future Generation Computer Systems*, *29*(1), 330–340. doi:10.1016/j.future.2011.08.001

Limited, V. (n.d.). *About Us - V2Soft*. Retrieved December 29, 2016, from https://www.v2soft.com/about-us

Lin, X., Sun, X., Lu, X., Deng, Q., Li, M., . . . Chen, L. (2004). Recent Advances in CFD Grid Application Platform. *Proceedings of the 2004 IEEE International Conference on Services Computing* (pp. 588-591).

Linuxgateway.in. (n. d.). How to configure VPN Service in Endian Firewall 3.0 Part – 4 - Linux Gateway. Retrieved from http://linuxgateway.in/configure-vpn-service-endian-firewall-3-0-part-4/

Litzkow, J., M., Livny, M., & Mutka, M. W. (n.d.). Condor-a hunter of idle workstations. *Proceedings of IEEE, 8th International Conference on Distributed Computing Systems* (pp. 104-111).

Loomis, C. (2010). *Review of the Use of Cloud and Virtualization Technologies in Grid Infrastructures, HAL-IN2P3*. Retrieved February 15, 2017, from http://hal.in2p3.fr/docs/00/68/71/59/PDF/stratuslab-d2.1-v1.2.pdf

Lösel, P., & Heuveline, V. (2016). Enhancing a diffusion algorithm for 4D image segmentation using local information. In *Medical Imaging 2016: Image Processing*. doi:.10.1117/12.2216202

Marchi, T. (2010, March 31). (PPT) *Internet 2020: The Future Connection - Mass Technology Leadership Council*. Retrieved March 05, 2017 from http://www.masstlc.org/news/91961/PPT-Internet-2020-The-Future-Connection-.htm

Martignoni, L., Paleari, R., Fresi Roglia, G., & Bruschi, D. (2010). Testing system virtual machines. *Proceedings of the 19th international symposium on Software testing and analysis (ISSTA '10)*, Trento, Italy (pp. 171-182).

Martins, J., Ahmed, M., Raiciu, C., Olteanu, V., Honda, M., Bifulco, R., & Huici, F. (2014, April). ClickOS and the art of network function virtualization. *Proceedings of the 11th USENIX Conference on Networked Systems Design and Implementation* (pp. 459-473). USENIX Association.

Mauch, V., Bonn, M., Chilingaryan, S., Kopmann, A., Mexner, W., & Ressmann, D. (2014, October). OpenGL-BASED data analysis in virtualized self-service environments. *Proceedings of the PCaPAC 2014* (pp. 234-236). Karlsruhe, Germany.

Maxam, M. A., & Gilbert, W. (1977). A new method for sequencing DNA. *Proceedings of the National Academy of Sciences of the United States of America*, 74(2), 560–564. doi:10.1073/pnas.74.2.560 PMID:265521

MediaWiki.org. (2014). Kernel based Virtual Machine. Retrieved from http://www.linux-kvm.org/page/Main_Page

Mell, P., & Grance, T. (n. d.). "Cloud Computing" by National Institute of Standards and Technology. Retrieved from www.csrc.nist.gov

Mell, P., & Grance, T. (2010). The NIST definition of cloud computing. *Communications of the ACM*, 53(6), 50.

Miller, R. J., Koren, S., & Sutton, G. (2010). Assembly algorithms for next-generation sequencing data. *Genomics*, 95(6), 315–327. doi:10.1016/j.ygeno.2010.03.001 PMID:20211242

Multi Data Palembang. (2008, February 13). Xen architecture overview. Retrieved from http://repository.mdp.ac.id/ebook/library-sw-hw/linux-1/cloud/xen/docs/XenArchitecture_Q12008

Narzisi, G., & Mishra, B. (2011). Comparing De Novo Genome Assembly: The Long and Short of It. *PLoS ONE, 6*(4), e19175. doi:10.1371/journal.pone.0019175 PMID:21559467

National Security Research Division. (2016). *The Global Technology Revolution 2020, In-Depth Analyses.* RAND Corporation. Retrieved March 5, 2017, from http://www.rand.org/content/dam/rand/pubs/technical_reports/2006/RAND_TR303.pdf

Nicolae, B. (2012). Bridging the gap between HPC and IaaS clouds.

Nunes, B. A. A., Mendonca, M., Nguyen, X. N., Obraczka, K., & Turletti, T. (2014). A survey of software-defined networking: Past, present, and future of programmable networks. *IEEE Communications Surveys and Tutorials, 16*(3), 1617–1634. doi:10.1109/SURV.2014.012214.00180

NVidia Corporation. (2013). NVidia grid k2 graphics board Specification. Retrieved November 23, 2016, from http://www.nvidia.com/content/grid/pdf/GRID_K2_BD-06580-001_v02.pdf

Openstack. (n. d.). Openstack software. Retrieved from https://www.openstack.org/software/

Otey, M. (2013, June 03). Top 10 Windows Server 2012 R2 Hyper-V New Features. Retrieved October 25, 2016, from http://windowsitpro.com/hyper-v/top-10-windows-server-2012-r2-hyper-v-new-features

Packtpub.com. (n. d.). VirtualBox architecture- Getting Started with Oracle VM VirtualBox. Retrieved from https://www.packtpub.com/mapt/book/Virtualization+and+Cloud/9781782177821/1/ch01lvl1sec14/Oracle+VM+VirtualBox+architecture

Paneque, L., & Katrib, M. (2011). HAMLET: Heterogeneous Application Middleware Layer for Extensive Tasks. *Proceedings of CIBSE2011* (pp. 11-23).

Pankaj, J., Palit, A., & Kurien, P. (2004). *The time boxing process model for iterative software development.* In *Advances in Computers* (Vol. 6, pp. 67–103). .

Pankert, G., Faggiano, A., & Taga, K. (2014, May). *The Future of the Internet Innovation and Investment in IP Interconnection.* Retrieved March 5, 2017, from http://www.adlittle.com/downloads/tx_adlreports/ADL_LibertyGlobal_2014_FutureOfTheInternet.pdf

Pedram, M., & Hwang, I. (2010). Power and Performance Modeling in a Virtualized Server System. *Proceedings of the 2010 39th International Conference on Parallel Processing Workshops (ICPPW)* (pp. 520-526).

Pepple, K. (2011). *Deploying openstack.* O'Reilly Media, Inc.

Pevzner, P., Tang, H., & Waterman, M. S. (2001). An Eulerian path approach to DNA fragment assembly. *Proceedings of the National Academy of Sciences of the United States of America, 98*(17), 9748–9753. doi:10.1073/pnas.171285098 PMID:11504945

Posted, & Kurth, L. (2013). VS16: Video spotlight with Xen project's Lars Kurth. Retrieved October 16, 2016, from http://www.xen.org

Protti, D. J. (2009, October 1). Linux KVM as a Learning Tool. *Linux Journal, 186.*

Raboso, M., del Val, L., Jiménez, M. I., Izquierdo, A., Villacorta, J. J., & José, A. (2011). Virtualizing Grid Computing Infrastructures into the Cloud. In A. Abraham, J. M. Corchado, S. R. González, & J. F. De Paz Santana (Eds.), *International Symposium on Distributed Computing and Artificial Intelligence* (pp. 159-166). Berlin: Springer. doi:10.1007/978-3-642-19934-9_20

Rani, C. R., Kumar, A. P., Adarsh, D., Mohan, K. K., & Kiran, K. V. (2012). *Location based services in Android*. International Journal Of Advances In Engineering & Technology.

Red Hat, Inc. (2014). A Complete Virtualization Solution for Servers and Desktops. Retrieved from http://www.redhat.com/en/technologies/virtualization

Ressmann, D., Mexner, W., Vondrous, A., Kopmann, A., & Mauch, V. (2014). Data management at the synchrotron radiation facility ANKA. *Proceedings of the PCaPAC '14,* Karlsruhe, Germany (pp. 13-15).

Rightscale.com. (n. d.). CloudStack Reference Architecture. Retrieved from http://docs.rightscale.com/clouds/cloudstack/cloudstack_reference_architecture.html

Rittinghouse, J. W., & Ransome, J. F. (2016). *Cloud computing: implementation, management, and security*. NY: CRC press.

Rosenblum, M., & Garfinkel, T. (2005, May). Virtual machine monitors: Current technology and future trends. *Computer, 38*(5), 39–47. doi:10.1109/MC.2005.176

Rouse, M. (2012, February). What is hot spot/cold spot? - definition from WhatIs.Com. Retrieved October 19, 2016, from http://searchdatacenter.techtarget.com/definition/Hot-spot-cold-spot

Sahoo, J., Mohapatra, S., & Lath, R. (2010). Virtualization: A survey on concepts, taxonomy and associated security issues. *Proceedings of IEEE Second International Conference on Computer and Network Technology (ICCNT)* Bangkok, Thailand (pp. 222-226). doi:10.1109/ICCNT.2010.49

Sanger, F., Nicklen, S., & Coulson, A. R. (1977). DNA sequencing with chain-terminating inhibitors. *National Academy of Sciences, 74*(12), 5463-5467.

Sarathy, V., Narayan, P., & Mikkilineni, R. "Next generation cloud computing architecture", 19th IEEE international workshop on enabling technology: infrastructure for collaborative enterprise (WETICE), pp. 48-53,2012.

Schmelzle, S., Norton, R. A., & Heethoff, M. (2015). Mechanics of the ptychoid defense mechanism in Ptyctima (Acari, Oribatida): One problem, two solutions. *Zoologischer Anzeiger - A Journal of Comparative Zoology, 254*, 27–40. doi:10.1016/j.jcz.2014.09.002

Schmelzle, S., Helfen, L., Norton, R. A., & Heethoff, M. (2009). The ptychoid defensive mechanism in Euphthiracaroidea (Acari: Oribatida): A comparison of muscular elements with functional considerations. *Arthropod Structure & Development, 38*(6), 461–472. doi:10.1016/j.asd.2009.07.001 PMID:19595788

Schopf, M., J., Pearlman, L., Miller, N., Kesselman, C., Foster, I., . . . Chervenak, A. (2006). Monitoring the grid with the Globus Toolkit MDS4. *Proceedings of Conference Series in Journal of Physics, 46*(1), 521-525. doi:10.1088/1742-6596/46/1/072

Schwermann, A. H., dos Santos Rolo, T., Caterino, M. S., Bechly, G., Schmied, H., Baumbach, T., & van de Kamp, T. (2016). Preservation of three-dimensional anatomy in phosphatized fossil arthropods enriches evolutionary inference. *eLife, 5.* doi:10.7554/eLife.12129 PMID:26854367

Seema, M., & Jha, C. K. (2015). Handling big data efficiently by using MapReduce technique. *Proceedings on International Conference on Computational Intelligence & Communication Technology IEEE* (pp. 703-708).

Sefraoui, O., Aissaoui, M., & Eleuldj, M. (2012). OpenStack: toward an open-source solution for cloud computing. *International Journal of Computer Applications, 55*(3).

Semnanian, A.A., Pham, J., Englert, B., & Wu, X. (2011). Virtualization Technology and its Impact on Computer Hardware Architecture. *Proceedings of the 2011 Eighth International Conference on Information Technology: New Generations (ITNG)* (pp. 719-724).

Sharma, S., & Veenu, M. (2015). Technology and Trends to handle Big Data: Survey. *Proceedings of 2015 5th International Conference on Advanced Computing and Communication Technologies* (pp. 266-271). doi:10.1109/ACCT.2015.121

Shibboleth Consortium. (n. d.). Retrieved from http://shibboleth.net/

Singhal, M., & Shukla, A. (2012). Implementation of location based services in android using GPS and web services. *IJCSI International Journal of Computer Science Issues, 9*(1), 237–242.

Singh, K., & Kaur, R. (2014). Hadoop: Addressing Challenges of Big Data. *Proceedings of International Conference on Advance Computing IEEE* (pp. 686-689).

Sitaram, D., & Manjunath, G. (2012). Moving to the Cloud. In Syngress (Ch. 9, p. 352).

Soltesz, S., Pötzl, H., Fiuczynski, M. E., Bavier, A., & Peterson, L. (2007). Container-based operating system virtualization: A scalable, high-performance alternative to hypervisors. *Operating Systems Review, 41*(3), 275–287. doi:10.1145/1272998.1273025

Soni, G., & Kalra, M. (2013). Comparative Study of Live Virtual Machine Migration Techniques in Cloud. *International Journal of Computers and Applications, 84*(14), 19–25. doi:10.5120/14643-2919

Soto-Navarro, R. (2012). Presenting Linux kvm. Retrieved from www.flux.org/slides/linux-kvm-presentation-flux.org.pdf

Stainforth, D., Martin, A., Simpson, A., Christensen, C., Kettleborough, J., Aina, T., & Allen, M. (2004). Security principles for public resource modeling research. *Proceedings of 13th IEEE International Workshops in Enabling Technologies: Infrastructure for Collaborative Enterprises* (pp. 319-324).

Stantchev, V., Barnawi, A., Ghulam, S., Schubert, J., & Tamm, G. (2015). Smart items, fog and cloud computing as enablers of servitization in healthcare. *Sensors & Transducers, 185*(2), 121.

Stojmenovic, I., & Wen, S. (2014, September). The fog computing paradigm: Scenarios and security issues. *Proceedings of the 2014 Federated Conference on Computer Science and Information Systems (FedCSIS)* (pp. 1-8). IEEE. doi:10.1145/2757384.2757397

Tan Jerome, N., Chilingaryan, S., Kopmann, A., Shkarin, A., Zapf, M., Lizin, A., & Bergmann, T. (2017). WAVE: A 3D Online Previewing Framework for Big Data Archives. In *International Conference on Information Visualization Theory and Applications - IVAPP 2017*, Porto, Portugal, 27.2.-1.3.2017.

TechTarget. (n. d.). Cloud Computing. Retrieved from http://searchcloudcomputing.techtarget.com/definition/cloud-computing

Tecmint.com. (n. d.). How to Create Virtual Machines in Linux Using KVM (Kernel-based Virtual Machine) - Part 1. Retrieved from http://www.tecmint.com/install-and-configure-kvm-in-linux/

Toth, D., Mayer, R., & Nichols, W. (2011). Increasing Participation in Volunteer Computing. *Proceedings of IEEE International Symposium on Parallel and Distributed Processing Workshops and Ph.D Forum* (pp. 1878-1882).

Turk, M. J., Smith, B. D., Oishi, J. S., Skory, S., Skillman, S. W., Abel, T., & Norman, M. L. (2010). Yt: A multi-code analysis toolkit for astrophysical simulation data. *The Astrophysical Journal. Supplement Series, 192*(1), 9. doi:10.1088/0067-0049/192/1/9

Ubuntu. (n. d.), MaaS. Retrieved from http://maas.ubuntu.com/docs/

Ubuntu.com. (n. d.). 16.04 LTS Ubuntu. Retrieved from https://www.ubuntu.com/download/desktop/install-ubuntu-desktop

Uhlig, R., Neiger, G., Rodgers, D., Santoni, A. L., Martins, F. C. M., Anderson, A. V., & Smith, L. et al. (2005). Intel virtualization technology. *Computer, 38*(5), 48–56. doi:10.1109/MC.2005.163

Urbah, E., Kacsuk, P., Farkas, Z., Fedak, G., Kecskemeti, G., Lodygensky, O., & Lovas, R. et al. (2009). Edges: Bridging egee to boinc and xtremweb. *Journal of Grid Computing, 7*(3), 335–354. doi:10.1007/s10723-009-9137-0

Vagrantup.com. (n. d.). Vagrant Installation. Retrieved from https://www.vagrantup.com/docs/installation/

van de Kamp, T., Cecilia, A., dos Santos Rolo, T., Vagovič, P., Baumbach, T., & Riedel, A. (2015). Comparative thorax morphology of death-feigning flightless cryptorhynchine weevils (Coleoptera: Curculionidae) based on 3D reconstructions. *Arthropod Structure & Development, 44*(6), 509–523. doi:10.1016/j.asd.2015.07.004 PMID:26259678

van de Kamp, T., dos Santos Rolo, T., Vagovič, P., Baumbach, T., & Riedel, A. (2014). Three-Dimensional reconstructions come to life – interactive 3D PDF Animations in functional morphology. *PLoS ONE, 9*(7), e102355. doi:10.1371/journal.pone.0102355 PMID:25029366 van de Kamp, T., Vagovič, P., Baumbach, T., & Riedel, A. (2011). A biological screw in a beetles leg. *Science, 333*(6038), 52–52. doi:10.1126/science.1204245 PMID:21719669

Venters, W., & Whitley, E. A. (2012). A critical review of cloud computing: Researching desires and realities. *Journal of Information Technology, 27*(3), 179–197. doi:10.1057/jit.2012.17

VirtualBox. (n. d.). Retrieved October 16, 2016, from https://www.virtualbox.org/

VirtualBox. (n. d.). Retrieved October 23, 2016, from https://www.virtualbox.org/

VirtualBox. (n. d.). User Manual. Retrieved from https://www.virtualbox.org/manual/UserManual.html

VirtualBox.org. (n. d.). Virtual networking (Ch. 6). Retrieved from https://www.virtualbox.org/manual/ch06.html

Virtualizationadmin.com. (n. d.). What is a snapshot? Retrieved from http://www.virtualizationadmin.com/faq/snapshot.html

Visionsolutions.com. (2016). Business continuity & disaster recover software, vision solutions. Retrieved October 17, 2016, from http://www.visionsolutions.com/Company/About-Vision-Solutions.aspx

VMware, Inc. (2007). Understanding full Virtualization, Paravirtualization, and Hardware assist. Retrieved from http://www.vmware.com/files/pdf/VMware_paravirtualization.pdf

VMware, Inc. (2011). VmWare ESXi™ 5.0 Operations Guide Technical (white paper). Retrieved from https://www.vmware.com/files/pdf/techpaper/vSphere-5-ESXi-Operations-Guide.pdf

VMware, Inc. (2013). Using vmware workstation. Retrieved from www.vmware.com/pdf/desktop/ws10-using.pdf

VMWare, Inc2006). Double-Take Replication in the VMware Environment. Retrieved from http://www.vmware.com/pdf/vmware_doubletake.pdf

VMware. (2016, October 13). VMware Virtualization for desktop & server, application, public & hybrid clouds. Retrieved October 16, 2016, from http://www.vmware.com

VMware.com. (n. d.). Knowledge Base. Retrieved from http://kb.vmware.com/selfservice/microsites/search.do?language=en_US&cmd=displayKC&externalId=1003882

Vouk, M. A. (2008). Cloud computing–issues, research and implementations. *Journal of Computing and Information Technology, 16*(4), 235-246.

Wang, C., Wang, Q., Ren, K., & Lou, W. (2010, March). Privacy-preserving public auditing for data storage security in cloud computing. Proceedings of IEEE INFOCOM '10 (pp. 1-9). IEEE. doi:10.1109/INFCOM.2010.5462173

Wang, A., Iyer, M., Dutta, R., Rouskas, G. N., & Baldine, I. (2013). Network virtualization: Technologies, perspectives, and frontiers. *Journal of Lightwave Technology, 31*(4), 523–537. doi:10.1109/JLT.2012.2213796

Wang, L., Von Laszewski, G., Chen, D., Tao, J., & Kunze, M. (2010). Provide virtual machine information for grid computing. *IEEE Transactions on Systems, Man, and Cybernetics. Part A, Systems and Humans, 40*(6), 1362–1374. doi:10.1109/TSMCA.2010.2052598

Wang, L., Von Laszewski, G., Tao, J., & Kunze, M. (2009). Grid virtualization engine: Design, implementation, and evaluation. *IEEE Systems Journal, 3*(4), 477–488. doi:10.1109/JSYST.2009.2028589

Weltzin, C., & Delgado, S. (2009). Using Virtualization to reduce the cost of test. *Proceedings of AUTOTESTCON '09* (pp. 439-442).

White, T. (2009). *Hadoop: The Definitive Guide. O'Reilly Media, Yahoo!* Press.

Wikipedia. (2016, November 23). Security Assertion Markup Language. Retrieved from https://en.wikipedia.org/wiki/Security_Assertion_Markup_Language

Wikipedia. (2017, April 6). Kernel-based Virtual Machine. Retrieved from https://en.wikipedia.org/wiki/Kernel-based_Virtual_Machine

Wikipedia. (2017, March 17). *Endian Firewall*. Retrieved March 19, 2017, from https://en.wikipedia.org/wiki/Endian_Firewall

Wikipedia. (n. d.). Cloud Computing. Retrieved from https://en.wikipedia.org/wiki/Cloud_computing

Wikipedia. (n. d.). Openstack. Retrieved from https://en.wikipedia.org/wiki/OpenStack

Wikipedia. (n. d.). Virtualization. Retrieved from https://en.wikipedia.org/wiki/Virtualization

Wikipedia. (n. d.). x86 Virtualization. Retrieved from https://en.wikipedia.org/wiki/X86_virtualization

Wilson, J., & Hunt, T. (2002). Molecular Biology of the Cell, A Problems Approach (4th ed.). New York: Garland Science.

Wind, S. (2011). Open source cloud computing management platform. Proceedings of the IEEE conference on open system (ICOS '11) (pp. 175-179).

Wohl, A. (2010). Software as a Service (SaaS). In *The Next Wave of Technologies: Opportunities from Chaos* (pp. 97-113).

Wu, F., & Sun, G. (2013). *Software-defined storage. Report*. Minneapolis: University of Minnesota.

Xen. (2009, December). How does Xen work? Retrieved from http://www-archive.xenproject.org/files/Marketing/HowDoesXenWork.pdf

Xen® Hypervisor The open source standard for hardware Virtualization, http://www-archive .xenproject.org/products/xenhyp.html

Xenproject.org. (n. d.). XCP Beginners Guide. Retrieved January 10, 2017, from https://wiki. xenproject.org/wiki/XCP_Beginners_Guide

Xenproject.org. (n. d.a). Xen Cloud Platform 1.6. Retrieved from http://www.xenproject.org/ downloads/xen-cloud-platform-archives/xen-cloud-platform-16.html

Xenproject.org. (n. d.b). Why Xen Project? Retrieved from http://www.xenproject.org/users/ why-the-xen-project.html

XenServer 7. (2016, December 29). Retrieved January 1, 2017, from https://www.citrix.com/ blogs/2016/05/24/xenserver-7-whats-new/

Xing, Y., & Zhan, Y. (2012). Virtualization and cloud computing. In Y. Zhang (Ed.), *Future Wireless Networks and Information Systems* (pp. 305–312). Berlin: Springer. doi:10.1007/978-3-642-27323-0_39

Yao, H., Zhao, L., Li, Y., & Yang, J. (2009). Using BOINC desktop grid for high performance memory detection. *Proceedings of 4th IEEE International Conference on Computer Science & Education* (pp. 1159-1162).

Yi, S., Li, C., & Li, Q. (2015, June). A survey of fog computing: concepts, applications and issues. *Proceedings of the 2015 Workshop on Mobile Big Data* (pp. 37-42). ACM.

Younge, A. J., Henschel, R., Brown, J. T., Von Laszewski, G., Qiu, J., & Fox, G. C. (2011). Analysis of virtualization technologies for high performance computing environments. *Proceedings of the IEEE 4th International Conference on Cloud Computing (CLOUD)* (pp. 9-16). Washington, DC, USA. doi:10.1109/CLOUD.2011.29

Yuen, E. (2012). Independent Third Party Assessments of Hyper-V. *Technet.com*. Retrieved from http://blogs.technet.com/b/server-cloud/archive/2012/07/09/independent-third-party-assessments-of-hyper-v.aspx

Zerbino, R. D., & Birney, E. (2008). Velvet: Algorithms for De novo short read assembly using de Bruijn graphs. *Genome Research*, *18*(5), 821–829. doi:10.1101/gr.074492.107 PMID:18349386

Zhu, J., Chan, D. S., Prabhu, M. S., Natarajan, P., Hu, H., & Bonomi, F. (2013, March). Improving web sites performance using edge servers in fog computing architecture. *Proceedings of the 2013 IEEE 7th International Symposium on Service Oriented System Engineering (SOSE)* (pp. 320-323). IEEE.

Index

W

X

Stay Current on the Latest Emerging Research Developments

Become an IGI Global Reviewer for Authored Book Projects

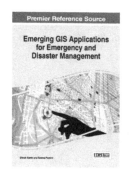

Premier Reference Source

Emerging GIS Applications for Emergency and Disaster Management

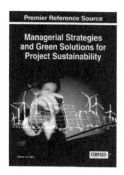

Premier Reference Source

Managerial Strategies and Green Solutions for Project Sustainability

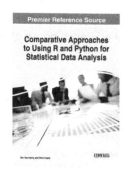

Premier Reference Source

Comparative Approaches to Using R and Python for Statistical Data Analysis

Premier Reference Source

Solutions for High-Touch Communications in a High-Tech World

The overall success of an authored book project is dependent on quality and timely reviews.

In this competitive age of scholarly publishing, constructive and timely feedback significantly decreases the turnaround time of manuscripts from submission to acceptance, allowing the publication and discovery of progressive research at a much more expeditious rate. Several IGI Global authored book projects are currently seeking highly qualified experts in the field to fill vacancies on their respective editorial review boards:

Applications may be sent to:
development@igi-global.com

Applicants must have a doctorate (or an equivalent degree) as well as publishing and reviewing experience. Reviewers are asked to write reviews in a timely, collegial, and constructive manner. All reviewers will begin their role on an ad-hoc basis for a period of one year, and upon successful completion of this term can be considered for full editorial review board status, with the potential for a subsequent promotion to Associate Editor.

If you have a colleague that may be interested in this opportunity, we encourage you to share this information with them.

Printed in the United States
By Bookmasters